Milk Craze

**FOOD
IN ASIA
AND THE
PACIFIC**

Series Editors:

Christine R. Yano and Robert Ji-Song Ku

This series showcases new works focused on food in the Asia-Pacific region and its diasporic iterations, highlighting the commonalities that the area and cultures might bring to the subject. Books under this series are disciplinarily diverse, drawing from the fields of geography, sociology, anthropology, history, globalization studies, gender studies, science and technology studies, development studies, ethnic studies, and cultural studies. The Asia-Pacific region evokes particular global relationships and domestic infrastructures—center-periphery, postcolonialism, imperialisms, and politicized imaginaries. The goal of the series is to bring food to bear in considering these relationships and infrastructures. We see a regional focus—including the inherent mobility of transnational flows, migration, and global capitalism therein—as productive elements, rather than as reifying limitation. By bringing together books that have a general topic (food) and an area focus (Asia-Pacific), FAP locates mobility itself as the framework from which scholarship may enrich our understanding of this complexly globalized world.

Milk Craze

BODY, SCIENCE, AND HOPE
IN CHINA

Veronica S. W. Mak

University of Hawai'i Press | Honolulu

26 25 24 23 22 21   6 5 4 3 2 1

Library of Congress Cataloging-in-Publication Data

Names: Mak, Veronica S. W., author.
Title: Milk craze : body, science, and hope in China / Veronica S.W. Mak.
Other titles: Food in Asia and the Pacific.
Description: Honolulu : University of Hawai'i Press, 2021. | Series: Food
  in Asia and the Pacific | Includes bibliographical references and index.
Identifiers: LCCN 2020026475 | ISBN 9780824886271 (hardcover) | ISBN
  9780824887674 (adobe pdf) | ISBN 9780824887681 (epub) | ISBN
  9780824887698 (kindle edition)
Subjects: LCSH: Milk consumption—China. | Milk consumption—Health
  aspects—China.
Classification: LCC HD9282.C62 M37 2021 | DDC 338.1/77109512—dc23
LC record available at https://lccn.loc.gov/2020026475

ISBN 978-0-8248-8798-8 (paperback)

Cover photo: Water buffalo cheese from Shunde is an indigenous
Chinese cheese recorded in the ancient literature. Photo by author.

To Born, Silex, and my parents

Contents

Acknowledgments

Milk Craze testifies to a change in my career pursuits. In 2009, I quit my job in food marketing and began research that explores the relationship between food consumption and production. Many people and institutions have contributed to making this adventure possible. It gives me great pleasure to thank all of those who have inspired and supported me at various stages of this project.

This project began as a doctoral dissertation at the Chinese University of Hong Kong (CUHK). I first arrived at the university feeling very lucky to have the chance to study with Tan Chee-Beng. Without his support, I would never have imagined going on to complete a research degree or becoming an anthropologist. The longer I know Chee-Beng, the more deeply I admire his scholarship and his commitment to his students. He has been a first-rate mentor. I am truly grateful for the many ways he has given me encouragement, prodding me in the right direction at the right time, and patiently working to help me clarify my thoughts. I must also thank Nancy Pollock for valuable suggestions, which helped me immensely as I revised the manuscript.

Of all my teachers in the field of anthropology, Sidney Cheung, who inspired me to start my first project in local "tea cafés," is most directly responsible for this book. Blending historical rigor and anthropological wit, he showed me the possibility of bridging anthropology and the culinary world. Gordon Mathews earns heartfelt thanks for his confidence in my teaching and research and for his leadership as department chair.

Joseph Bosco provided me with manuscript feedback that was full of his characteristic warmth and sharpness. David Palmer saw potential in me that I did not know I had and gave me the opportunity and impetus to meet that potential. Saroja Dorairajoo's confidence in my food research and teaching lit me up. Maria Tam, Erika Evasdottir, Wu Keping, and Wang Danning sustained me with their intelligence, spirit, and drive. Tracy Lu was in fact my first informant from Shunde. She kindly shared her own experience of homemade stir-fried buffalo milk with me. She was an incredible teacher beloved by students and colleagues alike and is deeply missed. I am grateful to all my colleagues in the anthropology department for their goodwill and encouragement, especially to Teresa Kwan, Huang Yu, Chen Ju-chen, and Sealing Cheng, for broadening my thinking, offering me teaching advice, and answering questions about publication. Grace Tsang, Leung Ming-wah, Kathy Wong, and Irene Chan's efficiency and unfailing good spirit are also heartening.

My interests in food and advertising started early with teachers in the philosophy department, who kindled my curiosity, taught me about critical thinking, and held me to high standards. I also owe a great debt to Cheung Chan-fai, my MA advisor, who planted the seed for my research on advertising, consumption, and phenomenology. I also benefited greatly from the passionate teaching of Lau Kwok-ying and Liu Chang-yuen on the thought of Foucault, Heidegger, Merleau-Ponty, and Nietzsche, and for transforming my understanding of the body, science, and morality.

In trying to learn about the food culture and dietary health of Shunde, I have been assisted by many people. First and foremost are the water buffalo cheese makers of Jinbang village and my friends in Daliang. Over the many years that I made visits to the village and the town of Daliang to conduct research for this book, I was warmly welcomed by them. They always answered my questions on the complexities and nuances of the milk culture with great patience. I especially wish to thank Yuk, whose sister's family became my host in Daliang. They introduced me to Jinbang village and have never stopped sharing knowledge with me about the past and present of its milk culture. My research in Shunde would not have been possible had I not also had the support of Chan Tak-wing of the Shun Tak Fraternal Association. He invited me to join the scholarship award ceremonies in several well-established secondary schools in Shunde, through which I was able to nurture connections with the local people. I am also grateful for the generous support of the assistant headmaster of Shunde

Liang Qiu Ju Vocational and Technical School in Daliang, Luo Meinuo, who graciously prepared a flat in a teacher's hostel and a quiet office space for my accommodation and writing. I especially wish to thank Huang Jianhua, Chen Zhentong, Wang Yinghui, and the many other administrative staff who helped me to arrange my student focus groups, as well as to thank them for sharing their experiences of milk consumption in everyday life. I also especially wish to thank Liao Xixiang and Luo Funan for sharing their incredible knowledge of Shunde cuisine with me.

This book is dedicated to my mentor and good friend, Sophie Leung, an experienced pediatrician and Honorary Clinical Associate Professor at the Chinese University of Hong Kong. Sophie read several chapters of my manuscript, sent me useful information, and invited me to medical and nutrition conferences. Her intellect, passion for health research, and promotion and charitable attitude to the poor are all greatly cherished. I am fortunate to have been introduced to her through Priscilla Lau, who taught me nutrition and continues to inspire me.

I am also grateful for the generous support provided by the United College Lee Hysan Foundation Research Grant and the Social Research Centre of the Hong Kong Shue Yan University. This research funding supported me throughout the later stage of this project, enabling me to revisit Jinbang village in 2017 and to complete manuscript revision. More importantly, I wish to especially thank Jimmy Yu and Cheung Yuet-wah, who provided me with a sense of the wealth of possibilities available and encouraged me to pursue academic research and writing against all odds.

Masako Ikeda, my editor at University of Hawai'i Press, has proven to be a careful and thoughtful person, and Wendy Bolton, my copy editor, has helped this project through the final stages. I also give my deepest thanks to Ellen Messer, an anonymous reviewer who revealed her identity. I appreciate the grace with which Masako and the entire staff of University of Hawai'i Press guided a first-time author. I also thank the anonymous reviewers from *Food and Foodways, Health, Risk and Society,* and *Ecology of Food and Nutrition,* who helped refine my thinking on topics that I would later focus on in this book. I wish to especially thank journal editors Carole Counihan for commenting on a critical part of chapter 1, Patrick Brown for helping refine a section of chapter 4, and Sunil Khanna for commenting on a section of chapter 5, which appeared in the three journals respectively in 2014, 2015, and 2017.

A writing career is a lonely one, but I have been blessed with much support and friendship. I am grateful to my copy editor, Scott McKay. Scott patiently read and edited every chapter of this book, raised provocative and important questions and sent me useful news and articles. His constructive criticism means a great deal. I have also presented parts of this research at the conferences and meetings of the Society for East Asian Anthropology, the Hong Kong Anthropological Society, the Taiwan Society for Anthropology and Ethnology, the Foundation of Chinese Dietary Culture, and the Association for Asian Studies. I thank commentators Sidney Mintz, David Wu, Midori Hino, Emiko Takei, James Farrer, Nir Avieli, Yang Chao-chin, Marc De Ferriere Le Vayer, David Schak, John Eng Wong, Kao Chiu-yin, May Chang, Tina Johnson, John Wong, Jessica Lin, and Suk-ying Lo for their comments at these meetings. I also thank the organizers of these meetings, especially George Wong, the Chairman of the Foundation of Chinese Dietary Culture, not only for his support of many of these wonderful meetings but also for his openness, encouragement, and hospitality. I also appreciated the sage advice offered by Chan Yuk-wah, Zhu Jiangang, Cheng Yu, and Duan Ying, who provided me with valuable insights on food, civil rights, and the health scenario in Hong Kong, China, and Southeast Asia.

On a day-to-day basis, I have been blessed with generous and supportive colleagues in the Sociology Department of Hong Kong Shue Yan University and the Marketing Department of CUHK. I thank all of my colleagues in the department for their professionalism and support, but I am especially grateful to Selina Chan, Yew-foong Hui, Flora Lau, Jessica Kwong, Zhang Men, Shen Hao, Fan Ting-ting, Kim Hwang, Samart Powpaka, and Julie Yu for their helpful advice on teaching and research. Cheung Yuet-wah, Jamie Jia, and Michael Hui earn hearty thanks for their leadership and counsel as department chairs. Candy Lam, Juliet Chau, Kerri Hung, Benson Chan, Cindy Wong, Yvonne Ling, Nova Tan, and Dylan Chen also deserve thanks for their helpfulness and unfailing support.

Most of all, I am grateful for my family's unwavering support. I would like to register my gratitude to my parents, who accompanied me to Shunde to take care of my son when I did fieldwork. Their close, affectionate relationship with Silex is a beautiful outgrowth of their willingness to help out. My son, who took his first steps at my field site, was born—and raised—during the writing of this book. His passion for creating and learning has been a vital source of inspiration and delight for me in the process of researching and writing. Yet, no one has lived with this project longer or more intimately than Silex's father, Born Lo. He has cheered me in my lowest moments and been a constant source of comfort. Born, thank you for teaching me how to follow my heart and to focus on things that really matter.

Introduction

The Cultural Politics of Milk Consumption in China

Agroup of anxious middle-class Hong Kong citizens suddenly became minor celebrities when they submitted a petition titled "Baby Hunger Outbreak in Hong Kong, International Aid Requested" to the White House website in 2013, bringing international media attention to what was portrayed as a local "milk famine." The petition stated: "Local parents in Hong Kong can hardly buy baby formula milk[1] in drugstores and supermarkets, as smugglers from mainland China have stormed into this tiny city to buy milk powder and resell it for huge profits in China. We request international support and assistance, as babies in Hong Kong will face malnutrition very soon" (White House 2013). Agitated by the potential health risks facing their babies owing to the formula milk shortages, coupled with their distrust in the local government's ability to resolve the problem, this group of web-savvy people asked the United States to intervene on their behalf (Chiu and Nip 2013). Some of these same parents also organized a series of online and street protests, successfully forcing the Hong Kong government to cap the maximum quantity of formula milk that may be taken outside of the territory at two cans per person (Government of Hong Kong SAR 2013*b*).

The "milk craze," however, is not limited to Hong Kong; rather, it is sending ripples around the world. In the same year, sales of infant formula milk in European supermarkets were also restricted to two cans per customer owing to bulk purchasing by Chinese travelers (Hatton 2013). Similarly, in 2015 Coles and Woolworths in Australia—the two largest

1

supermarket chains in the country—were forced to introduce a four-tins-per-customer policy. The shopping behavior of the Chinese people was even labeled as "crazy" after a video showing shoppers stripping supermarket shelves of an Australian brand of baby formula went viral (Pidgeon 2017). Despite having been characterized by anthropologist Marvin Harris as "lactophobic," the people of mainland China stunned the international community by being the second-largest consumers of milk products in the world in 2017[2] (Eagle 2017). Various Western commentators termed this rapid surge in milk consumption in China a "Milk Craze" (Graham 2017; Leong 2017).

The importance of milk, especially formula milk, in the daily lives of people in contemporary China can easily be felt in any corner of every city in China. As soon as you step into a drug store or a supermarket, you are certain to find stacks of colorfully packaged formula milk. When looking at the carefully designed labels on these cans—no doubt produced following hundreds of market research studies, big-data analysis, and market intelligence research—I am often puzzled by the various chemical names, formulas, symbols, and icons, as well as the product names and chemical abbreviations of the ingredients that appear on the packaging, all of which seem to be meant to represent the wholesome benefits of the modern, scientifically tested powdered milk sealed inside.

Nor is consumption of milk products simply a recent phenomenon in Chinese societies: in addition to drug stores, another site in Hong Kong that is saturated with milk and dairy products is the *cha chaan teng* (local-style "tea cafés" that vaguely resemble American-style diners). *Cha chaan teng,* an extension of home cooking for many families, are usually fully packed with hungry diners during breakfast hours. The most popular breakfast is the classic slightly sweetened oatmeal softly dissolved in warm evaporated milk, served with scrambled eggs and a piece of crispy toasted white bread. This is accompanied by a cup of hot Hong Kong–style "silk-stocking" milk tea.[3] Taking a closer look at the list of foods on a typical *cha chaan teng* breakfast menu, someone unfamiliar with the items would be surprised to discover the presence of milk in almost every single one, ranging from the milk powder added to the flour used to make bread to give it a softer texture to the generous splash of cream added to slowly cooked scrambled eggs to make them smooth and creamy. The belief in the nutritional power of milk as a breakfast food can also be seen in the habit of some health-conscious parents, who will give their young children an extra eight Hong Kong dollars to buy a bottle of Dairy Farm–brand fresh milk so that their children are assured of having good nutrition and enough energy at the start of a busy school day.

Although many Chinese people are now in the habit of drinking fresh cow milk or milk tea every day and regularly buy cheese, ice cream, and formula milk powder without much thought, an increasing number make such purchases with a degree of trepidation. One rarely noted fact is that the formula milk that the Chinese are "crazy" about is limited to three popular imported Western brands, namely Friso from the Netherlands, Mead Johnson from the United States, and Cow & Gate from New Zealand (*Mingpao* 2013; *Topick* 2015). Moreover, the decline in sales and popularity of indigenous water buffalo milk and cheese from Shunde in southeastern China reveals further that Western cow milk has become *the* milk for Chinese consumers (Chen 2015).

Understanding the process by which these consumer choices have come about is by no means easy. Chinese consumers, both in the mainland and in Hong Kong, resort to a variety of strategies to make "informed decisions" about milk products. Today, when making decisions regarding infant feeding, a new working-class mother will ordinarily consult with Western or Chinese medical doctors, health-care workers, relatives, and friends and will seek out nutritional information through social media and TV programs. Middle-class consumers of milk products will conscientiously compare the nutritional information on the different product labels, along with the price and their country-of-origin information when making their choices, taking into consideration their babies' perceived nutritional requirements as well as each brand's reputation for food safety.

I have opened this book with the "Baby Hunger Outbreak" petition to evoke a sense of the political and cultural pressures that shape middle-class family life and consumer behavior in contemporary Hong Kong and mainland China. In both societies, the choices one makes in purchasing milk products have become a contested ground for the politics of science, health, and identity building. Perplexed consumers ponder whether the nutritional and ecological benefits and brand image of a newly launched, technologically advanced imported formula milk line justify its premium price. They struggle over whether to buy milk from a local water buffalo dairy. They consider whether milk from Western cows will be fresher, safer, and more nutritious than milk from local cows or whether it will spoil more easily than the ultra-pasteurized milk from Inner Mongolia or canned milk powder from overseas. They deliberate over whether the locally produced flavored cow milk drinks, incorporating nourishing ingredients based on Chinese medical recipes, are better than the pure, fresh milk imported directly from Australia and New Zealand.

The milk craze phenomenon in China matters, both within China and beyond its borders. Not only does it create stress and exhaustion among Chinese parents, but it also creates social tension between local governments and citizens who press for political intervention. The Chinese thirst for milk has also had a number of unexpected environmental and health consequences. For example, as China is now the largest consumer of New Zealand milk powder (Inouye 2019), New Zealand has some 6.6 million dairy cattle squeezed into a country of 4.7 million people, transforming even the iconic, arid grassland of the Mackenzie Basin (made famous by the *Lord of the Rings* films) into a picture of emerald fields (*The Economist* 2017; Hutching 2018). The sudden increase in the number of imported dairy cows has produced tremendous amounts of bovine urine, which is rich in nitrogen, causing toxic algae to grow once it leaches into water. Nitrogen fertilizer, used to increase fodder yields so that more cows can be raised on less land, exacerbates the problem. One consequence of this is that now 60 percent of the lakes and rivers in New Zealand are polluted and unsafe for swimming (*The Economist* 2017). According to projections by Bai and his colleagues, by 2050 China's demand for milk will increase 3.2-fold. Meeting China's demand will increase global dairy-related greenhouse gas emissions by 35 percent and the amount of land used for dairy feed production by 32 percent, compared to 2010 levels. This may further contribute to climate change and intensify land shortages (Bai et al. 2018).

In addition to a significant environmental cost, the surge in milk consumption among the Chinese, as a kind of dietary change, entails new and significant medical costs. Although fresh milk and dairy products are rich in protein and calcium, both of which are essential for the functioning of the human body, their fat content is high. The increase in consumption of milk and meat products is tantamount to the Chinese population undergoing an overall nutritional transition to a high-fat diet. Coupled with a lack of physical activity, this dietary change is believed to be linked to rapid increases in overweight, obesity, and diet-related non-communicable diseases (DRNCDs) among Chinese adults (Caballero and Popkin 2002, 1; Du et al. 2002). Even worse, recent findings show that this trend in nutrition transition has expanded to include children. Based on data first collected from the China Health and Nutrition Survey (CHNS), a nationally representative survey of children aged six to fourteen from 2006 to 2011, children who followed the modern dietary pattern, loaded heavily with egg, milk, wheat buns, etc., were positively associated with later obesity, compared with children who followed a more traditional diet[4] (Zhen et al. 2018). Understanding the reasons behind this dietary change is crucial not only for scholars but also public health policy makers, so as to enhance the well-being and lower the mortality of urban residents.

Why Milk?

Based on media coverage of the milk craze and the existing literature, the basic outline of what is happening can be explained as follows: the goal of profit maximization led dairy farmers and the dairy companies in China to engage in unethical practices. After the melamine-tainted milk scandal in 2008, Chinese parents felt they could no longer trust made-in-China formula milk and began consuming milk products from outside the People's Republic of China (PRC). In addition, a series of food safety problems further demonstrated the inability of the Chinese government to reinforce its food safety policy (Agency France-Presse 2018; Pei et al. 2010; Xiu and Klein 2010; Zhu, Yang, and Zhang 2009). Therefore, Chinese parents felt they had no choice but to resort to buying expensive imported formula to feed their babies and young children. However, there is another, more fundamental question that people rarely ask: *Why are the Chinese drinking so much milk today?*

One of the most amazing facts I discovered during my study of milk consumption in China is that no one has asked the question, "How has milk, a globalized commodity, become China's drink?," in a systematic way, echoing the astonishment Melanie DuPuis experienced as she discovered that nobody had seriously addressed the "why milk" question in America (DuPuis 2002, 6). Anthropologists have long been interested in food choices and dietary change (Cwiertka 2000; Leach 1999; Messer 1984; Pelto and Vargas 1992). Explanations for the choice of consuming certain foods and dietary changes usually fall into one of two traditions of explanation—biological (or ecological) and cultural. Food is necessary for our biological existence, but, in all cultures, food is imbued with a variety of meanings. These competing modes of explanation are best represented by the debates over pork taboos among Jews and Muslims, and the prohibitions on beef consumption among Hindus (cf. Douglas 1966; Harris 1974, 1986; Harris and Ross 1987; Sahlins 1976). Marvin Harris, for example, argued that it is the economic contributions of the cow and not religious, cosmological, or other cultural factors that protect the animal from being slaughtered for food in India. Materialist perspectives and evolutionary perspectives consider the adaptive significance of a people's foodways (i.e., whether the behavior enhances survival and/or reproduction) as primary and maintain that the benefits of consuming a food should outweigh any costs, as measured in economic or Darwinian fitness terms (Brown et al. 2011; Harris 1979).

Indeed, many sinologists have sought to explain the non-dairy-consuming dietary practice of the Chinese using biological and materialist approaches, such as linking dietary patterns with supposed racial characteristics and analyzing the economic returns of systems of farming and animal husbandry. For instance, Hsingtsung Huang, through his historical studies of science and the technologies of milk and soymilk in China, explained the limited role of cow milk in the ancient Chinese diet using economic and evolutionary reasons. He rightly reminds us that the Chinese did not need to develop the necessary enzyme for the digestion of lactose (lactase, an intestinal enzyme that hydrolyzes lactose) after weaning for two main reasons. First, "throughout the long prehistoric period calcium was presumably supplied by the wealth of green leafy vegetables cultivated or collected from the wild. There was always plenty of sunshine to allow the synthesis of vitamin D needed for the utilization of dietary calcium. There would have been little selection pressure for lactose absorbers against non-absorbers even if milk had been freely available." Second, the commercialization of tofu in the Tang and Song dynasties provided rich protein and calcium sources to people of all walks of life (Huang 2002). As a consequence, even today, the lactase persistence of people in China is still remarkably low (5 percent compared to the 86 percent in the United States and 36.5 percent in India) (Nicklas et al. 2009; Tadesse, Leung, and Yuen 1992; Wang et al. 1984). As such, many scholars perceived that the Chinese were mostly lactase-insufficient and would have fit squarely into Marvin Harris's "lactophobic" category, making him "shocked to find others regarding it [milk] as an ugly-looking, foul-smelling glandular secretion that no self-respecting adult would want to swallow" (Harris 1986, 130–131). Yukio Kumashiro, a respected historian of Chinese agriculture, who translated the *Qimin Yaoshu* treatise into Japanese, also regards China as being unique in practicing what he called the "East Asian model of agrarian civilization" as opposed to the "lactic agrarian cultures" in the West (Yukio 1971, 445).

Ironically, in the past twenty years, China has rapidly grown into the fourth-largest dairy producer globally after the United States, the European Union, and India (DBS Group Research 2017). China is also the fourth-largest fluid milk market (12.7 million metric tons in 2018), following India, the European Union, and the United States (Statista.com 2019). Given that the current population in China has a low rate of lactase persistence, discerning readers will wonder why the rapid transformation of China from a "lactophobic" to a "lactophilic" country within fifty years is possible. Why do Chinese people, who might suffer from symptoms of lactose intolerance such as diarrhea, abdominal pain, flatulence, and bloating, drink so much milk today? In order to understand why and how milk consumption in China surged, a brief discussion of the genetic trait related to milk digestion and the symptoms of milk indigestion is needed.

Symptoms of Lactase Nonpersistence and New Milk Consumption Practices

Anthropological geneticists and biologists have long been studying how and why human populations vary in rates of milk digestion. Lactose is a double sugar (a disaccharide), made up of glucose and galactose, which must be cleaved into single sugars by a specialized enzyme called lactase in order to be absorbed (McCracken 1971; Wiley 2014). In general, infant mammals produce lactase in order to break down the lactose they ingest in their mother's milk and lactase production diminishes and stops around the time of weaning. As Kevin Laland and his colleagues point out, the lactose-intolerance allele was absent in ancient DNA extracted from early Neolithic Europeans, which suggests that the allele was absent or at low frequency 7,000 to 8,000 years ago (Laland, Odling-Smee, and Myles 2010, 145). The onset of the selection of the lactase gene took place 5,000 to 10,000 years ago with the spread of dairying, which also affected the present-day variation in the patterns of lactose tolerance in human populations. Northern Europeans and pastoralist populations from Africa and the Middle East have shown high frequencies of genetic mutation that function to keep lactase activity throughout life.

However, this does not mean that all other humans who have the ancient mammalian DNA sequence cannot drink milk. First, as biologist Nissim Silanikove and his colleagues pointed out, children who have lactase deficiency may not experience symptoms of lactose intolerance until late adolescence to adulthood (Silanikove, Leitner, and Merin 2015). Second, most people with lactose intolerance can tolerate some amount of lactose in their diet. National Institute of Health experts in America suggest that adults and adolescents with lactose malabsorption could eat or drink at least one cup of milk a day (12 g of lactose) without symptoms or with only minor symptoms (Silanikove, Leitner, and Merin 2015). Third, symptoms vary at the individual level. Some individuals have also reported that their intolerance varies over time, depending on health status, pregnancy, and adaptation to lactose intake (Hertzler and Savaiano 1996). Fourth, dietary practices can also minimize the experience of gastrointestinal symptoms. Increasing lactose consumption is possible if lactose is taken with meals, such as milk with cereal, or in small amounts throughout the day (Hertzler et al. 1996; Suchy et al. 2010).

Although these studies provide invaluable insight that people who are lactase nonpersistent can drink milk, they do not explain why Chinese people began to drink more milk, about 36 kg per capita, only after the industrialization of milk production in China. In order to answer the "invisible" questions of "why milk" and "how milk" in America, DuPuis proposed a holistic and interdisciplinary approach "to look at this food from production to consumption, from the birth of the industry in the mid-nineteenth century to the 'Got Milk' campaign, from the nitty-gritty details of milk production to the place of perfection in American social thought" (DuPuis 2002, 6). In this book, I address the "why milk in China" question, by further exploring a number of questions that might be termed historical or sociological: When did the Chinese start consuming dairy products? How did the Chinese people consume milk and how has this changed through time? Who consumes milk most and why? What does this milk obsession reinforce, obscure, or occlude? What does the milk craze story tell us about how the Chinese define good food, a good body, and good health today?

These historical and sociological questions raise an additional issue for anthropological interpretation: Can the study of changing marketing and consumption patterns of a single commodity at a particular moment in time shed some light on a wider range of cultural and social shifts? We have good examples of such analyses in Sidney Mintz's study of sugar and William Roseberry's study of coffee. Mintz's *Sweetness and Power* (1985) explores the link between the growing presence of sugar in the English diet from the seventeenth to the nineteenth century and the establishment of colonial power and slave labor in the Caribbean. His adoption of a political economy approach to study relationships of power between the production and consumption of sugar in Puerto Rico and the United Kingdom is particularly insightful for my study of the development of the milk market in colonial Hong Kong and modern China. In analyzing how a foreign food suddenly became a staple among the indigenous Caribbean people, Mintz argued that the capitalist class provided sugar for the emerging proletarian classes, who found sugar to be a kind of "drug food" with profound consolations in the mines and in the factories. He points out that the "sweet tooth" of the British working class is not natural, but was carefully cultivated by the colonialists to serve economic ends. He rightly noted, "the introduction of foods like sucrose made it possible to raise the caloric content of the proletarian diet without increasing proportionately the quantities of meat, fish, poultry and dairy products" (Mintz 1985, 193). Roseberry, in contrast, observed that upwardly mobile, financially successful consumers consumed gourmet coffee out of preindustrial nostalgia, fostering a boost in "yuppie coffee shops" in the United States. This new gourmet coffee market is supported by an exploitative relationship with the coffee producers in the Third World under the free market (Roseberry 1996). The range of issues relating to milk considered in this book is modest, but I share Mintz's and Roseberry's conviction that the social history of the use of new foods in modern nations can contribute to an anthropology of modern life (Mintz 1985, xxviii; Roseberry 1996).

The "Milk Regime" and the State–Corporate Alliance in China

This book is about the special significance of cow milk, a colonial product, in the growth of China's economy and in global capitalism. In seeking to understand the recent global phenomenon of the milk craze, which serves as an exemplar of the dramatic changes in the dietary patterns of the Chinese people in modern times, I find the framework of a food regime put forward by Harriet Friedmann particularly helpful. Friedmann points out that there was a widespread misperception of a food crisis in the early 1970s, which was explained as the result of natural disasters. In her investigation into this "food crisis," she found that the foods that were in short supply, such as wheat, were usually new, foreign food items, which formerly came to countries as "food aid" offered by developed countries, such as the United States and those in Europe (Friedmann 2005).

These export subsidies from the United States and other developed countries in the form of food aid changed the dietary patterns of many people in Asia and the Third World in the postwar period, transforming them from self-sufficiency to chronic import-dependence. The food aid program originating in the United States, the principal axis of the food regime, has created new food cultures that many countries have now embraced as part of their "heritage." Friedmann aptly argues, "for 25 years, the food regime that emerged after the defeat of the World Food Board in 1947 framed what seemed natural about agriculture, food, farm labor, land use, and international patterns of specialization and what was loosely called 'trade.' It unfolded as the expression of complementary goals of states, firms, social classes and consumers, dramatically chang[ing] patterns of international production and trade" (Friedmann 2005, 240).

We have a good example of this in historian George Solt's *The Untold History of Ramen,* in which he argues that the now "heritagized" ramen in Japan was in fact a result of food aid from America. The practice of consuming ramen started with the surplus supply and cheap *meriken-ko* (American wheat flour), combined with the return of war veterans from China with knowledge of that country's cuisine, which led to the flourishing of *gyoza* (dumplings) and *chuka soba* (wheat noodles in broth, which were eventually known as *ramen*) (Solt 2014). Foreign aid allowed the United States to "sell" goods abroad in return for inconvertible (or "soft") currency from the importing country, elevating the rank of the United States to leading export nation and fostering a perception that it was somehow naturally a "bread basket." Food aid transformed the United States from one among many exporters in the first food regime to a dominant exporter. For some Third World countries, however, food aid did not lead to commerce, but rather to dietary change and chronic import-dependence. The cheap wheat flour supplied by America in the form of food aid transformed Japan and many colonies and new nations of the Third World from self-sufficient to importing countries.

Similar to the way American food aid created a new ramen culture and culinary heritage in Japan, European food aid of dairy products to China during the 1980s paved the way for a new milk revolution. Beginning in 1983, China began receiving food aid from the World Food Programme and the European Union. This food aid included provision of 90,000 tons of skim milk and 30,000 tons of butter oil (Ke 2009, 64). Using skim milk, butter oil, and locally produced fresh cow milk, almost one million tons of recombined milk were produced. Between 1984 and the early 1990s, this new milk supply enabled the Chinese government to provide free milk to the needy, including newborn babies, the elderly, wounded soldiers, retired government officers, senior teachers, cancer patients, and other patients suffering from critical illness. This new milk policy was well received, especially among the well-educated middle class, who were increasingly aware of the Western science of nutrition and the nutritional value of cow milk. Even during the 1960s, dairy products remained a scarce commodity, restricted mainly to special use cases like hospitals and nurseries. As a consequence, it is not hard to understand that the provision of free milk products by the Chinese government became a sign of care from a modernizing state.

In addition to the food aid in the form of milk powder from Europe, Western dairy companies have long played a crucial role in promoting a milk-drinking culture and transforming the dietary pattern of people in China and other Asian countries. The practice and health beliefs surrounding the feeding of infants with diluted canned condensed milk, as a replacement for breastfeeding, would probably not have developed in Asian countries had there not been a surplus of military food supplies, including milk powder and canned milk, in Western countries in the immediate postwar era. One salient example is the aggressive promotion of canned, sweetened condensed skim milk for infant feeding in Indonesia beginning in the 1880s (Den Hartog 1986). It was not until 2018 that the Indonesian government finally prohibited brands from marketing condensed milk and derivatives as milk owing to the worsening obesity problem among young Indonesian children (Tay 2018). As Deborah Valenze points out, the globalization of canned milk can be traced back to the prewar period, when the production of cow milk in the Western world increased exponentially even before milk became truly popular as a beverage (2011). Because of the portability and longer life of milk in cans, whether condensed or powdered, the amount of condensed milk produced in the United States grew by nearly five times between 1890 and 1900, and the demand from Europe during World War I kept production climbing. As Valenze notes, the explosion of milk production and the surplus of milk in America happened as early as 1900 and was driven by the reorganization of the Western European and American capitalist economies. The milk-processing industry, threatened by a decrease in demand for canned milk and milk powder in Europe and America during the postwar period, benefited from the global network of food exports expanding to untouched markets. For example, Canadian farms and factories, as part of the British colonial constellation, supplied canned milk to the far ends of the British Empire: Hong Kong, South Africa, and even outposts in China and Japan.

Much like the case of canned milk, the decline in demand and the surplus in the supply of powdered milk in the Western world in the postwar era also contributed to a vigorous expansion of marketing activities and the fast spread of formula milk from Western dairy companies, such as Nestlé, into Asian countries during the 1960s (Sasson 2016). Even recently, in the 2000s, the sale and popularity of pricey formula milk with added DHA, tailored to the Asian market, was not simply a result of scientific breakthroughs in improving babies' cognitive performance, but rather the result of a carefully crafted marketing strategy adopted by giant pharmaceutical companies to expand their presence in the markets of Chinese societies. Since premium milk brands have lost their appeal in the West, pharmaceutical companies are keen to expand into the mainland Chinese, Hong Kong, and Southeast Asian markets, where parents are willing to spend as much as half of their salaries to buy the premium formula, which is promoted as an essential food to nurture the child's brain and physical capacity. These enhanced capacities are believed to be crucial for the child's future success, by enabling the child to become "internationalized" and achieve academic excellence.

Yet, this aggressive expansion by foreign milk companies into the Chinese market could not have been so successful were it not supported by the local governments and broadly aligned with certain elements of Chinese tradition. In China, the rampant increase in milk consumption began in the late 1990s, in tandem with the breakneck development of the dairy industry in Inner Mongolia. Although the dairy farms in China, mostly state-owned, began developing after the series of economic reforms in the late 1970s, the most rapid expansion in China's dairy industry did not happen until the late 1990s, driven by the central government's new economic policy emphasizing continual GDP growth and a fiscal burden-sharing policy. In order to increase local government incomes, a new kind of state–corporate alliance between the local government of the Inner Mongolia Autonomous Region and dairy companies was formed. Following its 2001 entry into the World Trade Organization, China opened its market to foreign milk products, such as inexpensive milk powder from New Zealand. In the face of this new competition, the Chinese government encouraged the consolidation of smaller dairies into ever-larger "dragon head" companies. The two largest of these, Yili and its offshoot and main competitor Mengniu, are both based in a suburb of Hohhot, now known as China's "dairy city." These large companies are well capitalized (including significant state and foreign investment), enjoy both economies of scale and government cooperation, and have captured the majority of China's dairy market. In other words, the rapid change in dietary pattern related to milk products coincided with the industrialization of the dairy industry in Inner Mongolia, which now constitutes an essential part of the bigger state modernization project of developing China into a global economic powerhouse (Fuller 2002; Fuller, Beghin, and Rozelle 2007).

The globalization of food products succeeds through the process of localization, whereby the people in a locality make adaptations to foods introduced from abroad to express their new, modern identities while at the same time reinforcing their local values and social norms. One example of this can be seen in David Wu's ethnography of McDonald's in Taipei (Wu 1997). Through critical engagement and close ethnography, Wu observed that a grandmother would patronize the same McDonald's at the same time each day, not so much for the standardized McDonald's food *per se* as for the physical space, in which she was able to wait for her grandson, and for the social space in which she was able to eat with him. In other words, McDonald's provided a means of maintaining her kinship tie with her son's family, thereby reinforcing local values and social norms.

This book is about the globalization and syncretism of food. Anthropologists, scientists, and food historians have done much to elucidate the relationships between the globalization of food, health, and modernity in China. But too often the efforts of those scholars who have studied milk consumption have shown a tendency to uncritically connect milk consumption with Westernization and changes in individuals' physical growth. According to such scholars' findings, drinking milk in China is one of the ways for the Chinese people to catch up in bodily height and in national strength with the imagined West.[5]

However, the assumption that cow milk is perceived as being "Western and modern" in China is not without empirical and analytical problems. My own ethnographic study of milk in China presents a more complicated and nuanced picture. I find the concept of syncretism particularly helpful in explaining the interaction between indigenous foodways and Western milk in China. The concept of syncretism was once utilized primarily in the study of religious change. Barnett (1953, 49) defines syncretism as a "compromise between the alien's form and the native's. . . . It is a conjunction of differences, producing something new. . . . Syncretisms are deliberate amalgamations or hybridizations." Sheila Cosminsky (1975) has also employed the concept of syncretism to understand the dynamics of the interaction between indigenous and Western medicine in a highland Quiche-speaking community in Guatemala. She found that two new concepts, *alimento* (nutritious food) and *fresco* (fresh or cool), were used to incorporate modern nutritional and medicinal information, but the community's notions of medicine and nutrition were neither wholly traditional nor modern, yet incorporated elements of both. This book will discuss how cow milk can be "Western" in form but "Chinese" in values, as revealed in the promotion of formula as a way of boosting children's cognitive capacity so that they can achieve better academic performance—a moral obligation for children that is based on traditional Chinese values. In other words, milk can be at the same time *Chinese* and "modern."

Based on this understanding, this book looks into how localized Western-style milk and the reinvented traditional milk products are used by the Chinese to perform various social roles while at the same time reinforcing local values and social norms. This book will therefore address the following interrelated questions: What are the (reinvented) "traditional" and "modern" consumption practices, production techniques, and health beliefs associated with different kinds of milk products, such as the fresh water buffalo milk, cheese, and *shuangpi'nai* in Shunde and the milk tea in Hong Kong? What are the historical, socioeconomic, and political conditions facilitating these developments? In China, imported cow milk is consumed not solely because it is rich in protein and calcium according to Western nutritional science, but also because it is classified as being *bu* (nourishing) within traditional Chinese medicine. More significantly, the very act of buying expensive imported formula milk establishes a social boundary between oneself and the "Other" that is unable to afford the same formula.

Milk and Critical Medical Anthropology

The industrialization and global expansion of cow milk would not necessarily have resulted in growth in consumption unless potential customers, and especially mothers, were able to identify a need for milk products or believed that those products could improve their lives. How do mothers choose whether to breastfeed, bottle-feed, or employ some combination of the two? How do mothers make decisions on whether to feed their children continually with dairy products as they grow up?

Infant feeding,[6] a seemingly private choice made by mothers, has now become one of the top concerns of the World Health Organization (WHO) and the United Nations' children's fund, UNICEF. Breastfeeding is advocated as a way of saving societal medical costs by protecting babies from preventable deaths arising from diarrhea and pneumonia. Breastfeeding also reduces mothers' susceptibility to ovarian and breast cancers (WHO 2019a). In many modern societies, mothers' decisions on infant feeding are, to a large extent, driven by their strong desire to build ideal identities as good mothers, capable workers, and decent individuals, by managing the development of healthy and "right" bodies for their children and themselves. Their decisions are also based on a rational calculation of the potential social and health risks and benefits of particular feeding approaches to the children and themselves.[7] The current literature on the choice between breastfeeding and bottle-feeding mostly focuses on the ideology of intensive mothering and its influence on women's decisions regarding breastfeeding. Successful child-rearing is defined as being "child-centered" (Lee 2008) and risk-averse (Furedi 2002). "Good mothers" are "risk managers," solely responsible for meeting their children's needs and for taking measures to minimize potential risks posed to their children by food and feeding-related consumer items (Afflerback et al. 2013; Avishai 2007; Furedi 2002; Hays 1996; Lee 2007, 2008; Murphy 2000; Stearns 2009). One prominent, explicit version of intensive mothering is the attachment parenting philosophy (Eyer 1992; Kukla 2005), which requires physical closeness—facilitated by breastfeeding, baby-wearing, and co-sleeping—said to promote bonding and facilitate immediate maternal responsiveness to the baby's cues. This ideology of intensive mothering may be one of the reasons for the relatively higher breastfeeding rate among more educated white women in the upper socioeconomic levels, who are usually more aware of health information concerning breastfeeding (Andres, Clancy, and Katz 1980; Nutt 1979).

However, the milk craze phenomenon among Chinese parents seems to run opposite to the Western trend of "breast is best," horrifying many public health policy makers. A resurgence of breastfeeding has obviously not occurred in Hong Kong and China. Hong Kong has one of the lowest rates of breastfeeding in the developed world (Callen and Pinelli 2004; Chan et al. 2000; Foo et al. 2005). In 2012, only 2.3 percent of babies in Hong Kong were being breastfed at the age of 6 months, one of the lowest rates worldwide (Government of Hong Kong SAR 2017a). The national exclusive breastfeeding rate in China also dropped dramatically between 2008 and 2013, from 27.6 percent to 20.8 percent. Do these low breastfeeding rates imply that mothers in Hong Kong and the PRC are not fully aware of the benefits of breastfeeding? Is the preference for formula milk because mothers would like to have more personal freedom and to return to work, as claimed by some lactation experts, rather than being attached to their babies (Chan 2018)? More broadly, does this mean that the theories on intensive mothering, which is usually assumed to be linked with breastfeeding or the concepts of health, are not applicable to the Chinese? We must also ask, what is at stake for the mothers themselves? What is being obscured in constructions of the problematic milk craze phenomenon in which Chinese parents are sourcing powdered milk throughout the world? If the task of the cultural anthropologist is to explicate the logic behind seemingly problematic behavior, how can ethnography illuminate something that on the surface might appear to be "crazy"—for example, paying half or more of one's salary to purchase Western-brand formula milk for babies who could just as easily be breastfed for free (Waldmeir 2013)? What is the experiential context in which these parents' zeal makes sense?

With these questions in mind, this is a book not only about the political economy of milk but also about child-rearing and bodily management in the context of a major historical transformation in Hong Kong and mainland China. In her study of dietary illness in America, Charlotte Biltekoff has rightly pointed out that some types of dietary illness, such as "hidden hunger," are invented, capturing the intertwined nutritional and social anxieties during World War II (2013). In Hong Kong and China, the nutritional intake for young children has been getting more and more attention as it is believed to be directly linked to the future competitiveness of those children. Following the 1997 handover in Hong Kong and the series of economic reforms in China, massive social and political changes have been affecting mothers' perceptions of their children's mental and physical development. In Hong Kong, since the transfer of sovereignty from the United Kingdom to the PRC, there has been a growing concern about the loss of competitiveness of Hong Kong as a whole— a situation variously attributed to the change in the language of instruction in schools from English to Chinese, the privatization of education, and the emergence of resource competition with new migrants from mainland China. In China, ever since Deng Xiaoping's Southern Tour in 1992, there has been a shift in emphasis in China's overall economic strategy, from reliance on secondary industries dependent on cheap labor to building tertiary industries dependent upon a knowledge economy (Greenhalgh 2011, 1). Teresa Kuan also aptly pointed out that the practices of child-rearing were (and continue to be) engineered and transformed by the state through the one-child policy, which was viewed by the government as the only solution to a demographic crisis that would have obstructed China's path toward modernization (2015, 7). The "quality education" (*suzhi jiaoyu*) reform movement occupies a significant position in realizing China's post-Mao-era goal of modernization—bringing China to its rightful place among the world's most powerful nations.

Although the *suzhi jiaoyu* reform movement did not take place in Hong Kong, well-educated middle-class parents there also exhaustively seek "scientific" techniques to provide the best nutrition and child-rearing method for their children, with the aim of producing high intelligence and strong bodies. Children in Hong Kong are trained and expected to become smarter, faster in learning, and more creative—the qualities demanded by a knowledge economy, and matching the new blueprint of Hong Kong as a "Smart City" (Government of Hong Kong SAR 2018). Also, in both Hong Kong and China, exam-centric education systems are firmly established. In the past decade, competition to succeed within these systems has started as early as the kindergarten stage and has greatly intensified.

This book is also an attempt to explore food and medicalization. The middle-class mothers I spoke to, who thought that they could not produce enough milk, are usually labeled as suffering from a "lack-of-milk syndrome," hiding the fact that they were under extreme pressure to help their children succeed academically while succeeding at their own jobs. Speaking on the situation in mainland China, Yunxiang Yan has noted that success has become "crucially important for the individual because only a person above persons can have all the power and privileges, which in turn accord the person dignity and social respect" (2013, 271). Although many of the middle-class parents in Hong Kong and China, who consider themselves more open-minded and liberal, no longer agree with the popular saying that "You don't want [your children] to lose at the starting line," they persist in industriously searching for the most appropriate kindergartens and schools for their sons and daughters to ensure that their potential can be fully developed against the backdrop of an increasingly stratified education system and society, and increasing downward pressure on the middle class. As Yupina Ng has reported, "Children in Hong Kong are raised to excel, not to be happy, and experts say that is worrying" (2017). So, what coping strategies are employed by parents in enabling their children to develop their full potential?

Here, formula milk becomes a rational solution to resolve the modern, contradictory expectations placed on mothers, who need not only nurture their babies and young children so that they can develop their full potential academically and physically, but also fulfill the labor market demands of being slim and pretty after returning to work (Shih 2016). The chemical symbols and the Oxford cap appearing on cans of formula milk communicate the health and social benefits of the product while at the same time reminding parents about the potential risks of *not* buying them. For example, on the label of a line of formula milk tailor-made for the Chinese market by the leading global formula milk company Mead Johnson, a large letter "A+" is prominently displayed, which not only represents the brand's trademark but also simultaneously serves as an auspicious sign of future academic excellence—a social and moral obligation for most children in Chinese societies (Tao and Hong 2013). Given the pairing of this auspicious symbol with the brain-shaped, three-dimensional molecular-diagram-like icon and the trademarked name itself—"DHA Brainergy 360," it would be impossible for members of the educated middle class to miss the message that the Omega DHA, ARA, and choline counted among the formula's ingredients can aid the cognitive development of infants and toddlers, especially in relation to four key aspects of growth—intelligence, mobility, emotion, and language. All these elements have been highlighted in TV advertisements for the product and are further elaborated in a well-organized table on the package itself. While the culture of competition was initially promoted by educational institutions—normalizing the need for preschool education—milk companies have found a niche in giving hope to parents that they can help enhance their children's cognitive development, provided that their children take up the daily ritual of milk drinking, ideally after breastfeeding for three months. This supports arguments made by both Foucault and Bourdieu—here the internalization of conduct (Foucault 1977), the way we act, serves as a marker of distinction (Bourdieu 1984).

This book is, thus, an attempt to de-medicalize two types of modern illness related to milk consumption, namely the "lack-of-milk syndrome" affecting mothers and the "picky-eating illness" among children. By adopting a critical medical anthropological approach, I argue that these two illnesses are constructed owing to the particular economic and political landscape in these two societies, reflecting hidden social problems. As Merrill Singer has noted, over the past fifty years, many ecologically oriented medical anthropologists, stemming from an adaptationist paradigm, construct "health and disease . . . [as] measures of the effectiveness with which human groups . . . adapt to their environment" (Lieban 1973, 10). Yet, in his study of the working-class people of nineteenth-century Manchester, Frederick Engels found that the "abusive," problematic, heavy drinking pattern among them was caused by structural factors—the prevailing class relations and the resulting poor living and working conditions, rather than by the quality or quantity of adaptation to those conditions (1958). Similarly, in Singer's own study of the high rates of heavy and problem drinking among Puerto Rican men, he found that these behaviors mostly occurred among unemployed men living in rented apartments in high-density, low-income, inner-city neighborhoods. Consequently, the high levels of alcoholism did not reflect individual illness, but rather the social problem of high rates of unemployment causing a loss of respect, dignity, and validation of their masculine identity. Heavy drinking became a means for the men to forget their problems and overcome boredom (Singer and Baer 1995, 322). As Singer points out, the shortcoming of adaptationism is that this understanding assumes the autonomy, self-regulation, and boundedness of local groups in local settings and fails generally to consider "processes that transcend separable cases" (Wolf 1982, 17), and especially capitalist penetration and the restructuring of labor relationships, knowledge, consumption, lifestyle, and habitat (Singer 1990, 30:180). In this light, the reading of disease rates as measures of environmental fitness can easily fall into the trap of victim blaming—a potential actualized in efforts to shift responsibility for health and illness on to the individual.

In *Milk Craze*, I seek to understand food consumption, illness experience, and structural violence in China in light of the larger political and economic forces that pattern interpersonal relationships, shape social behavior, generate social meanings, and condition collective experience. I will emphasize the importance of political and economic forces, including the exercise of power, in shaping health, illness experience, and health care. However, the mothers in the two societies are not blindly swayed by the narratives created by milk companies. Although the mothers that I knew did feel stressed to fulfill the roles of good mothers and good workers, they also knew and were aware of the cultural materials that they had to work with and the contradictions they were facing. These urban, middle-class mothers in Hong Kong and mainland China are fully aware of the benefits of breastfeeding and are caught in the dilemma of balancing their energy for breastfeeding and work or substituting formula milk. These mothers are also concerned about the premium they paid for the imported formula and are doubtful whether the expensive nutrition-enriched milk can really enhance their children's cognitive development. Through ethnographic study of how Chinese people consume dairy products in their daily lives and the meanings created through milk, I look into how the micro level is embedded into the macro level, as well as how the macro level is the embodiment of the micro level. As such, I root my study of "health-related issues within the context of the class and imperialist relations inherent in the capitalist world system" (Baer 1982, 1).

Ultimately, this book uses milk consumption as a lens to understand the ambivalent moral experience of people in contemporary life. Moral experience, as Arthur Kleinman explained, is: *what is most at stake for actors in a local social world* (2006). In our everyday life, we have something to gain or lose, such as status, money, life chances, health, good fortune, a job, or relationships. This feature of daily life can be regarded as the "moral mode" of experience. Moral experience refers to that register of everyday life and practical engagement that defines what matters most for ordinary men and women (Kleinman 2006). In the context of the food regime, the knowledge production and power of food and pharmaceutical companies, the modernization and internationalization project of state and local governments, and the inequality in the labor market, is there still any room to theorize human agency and moral experience without reducing lived experience to large-scale historical processes? What capacity do actors have to deliberate about and respond to the situation? What is the connection between the macro-level political reality and the micro-experience of the everyday food choices made by ordinary people? This is the understanding that ethnographic study of milk in Hong Kong and China can provide.

Telling the Story of Milk in China

I began this book with the story of the milk craze phenomenon because it represents a key site of contradictory bio-political knowledge and body control in post-Mao and post-colonial Hong Kong societies: the "good mother" fighting globally for a can of Western powdered milk. This opening story is not meant simply to praise or blame the milk companies, modern social institutions, or the government. Instead, it raises serious questions surrounding milk. What I will show is that in order to understand how people create the values attached to foods they consider to be good, we need to weave together the stories of milk production and consumption.

My aim in the first three chapters of this book is therefore to describe the rise in the production and consumption of modern, industrialized cow milk in colonial Hong Kong and modernizing China, as well as to contrast this with the decline in indigenous water buffalo cheese in Shunde. This change in "milkscapes," the metaphorical landscape of milk production, consumption, and its cultural associations, was a result of the interplay between each state's modernization plan and the profit-driven state–corporate alliance.

In chapters four and five, I begin to explore the inter-connections between the body and the hopes of better handling of the modern social, political, and environmental risks people in Hong Kong and Shunde face through milk consumption. In these two chapters, I argue that through their narratives on breastfeeding and formula milk consumption, mothers and fathers from different social classes in southeastern China express their love and perform their ideal roles as workers, parents, and citizens, while stigmatizing the breastfeeding mother as the "uncivilized" Other; and parents with picky-eating, less-attentive, and academically lower-performing children are seen as "losers." The book's conclusion points out the larger implications of this study: the need to rethink the meanings of body, dietary health, and science in post-Mao China and post-colonial Hong Kong.

The Research

My arguments are based on my analysis of data gathered in my ethnographic study of southeastern China, as well as the vast and varied marketing and public health materials that send messages to the public, whether on TV, in newspapers, in books, in social media advertisements, or in the informational brochures distributed in hospitals. To understand how milk-consumption practices and meanings really work in people's daily lives under different political and cultural contexts, we have to shift our focus from the big picture to local situations.

The two cities in which I conducted fieldwork, Shunde and Hong Kong, were chosen in order to understand the influence of the political-geographic differential and vertical social stratification of Chinese society on milk consumption. The first of these sites, Shunde, now part of the Foshan prefecture-level municipality, is located in the center of the Pearl River Delta in southeastern China, bordering Guangzhou to the north and situated close to Hong Kong and Macau to the south. The region is especially interesting because it is home to an indigenous milk tradition of ancient origin: the earliest settlers in Shunde are thought to have been an ethnic group called the *Yue,* who arrived more than two thousand years ago during the Spring and Autumn period (722–479 BCE). A reputable food historian in Daliang, Shunde, has claimed that the use of water buffalo cheese (*niuru*) as an ingredient and consumption of *fankuaiyu* (raw fish with rice) began with the ancient *Yue* people, based on records in the *Chuci,* or "Verses of Chu" (Liao 2009, 7).

Since my first arrival in Jinbang village of Daliang in the summer of 2009 for a preliminary study, I have returned several times. I lived in the village from the autumn of 2010 to the summer of 2011 for a period lasting nine months, and again spent the summers of 2016 and 2017 in the village. In 2011, I lived in a secondary school teacher's quarters located inside the school campus. This was an excellent site at which to conduct my research, and not only because it lies just a fifteen-minute walk from Jinbang village, where the artisanal water buffalo cheese makers are active. The site also offered a food stall, canteen, basketball court, and playground for students, all of which were ideal places for me to interact with the students who purchased and consumed dairy products, including ice cream, and spent time playing and socializing after their classes ended for the day. In addition to participant observation, I conducted focus-group research with over eighty students, interviewed ten teachers, and had numerous informal discussions with teachers, trainers, administrative staff, and other workers at the school.

The second field site for this project is Hong Kong, which operates under a special "one-country, two systems" political model. Under this unique political system, which treats Hong Kong as an independent jurisdiction, citizens enjoy a relatively greater degree of freedom of speech and mobility than their counterparts in mainland China. Hong Kong is located seventy-one miles south of Shunde, a distance that can be covered in about a two-hour drive. Interestingly, although water buffaloes have existed in Hong Kong for over a century, there was no indigenous milk culture in Hong Kong in ancient times, nor was there a group of aristocrats that would appreciate it. While Shunde, well known as the "Silver City of Guangdong," was probably the most prosperous financial center in southeastern China in the late Qing dynasty, Hong Kong was an obscure island inhabited primarily by fishermen, farmers, and stonecutters (Smith 1995). Despite lacking an indigenous tradition, Hong Kong is probably one of the earliest places to have Western dairy cows imported from overseas, as the first dairy cow arrived in Hong Kong from Britain in 1880, brought by John Kennedy, a British veterinary surgeon, less than four decades after Hong Kong came under British rule in 1842.

By comparing Hong Kong and Shunde, two geographically proximate but politically quite distant places, I seek to understand the impact of political factors on dietary change. To be more specific, the book will address the following geopolitical questions: Is there any significant impact of colonial rule on dietary changes? How did the different state policies in Hong Kong and China, such as media control, population policy, and education system, affect how their respective people think about food, health, and their bodies? Are there any differences in the factors affecting mothers' choices on infant-feeding method and how are these related to the different challenges faced by mothers in their daily lives in each jurisdiction?

In order to understand the transformation of traditional water buffalo's milk and the adoption of Western cow milk in the food system in Shunde, I interviewed all six water buffalo cheese makers and two water buffalo farmers in the Jinbang district, eight chefs and three master chefs in Shunde and two chefs in Hong Kong, who produced and trained young apprentices in both Western and Chinese culinary skills. In addition, I included doctors, nutritionists, food historians, culinary teachers, and chefs' association members as part of my ethnographic study, so as to understand how scientific facts are culturally and socially constructed. Altogether, I interviewed about one hundred milk consumers from sixty households and had numerous informal conversations with people who either produced or consumed milk, and who represented diverse socioeconomic backgrounds, in places where my informants gathered regularly, ranging from Chinese teahouses, Western restaurants, children's playgrounds, and traditional wet markets to modern supermarkets. During my fieldwork, I found that my identity as a mother who needed to take care of a one-year-old son gave me numerous advantages in doing fieldwork. For example, many of my informants, who were mothers themselves, were more willing to share their personal feelings and experiences with me because they believed that I could understand them. Many of them also generously offered me health advice on feeding and taking care of my son, who was energetic but skinny.

My aim with this book is to analyze the dynamics of dietary health knowledge creation and the construction of bodily ideals, not to give dietary advice, so I do not expect to change any of my readers' milk consumption habits. However, I do intend to change how people think about what it means to eat and feed right. As the anecdote of the "Baby Hunger Outbreak" petition presented at the opening of this chapter suggests, the people who choose, evaluate, and buy milk products are hoping to do much more than simply achieve better health. They see consuming milk or providing their babies or children with the "right" milk products as a way for them to pursue various social aims, and not just to better the health of themselves or their family members. While it might often seem that shopping and buying milk products represent personal choices relating to our own or our family members' health and wellness, I hope that this work will provide a fruitful starting point for thinking and rethinking food consumption, dietary health, and body management as a social duty, an act of moral judgment, and a form of power that is worthy of critical analysis.

Throughout this work, I have used the case study method and ethnographic observation to gather most of my material, restricting my sample size to a small number in Shunde and Hong Kong so as to get to know individuals and their families more intimately. Because of this qualitative method, I do not intend to generalize my cases to be representative of urban middle-class Chinese families in general. Although I often present examples as being representative, I would like to remind the reader that attending to the particular is theoretically and philosophically important.

1 | Milk, Body, and Social Class in Ancient China

Fresh turtle, and sweet chicken cooked with cheese
Pressed by the men of Ch'u.
And flesh of whelps floating in liver sauce
With salad of minced radishes in brine;
All served with that hot spice of southernwood
The land of Wu supplies.
O Soul come back to choose the meats you love!
    The Great Summons of *Chu Chi* (*The Verses of Chu*)

The study of variations in human consumption of milk and dairy products is often linked with biological arguments on the population-patterned genetic variations that can be tied to differences in historical subsistence patterns (Wiley 2014). Although dairy products were recorded in ancient Chinese texts, such as the *Qimin yaoshu* (533–544 CE) by Jie Sixie, there have been very few studies on milk consumption in ancient China (Sabban 2011; Wiley 2014) and, when mentioned, the practice has been explained as the result of the influence of foreigners living on the margins of China (Bray 1984; Elvin 1982; Sabban 2011; see also Schafer 1977, 105). As sinologist Francoise Sabban has suggested, thirty years ago milk consumption was a topic never considered by sinologists (2011). There was even a basic presumption among scholars that dairy products were considered "distasteful to most Chinese" (see Bray 1984, for instance).

I have opened this chapter with a beautiful song from southern China, *The Great Summons,* written by Qu Yuan (ca. 340–278 BCE), a patriotic poet and minister of the southern state of Chu during the Warring States period (475–221 BCE).[1] As part of his description of the "heavenly" good food on earth, which even the ghosts could not resist returning to the mundane world to enjoy, Qu Yuan wrote, "Cook the fresh tortoise and chicken with Chu cheese."[2] As this ancient song demonstrates, a considerable degree of indigenous Chinese milk production and consumption has existed in southern China since ancient times. This section will address the following questions: How were indigenous Chinese dairy products produced and consumed in ancient times? If nutrition therapy has been practiced in China since ancient times (Anderson 2000), what were the traditional medical beliefs of the ancient Chinese that affected how they consumed milk products? And, what other political, economic, and social forces shaped the indigenous milk culture?

In this chapter, I will explore these questions by, first, discussing the major types of dairy products that existed in ancient China. Second, I will compare and contrast traditional medical systems in ancient China, Greece, and India and how these health beliefs affected their respective milk consumption practices. Third, I will illustrate the rich milk culture in southeastern China through the example of the indigenous water buffalo cheese and milk cuisine in Shunde and analyze the forces that have shaped this milk culture. By the end of this chapter, I hope to demonstrate how the local milk culture of Shunde was affected not only by biological and ecological factors but also by global economic forces, such as the international silk and paper market in the early twentieth century; technological forces, such as changes in agricultural models; and social forces, such as the rise of a Chinese merchant class. These forces have intertwined and interacted, and continue to affect indigenous cheese production and consumption among the upper class in Shunde.

Classification of Milk in Ancient China

Historians Hsingtsung Huang, Edward Hetzel Schafer, and Michael Freeman are among the few scholars who have contributed significantly to the study of milk consumption in ancient China. All three have confirmed that China has a long history of producing and consuming fermented dairy products (Freeman 1977; Huang 2000; Schafer 1977). After poring through the ancient Chinese literature, Huang noted that milk has been used as a medicine since at least the Western Han dynasty (202 BCE–9 CE) and has been listed in all standard pharmacopoeias since the *Mingyi bielu* (Informal records of famous physicians) (Cooper and Sivin 1973, 227–234). In his celebrated work on fermentation and food science in ancient China, Huang provided a useful analysis of the major types of dairy products consumed in northern and central China, which are summarized below (Huang 2002).

Lao

This fermented milk drink was a type of sour milk or yogurt. *Lao* was significant in the diet of the ruling classes in northern China from the Han dynasty until the end of the Yuan (Mongol) dynasty (ca. 202 BCE–1368 CE) (Huang 2000, 250–253). The *Shiming* (Expositor of names) in the early second century CE states that "*lao* is prepared from milk juice; it makes one fat." *Lao* can also be produced in various forms, including *lu lao* (drained *lao*), *gan lao* (dried *lao*), *tian lao* (sweet *lao*) and *suan lao* (sour *lao*).

Su

Similar to butter, *su* can be made from cow, yak, water buffalo, or sheep milk. *Su* made from yak milk was considered the best and most precious, while *su* made from cow milk was perceived to be better than that made from sheep milk. *Su* was widely used in rolls, cakes, and pastries.

Tihu

Schafer noted that *tihu* strongly resembles clarified butter. It is a kind of oil produced by reducing *su* over heat, storing it until it has coagulated and then skimming small quantities of the butter oil from the top (Schafer 1977, 106). *Tihu* was considered tasty and precious and especially good for making cakes. Five kilograms of high-quality *su* could only yield three to four liters of *tihu*.

Rufu (Also Known as Ruping) and Rutuan

Rufu and *rutuan* are two kinds of milk curds listed in the Chinese food literature from the Tang (618–906 CE) and Yuan dynasties (1271–1368 CE), respectively. *Rufu* is curdled with vinegar, while *rutuan* is curdled by naturally forming lactic acid.

Rujiu (Literally, "Wine from Milk")

Also known as *kumiss, rujiu* is wine made from fermented mare's milk.[3] It was such an important food in the Han court that a group of mare milkers was assigned to collect mare's milk and process it into mare's milk wine (Bielenstein 1980, 34). Historian Michael Freeman also noted that in the Song dynasty the emperor had a special office for the production of *kumiss*. Some restaurants even specialized in serving it and it appeared many times in lists of high-end banquet foods. Thus, *kumiss* became "a well-established food in the Sung [Song] diet" (Freeman 1977, 156). Spence also pointed out that milk was one of the items for centralized purchasing for the imperial court during the Qing dynasty. "The Imperial Buttery (*chashanfang*) section of the Imperial Household . . . is a network of offices for meats, tea and milk, pastries, wines, pickles and fresh vegetables" (Spence 1977, 281).

Adoption of Milk and Traditional Concepts of Health

Accompanying each of the dairy product descriptions in the ancient literature are the health benefits of different kinds and prescriptions for their use in curing illnesses. This indicates that dairy products were used as a kind of medicine for remedial purposes rather than as everyday foods.

In Chinese cosmologies all aspects of an individual's lifestyle influence the individual's health status, and ideologies of individual and social health invoke concepts of balance, harmony, and wholeness. According to traditional Chinese medicine, human health is believed to be affected by cosmological or environmental forces, such as yin-yang, the five phases (*wu xing*) that constituted the basis of ancient Chinese thought (Porkert 1974), and the six qi (atmospheric influences, or "energetic configurations"): Wind, Cold, Summer Heat, Dampness, Hot Dryness, and Fire, a notion derived from the five atmospheric influences described in the *Huangdi Neijing* (literally, "The Inner Canon of the Yellow Emperor") (Leung 2009).[4] The six qi were later sometimes also called the "excessive influences" or "external pathogens" (yin). This was treated as a kind of syndrome caused by the imbalance of one's qi, or vital energy. Based on his decades of studies in Chinese societies, medical anthropologist Arthur Kleinman found that ordinary people were well versed in discussing the concept of qi in their everyday lives. Qi must be kept in good health, by harmonious balancing of all inputs to the body, so that a sort of dynamic equilibrium could be maintained—that is, so that the body could meet all of the constant variations and fluctuations of the environment (Kleinman 1976).

Diet, through the notions of hot and cold foods, interacts with climatic influences and individual temperaments to affect health. "Hot" or "cold" qualities (referring not to thermal temperature but rather to perceived intrinsic properties) are ascribed to bodily conditions, foods, and medicines. An individual's proper bodily functioning is maintained through consumption of a diet that has a balance of foods with these various qualities. Illness is perceived to be caused by an imbalance in the hot/cold equilibrium and results in specific reactions, such as headaches, digestive issues, skin eruptions, sore throat, lack of appetite, and infant milk vomiting (for example, see Tan and Wheeler 1983).

Theoretically, then, health is maintained through a conscious and constant balancing of one's bodily base, which demands daily attention to one's food consumption. Equilibrium encompasses a range of states, as individuals have different bases, according to their inherited characteristics, birth circumstances, sex, life stages, and the season. Diet, medicine, medicinal soups, and the environment all influence the bodily equilibrium. The base state of children is categorized as "hotter" and therefore less stable than that of adults, and so they tend to be more susceptible to "hot" illnesses (Tan and Wheeler 1983). Moreover, men usually have "hotter" bases than women and they demonstrate a greater degree of tolerance to changing conditions.

Chinese have a long history of consuming dairy products from a wide variety of mammals for their purported remedial functions. There are clear specifications of how milk from different mammals, including water buffaloes, cows, yaks, sheep, goats, donkeys, horses, dogs, and pigs, can be used to cure illnesses. Based on ancient texts such as the *Compendium of Materia Medica* by Li Shizhen, written during the Ming dynasty, milk was intimately related to health and consumed as medicine.[5] Different kinds of milk needed to be taken at particular times and in particular ways, based on one's medical condition. For example, cow milk was best when drunk warm. This was because, based on traditional Chinese medicine, hot milk was "heating," while cold milk was "cooling" (Li [1578] 2003). For babies, who usually had "hot" bodies, pig milk, which was particularly "cooling," was second only to breast milk in its efficacy. For children who had very "hot" bodies, a mixture of hot donkey milk and pig milk was most effective at cooling (Li [1578] 2003, 24:50). Babies or children who vomited their mother's milk were given boiled cow milk with ginger and spring onions. Goat milk was widely regarded as a salubrious beverage, of especially high value for nurturing the kidneys. For overexhausted and stressed people, goat milk, which was "warm," was the perfect choice, as it could nurture a cold and weak body. It nourished the heart and lungs and quenched thirst, while *bu*-ing ("nourishing") the qi ("wind") of the kidney and small intestine.

Following this traditional Chinese medical principle, dairy products, such as the *lao, su, tihu,* and *rufu* consumed in ancient China, were prized for both their taste and for their essential medical functions. *Su* made from cow milk, for example, was cooling and most suitable for cooling down "hot" bodies, but sheep milk *su* was deemed to have the opposite effect; it was considered warm and suitable for consumption by those who are sick or "cold." In addition, *su* made from cow milk is slightly cooling, for *bu*-ing one's organs, aiding digestion, curing ulcers, treating coughs, and brightening the hair. *Su* could be used as a medical ointment by melting and filtering it slowly. *Su* made from yak milk was highly treasured not only for its taste but also for its "neutral" heat property and its significant medical functions, including its ability to cure rheumatism and relieve the pain of bee stings when turned into an ointment. Last, but not least, *tihu* was used as a powerful tonic for bones and marrow and was considered conducive to a long life (Li [1578] 2003, 50:91–92).

The classification of food and bodily types based on the hot-cold principle is not unique to China. There is a rich body of research that has identified different frameworks based on humoral principles (impacting on food and health ideologies) throughout the world (e.g., Greenwood 1981; Messer 1981; and Tan and Wheeler 1983). The frameworks operating in Europe, the "New World," and the Middle East are believed to be derived from the Galenic system; parallel systems apparently exist in India and the wider South Asia, as well as in Southeast Asia and the Far East beyond

China (Messer 1981). Although the general structural principle may be shared worldwide, there are significant variations in the details and practices of these systems, both within and between cultures (Greenwood 1981; Tan and Wheeler 1983). For example, in the formal Ayurvedic ("science of longevity," the traditional Indian medical system) and Chinese systems, the hot-cold distinction is the major idiom for discussing moral, social, and ritual states, in addition to the specific qualities of foods and medicines (Harbottle 2000). Yet, at the folk level, only discrete elements of these beliefs may be adhered to, and these may be interwoven with other concepts (both traditional and modern) relating to food and health. Similarly, in Morocco, elements of the Galenic humoral system have been integrated with Islamic medicine in present-day pluralist practices, and a wide degree of intra-cultural variation in classifying foods has been demonstrated, according to individuals' personal knowledge and experiences (Greenwood 1981). Moreover, in Japanese popular health beliefs, only remnants of the Chinese hot-cold framework remain, consisting of "airs" of foods, which are thought to cause food poisoning if consumed together (referred to as *kuiase*)—for example, mushrooms and spinach (Lock 1980, 97).

Ancient Chinese medical beliefs and milk classification and consumption patterns bear some resemblance to those in ancient Europe and India, though with some significant differences. In ancient Europe, people believed milk to be blood in a "twice-cooked" state, and blood constituted one of the primary humors in charge of regulating the body (Valenze 2011, 59–60). The dietary rules of the Greek physician Galen of Pergamon (129–216 CE), who had developed the humoral calculus that informed European medicine for centuries, formed the basic structure of how ancient people thought about food. According to Galen, there are four qualities that could be found in various combinations and could be predicated of other substances, such as foods or human bodies. These four qualities, *blood* (hot and moist), *phlegm* (cold and moist), *choler* (hot and dry), and *melancholy* (cold and dry), appeared in different proportions in each person. Galen's theory went further, arguing that human beings and food could be distinguished from each other by their "complexions." For example, a man could be hot and dry or moist and cold. Barley soup is categorized as a cold and moist food, while ripe strawberries are cold and dry (Davidson 1999; Grant 2000).

Similar to the hot-cold classification of milk in China, in Galen's typology, milk is categorized as "cold," as its heat was believed to be extracted during the production process. To what extent those cold and moist properties could yield nutrition depended on the person consuming the food. However, unlike the Chinese belief system, in which cold foods can harmonize the hot body, according to Galen's theory, cold foods were used to balance cold bodies, especially those of the very young and the very old, who were by nature colder than people in the prime of life, and thus, for the young and old, milk proved especially nutritious. It harmonized with their already cool systems and contributed to the building of flesh and blood. But for those consuming it in midlife, the viscous liquid would most likely spoil in the process of digestion, sending putrid fumes upward to the brain and chalky deposits downward to the kidneys, where it would create blockages. Milk was most dangerous in cases where the person consuming it was ill: the weak and sickly, those who were melancholy, and those with headaches or pain were warned to stay away from it (Valenze 2011).

In India, similar to China and Greece, cow milk is also believed to be "cold." Rooted in the humoral medical traditions that are dominant in Asia, Ayurveda affects how people in South Asia think of milk and their bodies. In Ayurveda, the body is conceived of as having three semi-fluid *dosa*s (from *dosha*s; literally "faults") or humors: *vata* (wind), found mainly in the large intestine and involved in respiration; *pitta* (bile), located around the navel and involved in digestion; and *kapha* (phlegm), which is localized to the chest and involved in structural integration (Fields 2001; Meulenbeld and Wujastyk 1987). Individuals vary in terms of which *dosa*s predominate in their bodies, and the relative power of each *dosa* determines their "hotness" or "coolness." Furthermore, the relationship among the *dosa*s has a profound influence on an individual's health. If *dosa*s are out of place, or in too large or small quantities, an individual will become irritated (Wiley 2014).

According to the *Charaka Samhita*, the earliest foundational text of Ayurveda, cow milk is the best of all milks, while sheep milk is the least desirable. In the text, cow milk is described as "sweet, cold, soft, unctuous, viscous, smooth, slimy, heavy, dull and clear." It is wholesome, rejuvenating, and strength promoting. It promotes intellect, longevity, and virility. Cow milk can also be used medicinally as *rasayana* (Ayurvedic medicine) for healing and remedial purposes (Wiley 2014, 100). However, cold milk (*dhara sita*) aggravates all three *dosa*s and so should be taken warm (Guha 2006). Buffalo milk is considered heavier, sweeter, and more cooling than cow milk. Moreover, because of its high fat content, buffalo milk impedes digestion and the flow of energy through the body's channels and is thus recommended for those with "excess digestive power." In India, cow milk is clearly more highly valued in relation to the Ayurvedic humoral conceptualization of the body, as a more easily digestible form of milk, especially for children (Wiley 2014).

To summarize, dairy products have been consumed in geographically disparate ancient societies, but with different practices based on disparate medical systems. The consumption of milk in China, similar to the milk cultures native to Europe and India, can be traced back to ancient times. Coincidently, in ancient Greece, India, and China, milk was categorized as a medicinal food rather than as a beverage or daily food. In these three ancient societies, cow milk was categorized as a kind of "cold" food. In both ancient India and China, cow milk was to be consumed warm and was considered suitable for both young children and the sick. However, in ancient Greece, based on Galen's humoral system, "cold" cow milk was considered suitable for the "cold" children but not suitable for sick persons owing to their "hot" bodies.

If milk products have been produced and consumed since ancient times in China, what culinary techniques could make different kinds of milk into dairy products suitable for consumption by the lactase-insufficient peoples of southeastern China and able to be enjoyed for their taste and health benefits? In the next section, I will turn the anthropological lens to Shunde and discuss how the unique water buffalo milk cheese and cuisines developed. As there are hardly any related written records, I endeavor to give a record of the practice based on the oral histories of people from Shunde, including the cheese makers in Jinbang village and chefs from Daliang.[6]

Water Buffalo Milk Culture in Shunde

People in Shunde are well known for their advanced culinary skill in making fresh, light, refined, and highly crafted food in general and water buffalo milk products, like cheese, *shuangpi'nai*, and stir-fried and deep-fried water buffalo milk in particular. In this section, I shall first introduce the most popular indigenous water buffalo dairy products in southeastern China, including cheese and double-steamed milk pudding. Then, I shall explain how the production of these local indigenous water buffalo dairy products was driven by the Western markets for paper and silk and how they were re-invented as social markers of distinction under Mongolian rule.

Niuru

Niuru (literally, "cow milk") is a kind of cheese made from the indigenous water buffalo's milk. The snowy-white, round water buffalo cheese of Shunde is sold in the form of thin slices. Crispy and fragrant, *niuru* is usually packed in piles and bottled in salted water. It is probably the most ancient water buffalo dairy product in Shunde and is believed to have been consumed since the Ming dynasty.[7]

The high fat content of water buffalo milk has made it an ideal ingredient with which to produce good cheese and butter in southeastern China and in many other parts of the world. One renowned example is the pale ivory-colored, decadently creamy and flavorful water buffalo mozzarella (*mozzarella di bufala*) of Italy. Another example is the ghee (butterfat) of India, which is used in cooking. Both are traditionally made from river buffalo milk. In contrast, the water buffalo cheese of Shunde is made from swamp buffalo milk, the other subspecies of the domesticated water buffalo (*Bubalus bubalis*). Swamp buffaloes resemble wild water buffaloes and are used primarily as draft animals in rice paddies in China, Japan, and Southeast Asia.[8] The use of milk from the swamp buffalo is rare because of the low yield of milk from the subspecies, compared with that from cows and river buffalo.

In premodern Shunde, water buffalo cheese used to be consumed as a kind of medicine for nourishing and "cooling" the "hot" body. It was also regarded as a *bupin* ("nourishing product") consumed by wealthy people. This tradition continues even today, as water buffalo cheese is typically added to plain rice congee to produce a highly nutritious and easily digestible food for the elderly, babies, and young children. However, since the late twentieth century, *niuru* has become a highly affordable everyday food and it is both widely served in Chinese teahouses to accompany rice congee and promoted as a condiment for soup and cooking. Despite the labor-intensive production process, the price of the water buffalo cheese has held constant at 17 RMB per bottle during the past 20 years.

Silk Merchants and Water Buffalo Cheese

Why is there a tradition of buffalo milk consumption in Shunde that is not found in Hong Kong or other parts of southeastern China where water buffaloes are also raised? In the discussion of artisanal cheeses in the New World (Paxson 2010) or the Alpine cheese produced in northern Italy (Grasseni 2011), anthropologists emphasize the importance of *terroir,* the taste of place, which reveals a range of values—agrarian, environmental, social, and gastronomic. To study the *terroir* of water buffalo cheese in Shunde, I conducted an ethnographic study in the two places in Shunde where the earliest cheese is believed to have been made: Longjiang and Bijiang. Although the village/town of Daliang in Shunde is the most famous place for buffalo cheese (*niuru*) and milk cuisines today, Longjiang and Bijiang are the two places celebrated by most people as having the longest history of producing and consuming buffalo *niuru*.

Longjiang, which is on the northwestern side of Shunde, produced the highest quantity of *niuru* in the Qing dynasty (*Shunde Longjiang Gazette* 1967). Ecologically speaking, the geographical environment and ancient practices of agriculture of Longjiang provided a favorable habitat for water buffalo husbandry and the production of water buffalo milk. Longjiang, like many other places in Shunde, used to be crisscrossed with rivers and canals. In order to protect the fields from flooding during the wet seasons and to conserve water for dry seasons, the people in Longjiang started to build up layers of soil to form high and narrow earth dikes around the poldered fields (*weitian,* "encircled fields") starting from the Tang dynasty (Zhong 1982).[9] Individual farmers dug tanks where they grew lotuses and water chestnuts and raised fish and turtles. Sometime in the sixteenth century, people in Shunde and other parts of the Pearl River Delta began to grow mulberry and tea trees on the banks of the fish ponds to increase their incomes and to strengthen the banks. Even with heavy rain, the tanks would not overflow and harm the crops in the rice plots between the banks. This mulberry-grove-and-fish-pond model is highly productive both from economic and environmental perspectives—the silkworms and their waste formed part of the food for the pond fish, while the wastes from the fish served as natural fertilizers for the mulberries (Li and Min 1999). Before the modernization and urbanization of Shunde, nearly every family had at least one pair of water buffaloes. Water buffaloes enjoyed immersing themselves in the tanks, being tethered in the shade of the trees on the bank for hours, especially during the burning-hot summer. This relaxing daily routine for the water buffaloes, together with the abundant supply of clean grass as feed, are believed to be the two cardinal reasons why the water buffalo milk in Shunde is particular white and superior in quality (Qian, Huang, and Ma 2011).

The popularity of cheese consumption in Longjiang would not have been possible solely due to the availability of water buffalo milk; it also relied on the emergence of a rich, leisure class of fastidious eaters. Following Bourdieu (1984, 185), the consumption of cheese, a kind of eating habit, should be understood as part of the whole lifestyle of the upper social classes, who had the cultural and economic capital to develop, produce, and appreciate the taste of cheese. Since the Song dynasty, people in Longjiang and the nearby Longshan were so proud of their wealth generated from the silk industry and their cuisine that they "only identified themselves as Longjiang people or Longshan people and not as people from Shunde" (Su 2005). The prized silk from Longjiang was collected by the imperial court from the Ming dynasty to the Qing dynasty (*Shunde Longjiang Gazette* 1967). The rapid growth of the silk business in Shunde was driven by global, and especially British, demand for the silk traded through Macau (Li 1981). Longjiang's leading position in silk production was further signified by the invention of the silk production machine in Longjiang—the first of its kind in China—during the Qing dynasty.

Bijiang was another place in Shunde whose people were well known for their passion for the indigenous water buffalo cheese. Bijiang, one of the earliest settlements in Shunde, was formerly known as Baijiao, which literally means "hundreds of rivers." This can be understood by considering the text of a well-cited poem—"*Bijiang ershisi yong*" (Twenty-four chants on Bijiang)—written by Su He, a renowned scholar in the Qing dynasty. This poem is important for the study of the history of Shunde and is relevant to our discussion not only because it captures the social life of the people of Bijiang (Su 2005), but also because it describes the practices of buffalo cheese consumption during the period 1821 to 1850, as quoted below:

> Tea, tangerines, with no wine
> Accompanied with a piece of just-baked cake,
> which is being sold only in the town.
> Palatable is the home-made buffalo cheese,
> Yet, it is not as good as the famous *su*
> from the far side of the border.

Su 2005, 108–109, my translation

Su's picturesque poem is significant for our study of milk in China for two reasons. First, it shows clearly that water buffalo cheese was popular among the aristocrats in Bijiang. Second, it demonstrates that the Chinese milk culture was supported by a leisure class who, as reflected in the poem, had been influenced by the dietary culture of the Manchurian court during the Qing dynasty. Bijiang, even to this day, is known for its great number of wealthy merchants and powerful government officers with conspicuous lifestyles. Beginning during the Qing dynasty, Bijiang also became renowned for paper making. The abundant supply of river water supported key aspects of the paper-production process, including the soaking of fibers and draining. In addition to manufacturing and trading paper, Bijiang people produced pricey dried fruits, typically lychees and longan, which were served at formal banquets.[10] After becoming wealthy, people in Bijiang were eager to increase their political power and influence through securing official positions. There were over a hundred men who excelled in the government examinations and became officers. They led luxurious lives, built houses decorated with gold plates, and carried out conspicuous wedding ceremonies (Su 2005).

In explaining the culture of gastronomy, historian Michael Freeman gained his insights from the study of Chinese food in the Song dynasty. He argued that there were three factors at work in producing a "high" cuisine. First, there was a sufficiently diverse set of regional ingredients to allow cooks to experiment and create a broad range of possible menus. Next, the rise of a middle class yielded a large body of critical eaters beyond the ritual-bound environs of the royal court. Finally, the Chinese people held cultural attitudes emphasizing genuine pleasure in consuming tasty food (Freeman 1977, 165–166). My study in Longjiang and Bijiang provided ethnographic findings to support the theory that three factors—ecological, social, and cultural forces—are at work in shaping the indigenous Chinese milk culture in Shunde.

However, although Longjiang and Bijiang were known for their buffalo cheese culture in historical records, none of my informants in Shunde associated these places with *niuru*. Instead, Daliang *niuru* today is regarded as the most "authentic" and "traditional." Like Longjiang and Bijiang, Daliang was once also located in a floodplain area, crisscrossed with rivers and canals, growing mulberry trees on its dikes, and developing sericulture, firstly in Lumen district starting from the Ming dynasty. The silk industry in Daliang expanded between 1573 and 1619 due to the site's proximity to Guangzhou, the only international port in China at that time. This location provided a competitive advantage for Daliang's development into the "City of Silk in the South" and gave rise to a class of nouveau riche residents who displayed their wealth and built their social networks through hosting lavish banquets, which typically included water buffalo cuisine. Jinbang village in Daliang, the now well-known cradle of the authentic water buffalo cheese, will be the focus of the next section.

Artisanal Cheese Makers in Jinbang Village

Geographically, the village of Jinbang is located in the northern part of Daliang town. Little was known by my informants about the origin of Jinbang village, where most artisanal water buffalo cheese makers gather. The residents of the village only know that the early settlers came from different parts of China, as there were once thirty different surnames across sixty households. The villagers in Jinbang village used to live among fishponds and rivers, and water buffaloes could be seen everywhere, particularly in the area northwest of the current village, covering the area of what is now the campus of Liang Qiuju Vocational Technical School and the Foshan TV station building. Almost everyone used to travel by boat every day and the people in Jinbang district always won the dragon-boat racing competition.

Economically, the relatively low income and harsh rural life of most of the people in Jinbang contrasted sharply with the fortunes of the silk and silver merchants in the city of Daliang, the richest city in Guangdong Province during the late Qing dynasty. The hard lives of the people in Jinbang village are reflected in a popular verse of the time:

> If you have a daughter, do not let her marry into Jinbang village.
> Otherwise, her pair of sandals will be covered with cow dung and urine.
> If you have a pig and a cow, you will be tied up all your life;
> If you do not have any, you can be as free as the wind.
>   Author unknown, my translation[11]

Given this historical and geographical sketch of Jinbang village, it would be hard for one to imagine the extent of the changes that have taken place since the land reform of Daliang in 1984. Instead of fishponds and rivers everywhere, Jinbang today is a village within a modern city. It is located along a quiet street called Jinbang Shangjie, which lies between two busy, modern main roads—Fengshan Zhonglu and Jianhai Beilu in the northwestern part of Daliang. Villagers can also easily reach the city center by a fifteen-minute stroll. Today, the village of Jinbang consists of around fifty households, mainly comprising individuals from four clans bearing the surnames Li, Liang, Zhao, and Chen. Staying in a teacher's hostel in the north of the village during my fieldwork, I usually passed a small food market in the village in the course of my daily routine, walking along Timing Road, where the local government offices and community center are situated. Taking a right turn, I would enter a narrow alley filled with the sounds of Cantonese opera music. Most of the houses were two stories tall and made of red or green bricks. The front doors of most houses were open all day, with grandparents feeding their grandchildren at the doorway. The rich aroma of buffalo cheese hung in the air around Jinbang Shangjie, leading the way to the workshops of the cheese makers. There were a few retail shops, including two hair salons, a secondhand metal and leather shop, and three buffalo milk and cheese shops. Twenty years ago, there were more than twenty households making and selling water buffalo cheese and milk. At the time of my research, only six remained.

It is a tradition for the Jinbang village cheese makers to live near their workshops. For example, Auntie Lin's house, with a private well at the entrance, is situated to the right of her small, dim, and simply equipped workshop, where she works from 4:00 to 9:30 a.m. each day.[12] Similar to most buildings in the village, Lin's house is two stories tall, and she lives with her second son, daughter-in-law, and granddaughter. Born in the 1930s, she has been making cheese since she was sixteen. She was recommended by the local residents and cheese makers as the most senior water buffalo cheese maker. Most in the village respect her authority as the spokesperson on the history of Jinbang *niuru*.

Although many of the artisanal cheese makers spend most of their time at their small workshops with almost no electronic appliances, they are well connected to the global modern world. Lin is illiterate, but she is well aware of the deteriorating global environmental conditions and local food safety problems, mainly through her giant 48-inch TV, which she watches regularly. "Nowadays, the water in Daliang is polluted. The water from our well can only be used for washing, as it contains too many chemicals," Lin told me. To deal with this water pollution, Lin's son, a driver by trade, bought a water purifying machine, which cost over 3,000 RMB, close to one month of his salary. Between the water purifier and the giant TV stands a microwave oven. Every night before going to bed, Lin uses the microwave to heat a glass of buffalo milk for her granddaughter, to kill any germs. Another important step to safeguard against the city's pollution is sterilization of the family's eating utensils. Every night before dinner, all of the bowls and dishes are sterilized before use. Less well-off families use microwaves instead of utensil sterilizers.

In an interesting article titled "Cheese Makers Are Always Women," Carol Morris and Nick Evans point out that the stereotype of cheese makers in the United Kingdom as female was caused by hegemonic masculinity and the emphasis on women's femininity perpetuated in farmers' lives and through farming-related media (Morris and Evans 2001). Similarly, in Jinbang village, all of the water buffalo cheese makers are women who learned the techniques of cheese making from their mothers. The villagers, and especially the women, believe that cheese making is a domestic and inferior job. That is to say, even the cheese makers believe that cheese making is a job for those without "culture" and knowledge, and tend to look down upon men who take it up.

The cheese-making workshops have been built right next to the homes of the cheese makers, supporting their multiple roles in the family—as nurturer, mother, wife, helpmate, and homemaker. The setup of the workshop and the preparation procedures are strikingly similar among the six cheese makers, though they are from different families. Besides the core ingredients— buffalo milk and vinegar—the pieces of equipment that the cheese makers use are simple, comprising two coal stoves, a steel pot, a clay casserole, three small porcelain cups of different sizes, a wooden mold, and salt water.

Even though all of the cheese makers follow the same simple steps and procedures, their products differ in quantity and quality. Lin told me that the most difficult part is handling the temperature of the milk and vinegar. She usually puts a steel pot containing buffalo milk on a coal stove on her left-hand side to heat it to a temperature of 30–40 degrees Celsius. She keeps a casserole with vinegar on another coal stove in front of her. Coal is used not only for economic reasons but also for its ability to easily maintain very low heat. Lin uses a medium-sized cup to get some milk from the steel container and some heated vinegar and combines the two ingredients in a bigger porcelain bowl around 2 inches in diameter. Then, she swings the porcelain bowl and gets some heated vinegar, which she puts into a thin, small china bowl. With her left hand holding the bowl and two fingers touching the milk mixed with the vinegar, Lin swings the solution in a clockwise direction using her index finger, middle finger, and ring finger to mix it. Then, she uses her thumb to test whether the milk has started to curdle. Once the solution is well mixed and has reached the correct temperature, the milk curds nearly instantaneously. There are three different sizes of cups for measuring the milk, resulting in three different sizes of buffalo cheese: small, medium, and large. Usually, the cheese sold in bottles is of medium size. The large size is available only by special request. The smallest size is for those who intend to buy one hundred pieces as a gift.

Another important step that one needs to pay special attention to is the technical skill in water extraction during the cheese-molding process. Each piece of buffalo cheese is individually made by hand. First, with her left hand, the cheese maker holds the wooden mold embossed with the words "Jinbang *niuru.*" She then pours the solution into the mold, uses her right index finger to spread it out, and then uses her left palm to press the milk curds. The water is immediately extracted, with a "squeezing" sound, producing a thin layer of buffalo cheese. With one quick movement, this little piece of white and semi-transparent buffalo cheese is taken out of the mold and thrown into a big pool of salt water in a porcelain container. The piece of cheese, which resembles a snowy-white flower, floats on the salted water. Lastly, the cheese maker will pack the cheese in piles of ten pieces to let them dry completely before bottling.

The step of extracting the water before the shaping of the buffalo milk curd is essential. If the extra water is not squeezed out well, the shape of the cheese will be distorted and the cheese can break easily. In the past, as buffalo milk was precious, expensive, and considered to be good for health, the whey was collected and vinegar was kept. The cheese maker would boil the mixture slowly. After some water had evaporated, a layer of luscious oily cream was formed on top, similar to how *su* was made in the past. The people used to treat the cheese produced this way as a kind of delicacy to accompany rice. Today, most cheese makers would instead simply throw this mixture away. They said that they could no longer afford the time needed for the filtering and cooking. Furthermore, there is no lack of nutritious food available in present-day China.[13]

Dunnai, Shuangpi'nai, **and** *Jiangzhuangnai*

In addition to water buffalo cheese, the people in Shunde have long consumed double-steamed water buffalo milk in the wintertime as a kind of *dunpin* (double-steamed delicacy) for boosting health. As alluded to above, people in China are well known for consuming foods as medicine (Anderson 2005; Chen 2009). Foods range in their classification from being fully *bu* to simply being normal foods for sustaining the body, but eating *bu* is not always considered a good thing because nourishing foods can be too "hot" for those with "hot" bodies. One solution in making this protein-rich food ingredient *bu er buzao* (reducing its internal heat while preserving its nutritious value and positive energy) is to double-steam it.

Double-steamed water buffalo milk pudding (*dunnai*) is believed to be particularly good both for rejuvenating the body and for smoothing the skin. *Dunnai* has been prepared in the home in Daliang for generations. Other popular recipes for *dunnai* in Daliang include double-boiled steamed buffalo milk with egg and double-boiled milk with chicken. Moreover, steaming is particularly popular throughout Shunde cuisine as a whole. It is considered to be healthier than frying and able to preserve the real taste of the food. In Jinbang village, steamed water buffalo milk is a popular dish for dinners in the home. Double-steamed water buffalo milk pudding was further developed in the 1930s into *shuangpi'nai* (literally, "double-skinned milk") by milk merchants, originally for preservation purposes. Mr. Liu, a food historian, explained to me how a bowl of "authentic" *shuangpi'nai* used to be made:

> After the water buffalo milk is double-steamed in a porcelain rice bowl, a layer of skin is formed on top of the milk, which sticks to the edge of the bowl. A small pinhole is then made and the milk underneath the skin is drained out, allowing the skin to sink to the bottom of the container. Egg whites and sugar are then added to the milk and the mixture is double-boiled for twenty minutes. The resulting thick liquid is then injected back through the tiny hole in the skin, so that the skin floats up. A second layer of milk skin then forms beneath the first layer. The most difficult part to master in the whole process is to ensure that the first layer of milk skin does not detach from the bowl. With the silky milk skin on top, the milk pudding underneath becomes smooth and tasty.

Another indigenous Shunde buffalo milk product is *jiangzhuangnai* (milk pudding with ginger juice), which used to be consumed for its medicinal benefits. People in Shunde prepare this product by adding ginger juice and warm water buffalo milk, which will coagulate into a smooth curd almost instantaneously. Ginger has been used in China and India for over four thousand years for its antioxidant, anti-inflammatory, antiemetic, and gastro-protective effects (Biniaz 2013). Milk pudding with ginger juice was also formerly used as a cure for colds and flu, although it is now usually considered a kind of dessert in modern Chinese societies.

Milk, Health, and Social Distinction

The introduction of dairying—the domestication of animals for milk— in northern Europe has been regarded by many anthropologists and historians as a critical step in early agriculture, with dairy products being rapidly adopted as a major component of the diets of prehistoric farmers and pottery-using late hunter-gatherers (Copley et al. 2005; Craig et al. 2011; Evershed et al. 2008). The processing of milk, particularly the production of cheese, would have been a critical development because it not only allowed the preservation of dairy products in a nonperishable and transportable form but also made milk a more easily digestible commodity for early prehistoric farmers (Burger et al. 2007; Itan et al. 2009; McCracken 1971).

By a similar logic, this chapter therefore addresses one of the core questions: Why is there an indigenous cheese culture in Shunde but not other parts of southeastern China? My ethnographic study of Shunde demonstrates that the milk culture in China is supported by the most fundamental ecological factors. In his widely read book on Chinese foodways, *Food in China*, K. C. Chang remarked that "Chinese food is above all characterized by an assemblage of plants and animals that grew prosperously in the Chinese land for a long time" (Chang 1977, 6). As discussed above, great varieties of milk from domesticated mammals, including water buffaloes, horses, cattle, and yaks, have been consumed by Chinese in various parts of China from as early as the Shang and Zhou dynasties. My ethnographic study in Shunde further supports the importance of ecological factors in shaping the food culture of a place.

Yet, the story of the factors supporting a milk culture in China does not end here.

The popularity of water buffalo husbandry and the high availability of water buffalo milk is a basic but not sufficient condition to support the development of a cheese culture, because people in other places in the Pearl River Delta, including Hong Kong and Panyu, did not develop such a cheese culture. Yet, the people of Shunde have a long history of consuming water buffalo cheese and milk products for health, taste, and status reasons. The cases of Longjiang and Bijiang discussed above illustrate that the cheese culture has to be supported by a second, more crucial sociocultural, factor. In the Chinese context, a leisure class with the cultural capital to appreciate cheese was essential in making the milk delicacy a social marker of class distinction. We learn from ancient poems, agricultural treatises, and historical provincial records that buffalo milk products were regarded as local delicacies and essential marketable products consumed by members of the royal family, upper class, scholars, and gastronomes. This kind of conspicuous consumption, as first observed by Thorstein Veblen ([1899] 1994), is both social and private. At the social level, Veblen developed an evolutionary framework in which preferences are determined socially in relation to the positions of individuals in the social hierarchy, with the lower classes emulating the consumption patterns of those at higher points in the hierarchy. The social norms that govern such emulation change as the economy and its social fabric evolve over time. Privately, individuals of all social classes achieve status not only in the eyes of others but also in their own eyes, and this is reinforced by leading a desired lifestyle marking one's identity (Veblen [1899] 1994, 1:103).

Third, the case of milk culture in ancient China also demonstrates the importance of health beliefs and the indigenous humoral classification of milk in shaping its consumption. This linkage is, of course, not unique to China, as I have discussed similar systems originating in ancient Greece and India. As mentioned previously, milk occupies a unique position in traditional Chinese medical history. The recipes for preparing milk and dairy products in ancient China were intimately related to health beliefs that were built upon a distinctive yin-yang principle, which affected how dairy products were consumed. The yin buffalo milk consumed for cooling hot bodies and the yang sheep milk consumed by the weak are but two examples. *Niuru,* which was recorded in ancient medical texts, used to be taken for its medicinal functions, while *shuangpi'nai* and *jiangzhuangnai* used to be consumed as *bupin* during the wintertime to help smooth the skin and boost overall health.

Today, most anthropologists would agree that the dietary practices of a place are shaped not only by biological and environmental factors but also by historical, political, social, and cultural factors (see, for example, Levenstein 2003; Oxfeld 2017; Striffler 2005; Wiley 2014). My case study of Shunde provides ethnographic details on how these forces are at work in shaping the neglected milk culture in China. However, since the period of capitalist economic reforms, these medicinal and health-nourishing foods have been promoted as "snacks" for everyday consumption. In the upcoming chapters, I shall illustrate how the indigenous water buffalo milk products are being replaced by Western cow milk as the new markers of social distinction in the context of the globalizing economy and a modernizing state.

2 | Dairy Farm, British Milk Tea, and Soy Milk in Milk Bottles

O n the white-tiled wall of Ying Fat, a local tea café located on a busy street in Hong Kong's Kwun Tong district—one of the liveliest mixed industrial/residential zones in the city during the 1950s—is posted an art-nouveau-styled restaurant menu. The menu, which has been kept intact for the past five decades, depicts more than a hundred dishes and beverages offered by this local tea café. Underlying the menu are numbers reflecting accepted truths about the relationships between the individual food ingredients, their taste, their nutritional value, and their effects on health: that food is prepared with different ingredients that deliver a good or bad, an "authentic" or "artificial" taste; that each food comprises various nutrients needed by the body, delivers calories that provide energy; that each food also contains certain vitamins that are essential for disease prevention and for enhancing our bodies' health. However, these tenets about food, taste, and nutrition are only part of what lies behind this half-century-old menu.

One of the most interesting phenomena of the menu is that milk, a food item that rarely appeared on the breakfast tables of Hong Kong Chinese in the 1960s, appears in a significant number of the items on offer. Fluid milk, for example, appears in three forms at different price points, namely Dairy Farm–brand fresh milk, the most expensive variety; fresh milk in the middle; and the cheapest, so-called milk water.

The most premium variety of "milk" is the *da gongsi xian niunai* (literally, "fresh milk from the big company"), the glass-bottled fresh milk from

Dairy Farm—the first dairy farm established in Hong Kong in 1886. Drinks made with this type of milk are usually two to three Hong Kong dollars more expensive than those made with the second type—fresh milk from other brands. To assure the customer that the milk is authentic, fresh milk from Dairy Farm, the waiter will bring a sealed bottle of the refreshing, chilled milk to the customer's table and open a small hole in the bottle lid at the table so that the customer can drink the milk with a plastic straw.

The second type of fresh milk used is called "fresh cow milk." This looks similar to the Dairy Farm–brand fresh milk, except that it is not produced by the Dairy Farm company and is usually served in an ordinary drinking glass. Most of the "fresh cow milk" is made from milk packed in shelf-stable Tetra Brik Aseptic packages, which do not need refrigeration. As such, fresh cow milk is perceived by customers as being not as "fresh" and as wholesome as bottled "fresh milk," and thus it sells for a lower price.

The third type of Western-style cow milk available is *naishui* ("milk water"). In Chinese, the term *naishui* usually denotes breast milk. In local tea cafés, however, "*naishui*" is made by mixing water with sweetened condensed milk or unsweetened evaporated milk. Milky drinks made with evaporated milk were highly recommended by pediatricians as a food for infants from the 1930s to the 1940s (Radbill 1981). Similarly, from the 1940s to the 1960s, milky drinks made from evaporated or condensed milk were promoted as a substitute for breast milk throughout Asia. This is probably the reason that milky drinks are now referred to as *naishui*. In addition to fluid "milk," there are a number of "milk" drinks made from ingredients that may or may not include cow milk. For example, the fourth category of milk products is milk powder drinks, such as milk drinks made from Horlicks milk powder, chocolate milk powder, and almond milk powder, which include food ingredients like malt, cocoa, and almonds in addition to cow milk powder.

The hierarchy of milk products based on price range at a local tea café dating to the time of colonial Hong Kong not only illuminates the diversified types of milk in a Chinese society, but also expresses a number of beliefs about the values of food, science, health, and social order. Understanding the values of different types of milk products and the associated health beliefs requires that we investigate not only the evolution of nutrition and cultural knowledge but also the ongoing relationship between nutritional facts, taste experiences, and their moral implications.

My concern is not whether milk companies succeeded or failed in changing people's diets or health. Instead, I aim to investigate the cultural politics of food consumption, dietary health, and social change. Specifically, how did the foodscapes of Hong Kong, which previously had no tradition of indigenous milk production, change under British colonial rule beginning in 1841? What were the different health values and tastes associated with different categories of milk and soy milk? How did these values and meanings reflect the social and political conditions of Hong Kong under British colonial rule? The story of how Western dairy farms were first introduced into China is critical to understanding the cultural meaning and value of milk, as well as soy milk products. It concerns the formation of a social dynamic of dietary change and health that has since become part of our commonsense understanding of the world, obscuring the taken-for-granted notions of what dietary ideals are and what functions they serve. The entrepreneurs at companies like Dairy Farm and Vitasoy took special care to articulate the moral valences of milk or soy milk consumption and overtly embraced milk and dietary health lessons as a way of inculcating social values related to particular ideals of good bodies, good citizenship, and a strong nation. I explore each of these facets in turn, illuminating the politics of food consumption and dietary health, and lay a foundation for seeing subsequent milk-consumption practices, milk ratings and ranking, and discourses on milk products through a new lens.

The Science of Nutrition and the Colonial Dairy Farm

The globalization of Western cow milk started in the late nineteenth century and was closely associated with the expansion of European populations overseas and the emergence of nutrition science. Hong Kong is perhaps the first place in China where a Western dairy farm was established. During the late nineteenth century, Hong Kong was a small fishing village in southeastern China described by British Plenipotentiary Charles Elliot as "the chief basis of our [their] operation in China, Militarily, Commercially and Politically" (Tsang 2004, 17).[1] Surprisingly, although Hong Kong is only seventy miles south of Shunde—the hometown of Chinese water buffalo cheese prior to the arrival of the British colonists—there was no indigenous milk culture in Hong Kong. People in Hong Kong rarely drank water buffalo milk, nor had they developed the skill or taste for producing and consuming water buffalo cheese. Dairy cows had been transported to Hong Kong by 1847. This was just a few years after Hong Kong had been militarily annexed by the British in 1842 for its increasingly strategic location owing to the opium trade, which formed half of all British–Chinese trade (Liu 2009, 20–23; Tsang 2004, 17–18). Yet, during the demographic expansion of Europeans into the tropics, they faced more challenges than they had in their temperate zone colonies. In tropical Africa, Europeans died in droves of indigenous diseases or were languishing under blizzards and dust storms (Crosby 1988, 107). In Hong Kong, the mortality rate for the European settlers was especially high during the 1840s. As historian Tristram Hunt notes:

> For all that broiling sun, sea mist and lashing rain fostered not a clean Highland air, but a deadly "Hong Kong fever" which managed to wipe out scores of early colonists. Soldiers had the worst of it, as poor housing, bad diet, exhaustion, venereal disease and drink took their toll. Smallpox, malaria and cholera did the rest. The mid-1840s saw a mortality rate approaching 20 percent, with 100 soldiers from the 55th Regiment dying between June and August 1843, and over 260 men, 4 women and 17 children from the 95th burying them at a rate of fifty a month. (Hunt 2014, 223–260)

At the height of colonial anxiety over restoring the health of the settlers and boosting military morale, the lack of cow milk in the Asian colonies was framed as a strategic problem for the defense of the regions. The supreme position of cow milk in the food hierarchy of the time was supported by the state-of-the-art nutrition science that had emerged in the second half of the nineteenth century. The development of this nutrition science can be traced back to the "chemical revolution" in France in the late eighteenth century (Carpenter 2003). William Prout (1785–1850), an English physician, was one of the pioneers in arguing for the importance of milk in the human diet. He asserted that "the principal alimentary matters employed by man, and more perfect animals, might be reduced to the three great classes, namely, the *saccharine,* the *oily* and the *albuminous.*" These categories have come to be commonly referred to as carbohydrates, fats, and proteins, respectively, by later generations of scientists. For Prout, milk was the most perfect natural food as it contained all three. Thus, importing the Western dairy cow, as a way of domesticating nature and creating in the tropics an environment close to that of the European homeland, was a common objective of the nineteenth-century colonial powers (Osborne 2001).

Bearing in mind the discovery of the valuable nourishing chemicals found in milk, the Europeans placed a high priority on developing a stable supply of good quality cow milk at an affordable price in order to maintain the health of the European colonists living around the world. For example, in 1890 a French entrepreneur in Vietnam noted that "milk sells for at least twenty-five cents per liter, what milk—half coconut powder, half water— and people pay as much as forty cents for it" (Peters 2012, 190). In the earliest years in Hong Kong, which was inhabited by around 618 Europeans in the year 1847, milk was obtained from the native water buffaloes or from the few cows owned by the Europeans in the lower part of Victoria Peak, where most of the colonists were staying (Cameron 1986, 14). Dr. Ayres, the colonial surgeon for the period of 1873–1897, observed that the cows owned by well-off Europeans or Chinese were raised in conditions that were far from ideal. Cows were only found in the basements of their estates, but goats and sheep, like pigs, might be found on any floor. Milk from these sources was sold for between twenty and twenty-five cents for a twenty-four-ounce bottle, making it a commodity within reach of the rich alone in Hong Kong. Less well-off Westerners and others might do with the local supply of water buffalo milk, a product perceived by the Europeans as being much less readily digestible, especially by children, than cow milk (Cameron 1986, 30).

In order to create a stable, more affordable supply of unadulterated Western cow milk, European colonists in East, South, and Southeast Asia established dairy farms and Western cow-milk-supply networks in the Asian colonies in the early colonial period. For example, in Indonesia, the Dutch built dairies in the cooler mountain areas as early as the seventeenth century and set up milk stables in towns as the European populations grew in size in the nineteenth century (Den Hartog 1986, 72–78, 82–83). Similarly, in India the British colonists maintained their own cows for their milk and dairy products (Wiley 2014). In Vietnam, Tamil migrants from India offered the French goat milk during the early colonial period. By the late nineteenth century, although the French were unsuccessful in running their own dairy farms, there were many Tamil-owned dairies in Saigon that supplied bottles of milk door-to-door to the French colonists, with milk produced by cows imported from South India (Peters 2012, 190).

In Hong Kong, the establishment of the first industrialized dairy, named "Dairy Farm," in 1886, was driven not only by business concerns but also by a social purpose suffused with moral intent. Dairy Farm was founded by a Scottish parasitologist dubbed "the father of tropical medicine," Patrick Manson, who was famous for his discovery that the mosquito served as a vector in transmitting the malaria parasite. After participating in a tour led by Dr. Ayres and learning about the poor hygienic conditions of the dairies and meat production operations of the Chinese suppliers, Manson found Hong Kong was facing "every prospect [of] a milk famine" when the population of Westerners suddenly swelled to 125,000 from 87,000 in 1859, mainly owing to an influx escaping the Taiping Rebellion in Shanghai (Cameron 1986; Manson-Bahr and Alcock 1927). Manson declared in his proposal for a dairy farm that, "From a hygiene point of view the milk supply of a community is second in importance only to its water supply." As Western cow milk was seen as being the "staff of life," especially for young children and the sick, Manson felt that building a dairy farm was especially important for the benefit of the less-privileged Europeans in Hong Kong, as it could "supply a thoroughly reliable article and at such a price that what hitherto has been the luxury of the rich may become, what milk ought to be, one of the principal elements in the food of the poor in all communities" (Manson-Bahr and Alcock 1927).

By classifying the Western cow as the only healthy source of potable milk, which was particularly essential for babies and the sick, the building of what later became Dairy Farm took on a moral imperative that enabled it to draw resources and support from merchants and government officials. Establishing a Western dairy farm in a warm and wet tropical colony like Hong Kong would probably not have materialized had it not gained financial, technological, and social support from a merchant–government group. This nexus of wealthy businessmen, which formed the Board of Directors of Dairy Farm, included Catchick Paul Chater, who also built the first electric power station in Hong Kong; Granville Sharp, who provided the financial capital; Mr. Phineas Ryrie, the senior unofficial member of the Legislative Council of Hong Kong; and William Henry, the secretary to the China Trader Insurance Company (Cameron 1986, 34; Sayer and Evans 1985, 50–58).

Hong Kong, located in a subtropical region with hot and humid summers and vulnerable to a regular onslaught of typhoons, would probably not have been an ideal place to build a dairy farm raising cattle adapted to living in different habitats, such as those purchased from the United States, Australia, England, and Holland, were it not for the motivation of European demographic expansion. Although Dr. Manson was well resourced financially and politically, starting and running a dairy farm from scratch was far from easy. As pointed out by agricultural researcher Huitema, the main difficulty of milk production in the tropics is that the animals are often unable to regulate their body temperatures within normal limits. This has a negative impact on lactation (Huitema 1982, 262). Given his government connection, Manson had the privilege of choosing the site at which to build the dairy farm. To overcome the problem of low levels of lactation in Hong Kong during the hot summers, Manson selected a southwest-facing, steeply sloping piece of land of 300 acres in Pokfulam on Hong Kong Island as the site for the new dairy farm. This helped keep the cows in better condition physically as they could enjoy the cool, southwesterly breeze in the hot summertime, although in those days this meant that all foodstuffs and building materials had to be shouldered up from the seashore to the top of the hill by workers. The Dutch had built their dairies in Indonesia in the cooler mountains for similar lactation reasons in the nineteenth century (Den Hartog 1986, 72–78, 82–83).

As briefly alluded to above, the British colonial government also played an important role in boosting the local supply of Western cow milk as a means of strengthening the physical bodies of members of the ruling class. Special services, including land rental, road construction and repairs, provision of water supply, immunization, and dairy-product quality inspection, were offered by the government (Cameron 1986). In addition to this, the British government supported Manson and the London Missionary Society in establishing the territory's first medical school—the Hong Kong College of Medicine for Chinese—in 1887 as a means of ensuring the strength and vitality of both the European and Eurasian settlers and the local people of Hong Kong. This was an essential moment in the spread of nutrition science in Hong Kong's history, as it was decided that instruction would be based on the principles and scientific rigor of modern Western medicine (Lai et al. 2003). The College, which later became the Medical Faculty of the University of Hong Kong, was the only medical school in Hong Kong until the founding of a second medical faculty at the Chinese University of Hong Kong in 1981. In other words, the first industrialized dairy farm came hand in hand with the establishment of the Western medical system in Hong Kong, which came to gradually transform how the Chinese would understand milk, nutrition, and their bodies.

Milk Bottling and Vitamins in Soy Milk

The discovery and spread of the Western science of nutrition not only elevated the position of cow milk in the colonies of Asia, but also that of soy milk, leading to its industrialization in the 1930s. Liquid soy milk was first invented in China during the earlier part of the Han Dynasty (202 BCE–9 CE). The liquid was not initially consumed as food because raw soy milk is not easily digested owing to the presence of protease inhibitors, flatulence-causing oligosaccharides, and lipoxidase (Huang 2008, 52). Thus, contrary to the conventional belief that soy milk is an ancient Chinese food, it only became a part of the Chinese diet in the eighteenth or nineteenth century, when it was discovered that prolonged heating of the milk made it palatable and easily digestible.

Although soy milk and *youtiao* (a Chinese fried dough), usually sold as a street food by migrants from northern China, had become one of the most common breakfast foods or snacks for working-class people in Hong Kong between the 1930s and 1960s, many people thought of them as "poor people's foods" with low nutritional value. It is therefore unsurprising that during the turbulent 1940s, when tens of thousands of Hong Kong people died under the Japanese occupation, the suggestion of including soybeans as a food staple in the reinforced concrete food stores, in addition to rice, groundnut oil, a limited quantity of meat, and fuel oil, was rejected. As Sir Percy Selwyn Selwyn-Clarke, then director of Medical Services (1937–1943), recalled in his autobiography, "my recommendation to lay in the latter [soybeans] as a source of protein was at first opposed by some of my Chinese colleagues on the legislative council, who protested that it was only of use for feeding pigs. It was a Chinese industrialist, however, Mr. K. S. Lo [Lo Kwee-seong], whose early appreciation of soy products was to prove of such value in Hong Kong and far beyond it" (Selwyn-Clarke 1975, 62).

If the promotion of cow milk, introduced by the Europeans into colonial Hong Kong during the late nineteenth century, was a project driven by a moral intent for a defensive purpose, the industrialized soy milk, developed in the 1930s, was motivated by the perceived need to strengthen the bodies of the Chinese, especially during the second Sino–Japanese

War (1937–1945). As recounted by Lo Kwee-seong, the founder of Vitasoy, the industrialization of soy milk in Hong Kong was meant to provide a low-cost food with high-quality nutrients that most Chinese could afford. For him, the development of soy milk was a kind of patriotic calling inspired by witnessing malnourishment among the large number of refugees from China living in squalid camps during the Sino–Japanese War in the late 1930s (Hsieh 1982). During his volunteer service, in which he provided the refugees with daily necessities such as toothbrushes and toothpaste, Lo discovered that many of them suffered from beriberi—a disease caused by a lack of vitamin B1 that affects the nerves and causes pain and weakness, and sometimes heart failure (*Encyclopedia Britannica* 2019). Lo had first learned of the nutritional value of soy milk at a talk given by Julian Arnold, titled "Soybeans—The Cows of China," during a business trip to Shanghai in 1937. Understanding that soy milk was rich in high-quality protein (similar in its proportions of amino acids to that of meat and dairy products), minerals, and vitamins and containing a good balance of carbohydrates and fats, Lo got the idea of using soy milk as a low-cost, nutritious food to improve the health of the refugees. To help them produce soy milk by themselves, Lo and his friends bought the refugees a few hundred pounds of soybeans, a pot, a stone grinder, and filters made from mosquito nets, and showed them how to make the nutritious soy milk. According to Lo, before long many of the beriberi patients could walk. Encouraged by this positive result, in 1940, he set up the first soy milk factory in Causeway Bay, right in front of the foreign dairy giant, Dairy Farm, which produced fresh cow milk, mainly serving the Europeans and the rich during that time.

Taking up the moral role of educating the public about the new science of nutrition and using it as a tool to market his newly created soy milk products, Lo tried to shift the categorization of his soy milk products from "traditional Chinese foods" to "modern milk products" by naming them *weitanai* ("vita-milk") and bottling the liquid in an easily recognized glass milk bottle. The word *vita* means "life" in Latin and is an abbreviation of the term "vitamin," giving the modern soy milk a scientific aura, while naming the beverage *nai* (milk), rather than using the more common Chinese term of *doujiang* (bean liquid), and placing the milk in easily recognized milk bottles, removed Lo's modern soy milk from the soy product category, which was perceived as including traditional, Chinese, and lower-class foods, recoding the beverage as a premium, modern,

"Western"-style milk. To further strengthen the association of Vitasoy with cow milk, Lo even adopted the same door-to-door delivery methods as Dairy Farm. Following Dairy Farm's strategy of running Western restaurants, Lo began operating a small restaurant—"Vita Café"—selling Vitasoy milk and Chinese desserts in Mong Kok in the Kowloon peninsula of Hong Kong (Cai 1990, 30–31).

Given the long tradition of soy-food consumption, the moral motivation, and well-conceived marketing strategy, it was a surprise to Lo when he only sold nine bottles of soy milk during the first day of his business operation. The failure of Vitasoy soy milk during the late 1940s can be understood from both cultural and historical perspectives. At that time, most people in Hong Kong did not consume soy milk on a daily basis because it was considered a "cold" food. Soy foods and soy milk are classified as "cool" foods according to the Chinese humoral system stressing the inherent hot/cold characteristics of foods (Li [1578] 2003, 595). As noted by sociologist Eugene Anderson, people in modern societies, both East and West, still make food choices and design recipes based on the Galenic hot/cold, dry/wet division of food (2005, 142). This is the reason why the "cool" soy milk and "hot" *youtiao* eaten together at breakfast came to be thought of as a perfect match by Hong Kong people. The lasting influence of this humoral system in Hong Kong can also be seen in the anecdote of an old lady who accused Lo of being "immoral" for selling unhealthy food, as she believed that soy milk was "too cold," and thus "unhealthy" (Cai 1990, 20). Even as late as the early 2000s, in a study by Sidney Mintz and Tan Chee-Beng on the consumption of soy foods in Hong Kong, the authors found that it was widely considered inadvisable for old people to eat too much bean curd or soy milk because of their associated "coldness" (Mintz and Tan 2001, 125). In the study, one informant mentioned that her mother usually served soy milk with a piece of ginger (classified as "hot") in order it to reduce the "coolness."

Lo's failed effort to position Vitasoy milk as cow milk in the 1930s also demonstrated that most consumers were unconvinced by the innovative marketing message of the nutritional value of Vitasoy, or, more broadly, of the relevance of the newly established milk culture in colonial Hong Kong. The turning point for Vitasoy in winning the hearts of the younger generations and finally triumphing over Dairy Farm happened in the mid-1970s, thanks to a shift in technology and marketing. With the adoption of the ultra-high-temperature (UHT) processing technology developed in

Sweden, Vitasoy could now be packed in the lighter, unbreakable Tetra Brik Aseptic packages and sold on supermarket shelves, making it a perfect outdoor drink.[2] With its new easy-to-carry product feature, Vitasoy was re-categorized from a nutritious, growth-enhancing "milk" to a thirst-killing, cosmopolitan "soft drink," whose marketing provided hope of taking on a new, modern identity for people of different social classes. A new series of advertisements beginning in 1975, bearing the new colloquial Cantonese slogan "Vitasoy—More than just a soft drink"—was tremendously successful. To build up the "modern," "Western" brand image of Vitasoy, the firm hired celebrities—such as artist Josephine Siao Fong-fong, whose rendition of English songs since the 1960s crystallized her image as a cosmopolitan, modern woman, and "Wynners," a local version of the British rock band The Beatles—to endorse the product in its advertisements in order to appeal to younger consumers, who were increasingly fascinated by globalized Western movies and rock culture (McIntyre, Cheng, and Zhang 2002). Through these marketing strategies, Vitasoy milk changed from symbolizing health and science during the 1950s and 1960s to become a modern, outdoor and leisure-oriented "soft drink," consumed for fun, happiness, and relaxation during the 1970s. As we have seen, this re-categorization was made possible by the clever manipulation of cultural symbols in marketing, the globalization of the soft-drink culture, and the availability of modern packaging technologies.

The success of Vitasoy's repositioning in the hearts of a younger group of middle-class customers in the 1970s as a "soft drink" needs to be understood against the backdrop of the political and social conditions at that time. The image of a modern lifestyle, imbued with the ideology of freedom, fun, pleasure, and leisure, projected in the Vitasoy advertisements was well received by new middle-class nuclear families, made possible by the high degree of political stability and social security brought by the "Big Bang" of social reforms, which included the 10-year housing plan and the nine-year free education plan implemented after the violent 1967 riots (Tang 1998, 65–67).[3] This new middle-class and local Hong Kong identity manifested in a diversification of leisure activities and in the internationalism of the culture of drinking and eating out that became popular among Hong Kong people. Owing to the high density of housing, outdoor activities such as swimming and picnicking became weekly weekend rituals for the newly formed nuclear family. The 1970s was also the period during which the first generation of Hong Kong people experienced an economic boom, negotiating a modern, international Hong Kong identity for themselves by setting themselves apart from the mainland Chinese and the Taiwanese. A sense of belonging began to unfold in popular culture, where Cantonese popular music—or *Cantopop* as it is known to the West—became mainstream (McIntyre, Cheng, and Zhang 2002). The formation of a local identity was escalated by increasing interaction with the "Other"—the new immigrants from mainland China. During the period from 1976 to 1980, more than a hundred thousand immigrants from mainland China migrated into Hong Kong. These new arrivals, who were considered by many local Hong Kongers as a threat to their livelihoods, were looked down upon and nicknamed "Ah Chang" for their "uncivilized" ways (Wu, Zhang, and Ceng 2012, 124).[4] In these circumstances, Vitasoy milk became an icon of a distinctive new Hong Kong identity and social class. No longer did Vitasoy symbolize a Western cow milk substitute or nourishing, energy-rich food to satisfy the nutritional needs of the unprivileged masses. Instead, by the end of the 1970s Vitasoy had become a modern "soft drink" for a new leisure class of middle-class people who were fun-loving, outgoing, curious about other cultures, and differentiated from the poorer new migrants and people from other less economically advanced countries.

The High and Low Tastes for Milk Tea

Similar to fresh cow milk, black tea drunk with milk and sugar was once consumed exclusively by the British colonists and a privileged group of local elites as a cultural marker of distinction in early colonial Hong Kong, dividing those with power from those without. The act of drinking black tea with milk and sugar, a national ritual in Britain, and in George Orwell's words "the mainstay of civilization" (Orwell 1946), is a modern phenomenon. Surprisingly, as early as 1660, green tea imported from China was the first type of tea to be embraced by the British, as well as physicians, for its supposed medicinal virtues. One of the reasons for this early popularity of tea was its salutary effect in countering alcohol intoxication. This belief can be traced to a mention by the Venetian author Giovanni Botero, who in 1589 wrote, "The Chinese have an herb from which they press a delicate juice which serves them instead of wine. It also preserves the health and frees them from all those evils that the immoderate use of wine doth breed in us" (Hohenegger 2006, 106). In the seventeenth century, tea consumption was supported by the British reformers of the temperance movement, who were devoted to the eradication of alcoholism in society. Tea, together with coffee and chocolate, as recalled by Thomas Rugge, had come to be "sold in almost every street in 1659," and beloved by the intellectuals who gathered at coffeehouses (Sachse [1659] 1961, 91:10).

Tea served with milk first appeared in Hong Kong at Western private clubs, hotels, and Western restaurants, where it acted as a marker of strict racial distinction between the local Chinese and British colonists in terms of economic activity, place of residence, and forms of entertainment in the early years of colonial rule. The earliest well-known private club to offer banqueting and restaurant facilities was the Zetland Hall in Central district, established in 1846 by the Zetland Lodge of England, which was patronized exclusively by members of the Masonic Lodge of England and elite British colonists (Zetland Hall 2020). The new Zetland Hall claimed to focus on serving the social and welfare needs of the "non-Chinese" (Cheng 2003). While foreigners were free to roam the Chinese parts of the island and visit their restaurants, the Chinese were not permitted to enter Zetland Hall and other Western restaurants in hotels, such as the restaurant in the sumptuous Hong Kong Hotel, which was established in 1893. At that time, Western-style black tea, which had originated in China, was served exclusively in such private clubs, Western restaurants and hotels, to be enjoyed exclusively by the colonial elites in spaces where the Chinese were prohibited to enter (Cheng 2003).

Given the context of supremacy and exclusivity in Western culinary spaces in colonial Hong Kong, the first opportunity for the Chinese community to sip cups of British-style tea made from bags of imported Ceylon black tea mixed with white refined sugar and fresh cow milk was a key historical moment, marking the successful crossing of a social boundary between the ruler and the ruled and between high and low culture. British-style milk tea was served to the Chinese for the first time in a public space in 1895, when the first Chinese-owned hotel, Lujiao Hotel, was built in Central.[5] This event reflected the increasing economic power being consolidated by Chinese businessmen in the late nineteenth century (Liu 2009, 75). The symbolic association of British-style milk tea with "Western-ness" or "British-ness" transitioned to include a "Western-style and modern Chinese-ness" when Tai Ping Koon—the first *fancaiguan* (Chinese-owned Western restaurant), specializing in the creation of "soy sauce Western cuisine" in Guangzhou—relocated to Hong Kong during the turbulent Sino–Japanese War in the 1930s (Xu 2007, 5, 108).[6] Xu Laogao, the founder of Tai Ping Koon, quit his job as a corporate chef for Ji Cheong Hong, an American trading and business firm in the "Thirteen Factories" in Canton,[7] following a big quarrel. Instead of finding a job in another trading firm, Xu earned his living by selling Western-style roast beef served with soy sauce on the street. He won the hearts of many because of his creativity in cooking "Western" food according to Chinese cooking principles. His "Western" food was so popular that he was able to open his first *fancaiguan* in the strategic trading center and transportation node of southern China—Tai Ping Sha in Canton—and named his shop after the place. British-style tea-bag milk tea only began to be served in Tai Ping Koon following Xu's family's move to Hong Kong. As suggested by the veteran restaurateur, having a cup of British-style milk tea brewed from imported tea bags in Tai Ping Koon implied one's cultural and economic capital, as Tai Ping Koon was an iconic place patronized by stylish and famous Chinese opera artists, sportsmen, prestigious politicians, and upper-class gourmet lovers (see also Xu 2007).

Hong Kong Silk-Stocking Milk Tea and the Lion Rock Spirit

By now, we may readily grant that there were two main paths leading to the cultural practice of preparing the upper-class "high taste" of milk tea that was once a marker of the rich and powerful European social class. First, the practice of adding milk and sugar to black tea trickled down from the European colonists to the compradors (Chinese merchants who worked as intermediaries between foreign traders and the China market) and merchants with whom they had frequent contact through Western institutions like private clubs and hotel restaurants. Second, the upper-class Chinese began to patronize the exotic and fashionable Chinese-run *fancaiguan*.

However, what triumphed over the mild British-style milk tea to become the most "authentic" taste of tea in Hong Kong was the strong, silk-stocking milk tea made by the working-class street hawker stalls (*daipaidong*) and local tea cafés.[8] Today, with many locals considering milk tea a beverage they "cannot live without," the city empties 2.5 million cups of milk tea each day (DeWolf et al. 2017). In 2004, the images of milk tea and a pineapple bun with butter (*boluoyou*) were voted as the best designs to represent Hong Kong (*Apple Daily* 2004). In 2014, after five years of consultation and application, three of the most popular foods served at *cha chaan teng*—milk tea, Hong Kong–style egg tarts, and pine-apple buns—were successfully listed as an intangible cultural heritage and recognized by the Hong Kong government. Today, many local restaurants from the low-end to upper-middle range and even international fast food chains such as McDonald's offer Hong Kong–style milk tea. Hong Kong–style milk tea has also gone global, and can be found in cities such as London, Paris, Tokyo, and Singapore, as well as other cities where large numbers of Hong Kong people have migrated. International KamCha (Hong Kong Style Milk Tea) Competitions were held regularly by the Association of Coffee and Tea of Hong Kong with support from the Hong Kong Trade Development Council in Hong Kong, Shenzhen, Shanghai, Guangzhou, Toronto, and Sydney. Winners from each district would gather in Hong Kong to compete for the final Championship.

The aromatic, velvety smooth consistency of silk-stocking milk tea, as related by many milk-tea masters in my research, is the result of an art of tea blending and brewing that is totally different from the method used to produce the older British-style milk tea.[9] As Lam Chun-chung, the tea master and the son of the founder of a century-old tea café, Lan Fang Yuen, explained to me:

> Our milk tea is made from a blend of five to six types of black tea, including broken orange pekoe, broken orange pekoe fannings and tea dust produced mostly in Assam, India, Ceylon tea from Sri Lanka, and other teas from Java, and China. The broken orange pekoe is essential in producing the alluring fragrance but will be lighter in color and taste. Pekoe fanning gives the milk tea a richer and stronger taste. The black tea dust, though lowest in cost, is essential for making a cup of authentic Hong Kong–style milk tea. By adding the Ceylon tea dust to the blend of the other five different types of black tea, we can produce a better aroma, and a richer and stronger taste. In addition, the richness of the tea is created by pouring the tea into and out of two tall teapots eight times before serving it in a thick tea cup with canned evaporated milk.

Throughout my fieldwork, many of the tea masters, food critics, and passionate milk-tea drinkers bemoaned the disappearing taste of authentic local-style milk tea. The tea masters and entrepreneurs attributed the declining standard of Hong Kong–style milk tea to fast food chains, like McDonald's and Café de Coral.

To educate the public about the "real" taste of milk tea and the Hong Kong spirit hidden in the food, equipment, and practices of a milk tea café, some tea café entrepreneurs and local tea merchants started making astute use of appeals to the past in their books, media interviews, and writings beginning in the early 2010s. Incidentally, two recently published books on tea cafés in Hong Kong, written by entrepreneurs Simon Wong Ka-wo and Lau Wing-bo, play on the enduring fascination with the past by incorporating the founding myth of Hong Kong—the Lion Rock Spirit—in their discussion of the foods served in their *cha chaan teng*. Both proclaimed in their books that the local tea café *is* the embodiment of the Hong Kong spirit and is essential to sustaining the city's future growth (Huang 2011; Yinlong yinshi jituan 2013).[10] The Lion Rock Spirit refers to the perceived core values of the Hong Kong people, who are considered to be hardworking, persevering, cooperative, and imbued with a great sense of solidarity (see also G. Chan 2015; Y. Chan 2014). The term "Lion Rock Spirit" came from the RTHK TV series *Below the Lion Rock*, which aired from the 1970s to the 1990s and portrayed the joys and sorrows of lower- and working-class people in their daily lives. During the 1960s and 1970s, many families lived in squatter huts and squalid public housing. Their shared hardships had the effect of knitting relatives and neighbors into one large family. This spirit is believed by many Hong Kong people to be the core set of values that enabled them to achieve the economic miracle of the 1970s and 1980s and transformed Hong Kong into a cosmopolitan Asian financial center.

As suggested in his book's title, *Chongchu Xianggang Hao Weilai* (Brewing for the future of Hong Kong), Simon Wong asserts that the Hong Kong spirit, as manifested in a cup of milk tea, is a panacea that can resolve current problems and lead to the future success of Hong Kong. Wong is a second-generation proprietor of a tea café business, an influential tea merchant and the chair of the Association of Coffee and Tea of Hong Kong. His book includes a wealth of detail on how the essential elements involved in making a good cup of Hong Kong–style milk tea reflect the Hong Kong spirit—creativity, adaptability, and cooperativeness. These elements include the blending of tea leaves, the choice of milk, and the equipment and utensils used in local tea cafés, each of which will be discussed below.

First, Wong claims that the core of the Hong Kong spirit—creativity—is reflected in the way that the different grades of tea leaves are blended, thus producing the strong, pungent taste and texture of the local silk-stocking milk tea that is noticeably distinct from British-style tea. As Wong explains, during the 1950s, the hardworking and thrifty workers at the pier would collect the leftover Ceylon black tea fanning and tea dust. Instead of following the usual practice of throwing them away, they instead used these to make themselves a cup of strong and aromatic tea during their precious tea break at a quarter past three in the afternoon. This innovative secret recipe inspired the small tea stall owners, who in attempting to economize, began developing their own house blends. This creative recipe, incorporating low-end tea dust in the brewing of Hong Kong–style milk tea, is in line with what we have learned from tea master Lin and supports Wong's argument that the blending of tea represents the innovative characteristics of the Hong Kong people, who are able to come up with creative solutions when faced with economic or resource constraints.

The second core value of the Lion Rock Spirit is adaptability. The high degree of adaptability of Hong Kong people is reflected in the equipment and ingredients used in making a good cup of tea. The purpose of the unique tall and slim design of the aluminum teapot in Hong Kong is to fit into the limited spaces available in the small street stalls, to ensure that the tea leaves and tea dust will be fully covered with water, and kept in almost air-tight conditions for the best aroma and taste to be drawn out (Huang 2011, 69).[11] A cotton tea infuser tailor-made to fit the pot is also used, which finely filters the tiny broken tea leaves, fanning, and even the tiny tea dust. To overcome the operating and storage-space limitations of *daipaidongs*, tea glasses that can be stacked and condensed milk that can be safely stored at room temperature are used, breaking the British ritual of serving afternoon tea with fresh milk.

The third characteristic, cooperativeness, is closely related to the Chinese notion of *ren qing wei* (literally, "human love taste," meaning something like the taste of love). The spirit of cooperativeness is reflected in the daily operations of the tea cafés and *daipaidongs*. According to Lau Wing-bo: "*Ren qing wei* is a kind of feeling, giving you a mental space to slow down from a hectic daily life, an intimate, warm feeling that is at the same time a private space for individual freedom and autonomy. It is a feeling of home" (Yinlong yinshi jituan 2013, 21).

The harmonious relationship between the customers and staff in a tea café or *daipaidong* could be easily observed in the past. In a local tea café, the customers and staff members usually spoke with each other in familiar terms as if they were a family. The local remedy of a lemon boiled with Coca-Cola would be suggested to a customer if he mentioned that he was suffering from the flu. During peak hours, some loyal customers would even help out with serving. In the context of a *daipaidong*, a customer could take a seat at a *chashuidang* (literally, "tea water stall," or a sideways tea café) to enjoy an authentic cup of milk tea while at the same time ordering a bowl of noodles from the noodle stall nearby. The open, flexible, and cooperative attitudes of the tea café and noodle stall managers enabled them to increase their sales and incomes while providing greater convenience to their customers. Not only the staff of the *daipaidong*s and tea cafés, but also the customers were highly cooperative. Seldom would the customers complain, despite the heat, noise, and sometimes poor hygiene of the tea stalls. Many of the customers would make new friends by talking with one another during their meal times despite coming from different social backgrounds.

Fourth, skillful adoption of the wisdom of Eastern and Western cultures was frequently mentioned as a key aspect of the competitiveness of the Hong Kong people, especially before the economic reforms in China. Wong and Lau contend that the production and designs of the milk drinks and food in *cha chaan teng* express the flexibility and artful combination of the knowledge of East and West. Prior to the Chinese economic reform in 1978, Hong Kong, as a British colony, acted as the window through which China learned about the West. The making of silk-stocking milk tea, Western-style fried rice, and Chinese-style steaks is said to incorporate the culinary wisdom of East and West. Locally invented drinks like boiled Coca-Cola with ginger and *yeunyeung* (Mandarin for duck)—tea mixed with coffee—are exemplars of the innovations produced by mixing Eastern and Western culinary concepts, following the Chinese traditional principles of health. Newly introduced popular food items from around the world, such as Macanese pork-chop buns, Japanese *udon*, Taiwanese-style bubble tea, and Malaysian-style pandan cakes show the high adaptability of Hong Kong entrepreneurs in inventing foods that are at once global and local.

The vitality of the local *cha chaan teng* was tested during the large outbreak of severe acute respiratory syndrome (SARS) in 2003.[12] During the SARS and post-SARS period, more than 2,000 restaurants and catering services closed down. Contrary to this trend, the number of *cha chaan tengs* actually expanded from 4,000 in 2003 to 6,000 in 2010. Following the September 2008 financial crisis, many hotel restaurants and high-end Chinese and Western restaurants were affected, but the business of the *cha chaan teng*s grew and even began attracting new middle-class customers. Yet, despite this success, Wong expressed his worry about the disappearing Hong Kong spirit: "This inclusive attitude and Hong Kong spirit seem to be disappearing. Instead, people nowadays are arrogant, fighting with each other, finding faults in everything and opposing everything" (Huang 2011, 4).

Wong asserts that the current challenges faced by Hong Kong people, such as the increasing number of conflicts between different political parties and between Hong Kong and China after the handover, were due to the growing lack of cooperativeness, inflexibility, and uncompromising attitude of the new generation of Hong Kong people, whom he feels have probably lost all of the good qualities of the Lion Rock Spirit. In such a conception, the *cha chaan teng* is more than a restaurant serving a particular style of food, but, rather, in Wong's and Lau's estimation, a cultural phenomenon that represents the Lion Rock Spirit of the people who created the extraordinary success of Hong Kong.

As the milk tea discourses just discussed have redefined a good cup of milk tea, they have simultaneously produced a set of ideas about what a good tea drinker or even a good person should be. In this context, by being informed about the Lion Rock Spirit embedded in the food and drinks in a tea café, the eater or drinker should actively engage in the local food culture, rather than simply being passive consumers of industrialized milk tea and globalized food. These dietary ideals reflect notions of good citizenship in Hong Kong—being cooperative, harmonious, flexible, creative, and hardworking. Citizenship in Hong Kong was never intended to be a nation-building exercise (Turner 2004). Hong Kong became a Crown colony in 1843 and remained essentially a safe harbor and trading center to support British economic and military interests in East Asia. Successive British administrations had denied basic citizenship rights in the colony, and it was not until the final stages of negotiations for the transfer of sovereignty that the conditions for citizenship arose. This meant that the people of Hong Kong had learned to be self-reliant, cooperative, flexible, and pragmatic long before the emergence of neoliberalism around the world (Lau and Kuan 1988). By culturally constructing stories about milk tea and tea cafés and linking them to the founding spirit of Hong Kong, Wong and Lau neutralize the submissive and passive political attitude of

Hong Kong people and emphasize the "good" qualities of the local people—creativity, flexibility, adaptability, pragmatism, and tolerance. This mythology aims at altering the symbolic associations and culturally constituted uses of milk tea in order to stimulate consumption, to promote political stability, and less noticeably, to educate the public on what a good person should be.

Yet, as we shall note shortly, young people in Hong Kong have not passively internalized the docile Lion Rock Spirit and the moral value of tolerance promoted by the tea merchants and entrepreneurs, but have actively created an entirely different set of meanings for milk tea and the local tea cafés as the expression of a modern identity, social class, and even an alternative version of the Lion Rock Spirit. Interestingly, they also prefer the strong and fragrant silk-stocking milk tea to the expensive but weak British-style tea-bag tea served in five-star hotels, not so much as a result of acculturation in the family, but more due to the new meanings that the local milk tea has been imbued with in the current wave of local art and pop culture, which we now turn to.

Redefining a Good Cup of Milk Tea: Knowledge, Responsibility, and Pleasure

The online magazine *Milktealogy* is a good example to illustrate how modernity, morality, and the self-identity of the young generation are expressed through their scientific study of and bodily engagement with milk tea. The establishment of the *Milktealogy* magazine in 2014 by two young illustrators and self-made food critics, twin brothers Haze Tsui and Long Tsui, was meant "to conduct an exploration of *cha chaan teng* culture, and by extension, the Hong Kong way of life" (Yung 2015). Through their online magazine, the Tsui brothers successfully transformed milk tea from a simple beverage consumed daily to both a science and an art. They have redefined the standards for aesthetic judgment of a cup of Hong Kong–style milk tea by designing a new grading system, creating new meanings for local-style milk tea through humorous comic strips about milk tea and office life, and building a new type of local identity by expressing the morality of slow tea drinking and the responsibility to support local culture.

The Tsui brothers are probably the first to attempt to study milk-tea making as a "science." They established a database by systematically collecting ratings for the milk tea from over a hundred small tea cafés, most of which are unknown to the general public. As implied in the suffix "logy" in the website name, Haze and Long argue that the tacit and explicit knowledge in silk-stocking milk-tea making can and should be studied seriously as a kind of "science" like oenology, the science of wine making. Since 2014 the pair have been collecting data not only on milk tea, but also on the histories of and anecdotes about more than a hundred tea cafés and *daipaidong* spread throughout Hong Kong, most of which are small, family-run shops.

Their aesthetic standard for judging and grading a cup of milk tea is based on seven quantifiable criteria, each involving a scale of one to five: hotness, visual appearance, aroma, smoothness, proportion (between the tea and milk), richness, and aftertaste. Although veteran local food writers and popular hosts of TV programs, such as Cai Lan, Craig OuYang, and Susez Wong, have also introduced and commented on the tea sold at a few of the locally famous *cha chaan teng* based on taste and mouth-feel (e.g., see OuYang 2007), their judgments were not based on a set of standardized criteria, making comparisons difficult. Yet, as wine scientist Emile Peynaud has pointed out, taste judgment of a drink such as wine can involve many tasting problems and perceptual errors (2005). The judgment and grading of milk tea are also similarly affected by the physiological and emotional state of the judge and factors in the external environment. The merit of the reports created by the two Tsui brothers is that they give a detailed account of the phenomenon of taste by recording their judging process, as we can note from one of their accounts:

> The milk tea from Keung Hing is served in a traditional porcelain cup with two red lines and a tea spoon. The initial taste is smooth but bland. However, when I slow down my mental pace, relax and wait, the taste of the tea slowly comes out. Sitting in the outdoor tea stall, looking at the fading color of the tea stall sign, viewing the old but energetic public estate, the aftertaste of every sip of tea in my mouth starts to turn strong and rich. (*Milktealogy* 2016)

Although the milk-tea grading system seems to provide an objective and quantitative judgment based on holistic evaluation, the "aftertaste" of the milk tea is affected by the emotional state of the taster, who is embodied in a physical environment with a unique set of personal history and memories. In addition, the Tsui brothers note that how the staff take care of the customers also affects the taste of milk tea, an example of the *ren qing wei* discussed above.

By portraying milk tea through their amusing and artistic illustrations, as the social space and source of joy and energy for middle-class office workers, the Tsui brothers succeed in gentrifying the traditional milk-tea culture and transform milk-tea drinking from a local, working-class, and nostalgic activity to a chic, modern, and cosmopolitan practice. The professionally drawn comics depicting the everyday lives of office workers appear in the online magazine and communicate a consistent theme—how "milk tea makes my day!" The main protagonists in the comics are two fictional milk-tea addicts—Benny and Miss M. Benny is a middle-aged Eurasian man with a trendy haircut, wearing a well-tailored tight black suit and shiny, black-leather shoes. Like many of the office workers in Hong Kong, Benny leads a monotonous and hectic working life. His biggest fantasy and source of enjoyment is to have a good cup of milk tea or to eat at a tea café in the company of female beauties. However, he suffers various embarrassing moments during his dates owing to his unfamiliarity with the tea café culture. In contrast, Miss M., with a pair of clear, big eyes, and long, dark hair, is an attractive, pleasant office lady who is interested in food and traveling and is active in online shopping and office gossip. Her biggest wishes are to meet Mr. Right and to find the best cup of milk tea. Milk tea, as depicted in the comics, is not only a drink but a social space for human interaction, an exciting event, and an idiom to express one's feelings, identity, and lifestyle. These comic scenes incorporating modern office settings and politics resonate with the young professionals and office workers who often need an energy boost and break from their routine, stressful lives, and from what Harry Braverman calls the "degradation of work" caused by the monopoly of capital (Braverman 1974).

As emphasized by Haze and Long at Milktealogy.com, the purpose of their never-ending, self-driven project is to record the disappearing tastes, stories, and history of milk tea because of their love of the culture and local communities of Hong Kong. They have posted anecdotes about the struggles of the tea shop owners, the invention or reinvention of their milk tea, and the other signature foods of local tea cafés, such as egg tarts and satay noodles, and the way the staff wholeheartedly serves customers.

In providing gastronomic information on milk tea and Hong Kong local foods, Haze and Long also unveil their own views on what an ideal market should be. As they stated in one interview:

> "The so-called free market is actually not that free at all. It's all under the shadow of corporate monopoly," Long says. "Economic efficiency shouldn't always come first. We don't want to see a day when machine-made milk teas all made with the same formula are all that's available. Even if they can replicate the taste, they won't be able to retain the culture and flavor." (Yung 2015)

Rather than being cooperative and flexible in adapting to changing government policies and keeping silent in the face of social changes, the twin brothers, through their humorous comic strips, illustrate their resentment over the astronomical rents that forced many of the distinctive small tea cafés to close. So, through *Milkteaology*, they pursue what they believe is a moral mission to keep the *cha chaan teng* culture alive. In their words: "We do not have the experience to start a *cha chaan teng* or make a cup of milk tea, but we are using what we are good at—art and creation, to play a part in preserving the culture" (Yung 2015).

Viewing the preservation of the *cha chaan teng* and other local cultures through art as their moral calling, they wish to make a change and bring hope to society through their online magazine. Their posts express their strong support for local culture, including protecting the local language (Cantonese), festival foods, and literature, and occasionally touch on politically sensitive subjects like the 2014 Umbrella Revolution.[13] They also support fundraising activities for local movie productions, homegrown music, and community services. All of this has made their online magazine popular not only among Hong Kong and international gourmet lovers but also among socially conscious young people who, on the one hand, are looking for MacCannell's sense of "backstage scenery" and authentic cultural experiences in local food, while on the other hand caring about the local community (MacCannell 1973).

Here, as we have seen in the discourses on milk tea and tea cafés in Hong Kong, no matter whether in print or online, the milk-tea culture incorporates elements of knowledge, memory, and pleasure. The process of enjoying a good cup of milk tea is understood to emerge from a nexus of knowledge about the background of the particular tea café, method of tea brewing, and the collective memories behind the foods served. But the moral aspect of a good cup of tea surrounding the knowledge-memory-pleasure nexus was not as great a departure from the narrative of the supply of Western cow milk that began during early colonial times. Despite their rejection of elitism, local discourses of milk-tea consumption, casting off the original British rules for tea making and drinking etiquette, and instead emphasizing the ethics of the Lion Rock Spirit and a celebration of pleasure, did not lead to a redefinition of the right way to drink milk tea. Neither did these discourses diminish the empirical role played by food in normalizing social classes and in constituting the definition of a good person. While the entrepreneurs emphasize self-made, well-disciplined docile citizens—the celebrated values of colonialism and neoliberalism—in their narratives of the Lion Rock Spirit, the new generation stresses instead the existential taste experience and documentation of the unofficial history of a place, while at the same time normalizing a proper ritual of drinking the tea—slow tasting, which likely will have the effect of further normalizing class difference and excluding members of the working and lower classes, who can hardly spare the time and energy to take part in such a ritual.

Colonial Rule, Social Hierarchy, and Dietary Changes

This chapter used the rise of fresh milk, soy milk, and milk tea during the colonial period of Hong Kong's history to ask some of the core questions surrounding the globalization and cultural politics of food—how is global food adopted in new markets and what are the new meanings created through its adoption? I have discussed how the introduction of Western cow milk by a Scottish physician to colonial Hong Kong was not so much due to environmental or economic needs, as proposed by cultural materialism (Harris 1974; Harris and Ross 1987), but to political and social reasons. Through the classification of water buffalo milk as an "inedible" food and Western cow milk as the "staff of life" necessary to maintain the physical and mental health of the European population in Hong Kong, Patrick Manson successfully drew on financial resources and government support in building a dairy farm and importing Western dairy cows into Hong Kong, which has a subtropical climate not suitable for dairying. The institutionalization of Western cow milk production came in tandem with the establishment of Western medical education and the spread of nutrition science, changing how the Chinese perceived their own bodies and health and the way they understood the new hierarchy of milk products.

The milk drinks appearing on the menu of a century-old tea café, discussed in the introduction to this chapter, are a microcosm of colonial Hong Kong, reflecting the new social hierarchy established under colonial rule. As we have noted, the new social order, which privileged nutrition science and Western milk, was reflected in the hierarchy of "milk": ranging from the superiority of Dairy Farm bottled fresh milk, which was formerly consumed almost exclusively by the European population, to the diluted "milky water" made from condensed milk, which was consumed by the locals as a precious food supplement. Notably excluded from the "milk" category, and the social hierarchy, is soy milk, which is not served in most tea cafés nowadays. In this way, the local tea café acts as an institution normalizing proper eating habits and leads to social class formation, by defining the meaning of high-quality "milk," "healthy" foods, and what is considered to be an "authentic" cup of milk tea. These hierarchical classifications of food are created and maintained by social institutions (Douglas 1986). Moreover, these classifications embody and reinforce the power relationships in-between (Foucault 1973), such as between the British colonial government and the people, between the Western industrialists and Chinese entrepreneurs, and between Western and local food.

This chapter also shows how the cultural dimensions of globalization act in the rejuvenation of local culture (Appadurai 1996) rather than in cultural homogenization (Ritzer 2019). The globalization of Western food science, instead of "undoing" local food cultures (Featherstone 1995), can re-categorize and rejuvenate local cultures, and, consequently, create a culture of differences. In the case of Hong Kong, the globalization of Western cow milk, soft drinks, and the technology of food packaging escalated the movement of ideas from Western medical science, people, commodities (cows and dairy products), technologies (sterilization, bottling, and packaging), and capital (financial, social, cultural, and symbolic), which in fact also fueled the development of the local soy milk industry. The emergence of nutrition science creates new ingredients for the imagination of the "healthy" "Western" diet, characterized by plentiful dairy products and the absence of Chinese soy milk, while proving new forms of cultural capital for local inventions (such as diluted milk water and local milk tea) and establishing a new hierarchy of food.

Moreover, the discourse on milk-tea culture in Hong Kong in some senses offers the local people a new way to think about what makes a good citizen and a good society. Sociologist Georg Simmel once remarked that "one nowhere feels as lonely and lost as in the metropolitan crowd" ([1903] 2002). The milk-tea culture promoted a sense of connection and human relationships with others through the *ren qing wei* of the local tea café staff, which brought meaning and solace to people's fast-paced, stressful, technical, and lonely urban lives. This is a foodway ideal that celebrates love, sensuality, intuition, and tradition, ways of relating to food that, unlike the Dairy Farm fresh milk, could not be calculated in terms of nutritional value. It also endorsed and promoted pleasure. Enjoying milk tea and food at an authentic tea café, taking photos of the cups of milk tea and food, and sharing the traditional tea café food culture online, as well as the production of comic strips are part of the "prescription" for eating the right "authentic" local food.

Despite having its origins in a "low" cuisine, the milk-tea culture foregrounded the ethics of proper eating and drinking, celebrating the ways in which choosing good local food is a moral act. But the discourse on milk tea provided rules about where and what to eat that were no less normative in regard to social class differences than those rules prescribed by standards of nutrition, possibly more so. The celebration of the sensory pleasure of eating the right kind of local food and the experience of *qing* (love) in a tea café mandated the feeling of enjoyment obtained from eating "authentic" local food, normalizing social class differences in the ability to participate in leisure activities. Yet, the case of milk tea also heightens the generational difference in the cultural meaning attributed to it. Against the background of social and political change since the handover of Hong Kong, which made identifying the cultural identity of the people more problematic than ever, the focus on the ethic of the cooperative Hong Kong spirit, as shown in the discourses of the older generation of tea entrepreneurs, and the ethics of supporting local culture, freedom, and identity, as emphasized by members of the younger generation, actually serve to heighten the moral valence of the value of drinking milk tea and eating traditional local foods across generations. They create higher stakes in making the choice of whether to support local autonomy or national stability under the rule of the Chinese Communist Party. This reminds us that there is no such thing as food choice or dietary health apart from social ideals, and food assessment is inseparable from a moral hierarchy that is inevitably classed. But the stories of Dairy Farm, soy milk, and milk tea in early colonial Hong Kong are just the beginning of the dramatic dietary change—from lactophobia to lactophilia—in China. In the decades that followed, while the definition of a good food, good diet, and a good person continued to evolve, food discourse maintained its ethical function, providing a lesson in eating right that connected food, personhood, and citizenship. The most significant expansion of milk consumption in China took place after the economic reform, as nutrition concerns converged with food uncertainty and global aspirations to make drinking milk a modern duty for every Chinese.

3 | Global Capital, Local Culture, and Food Uncertainty

On April 23, 2011, a TV program titled *"Niuru renjie"* ("water buffalo cheese-making family"), which told the story of the decline of the traditional cheese-making industry in Shunde, was broadcast by Foshan TV. With the economic opening up and transformation of Daliang as a backdrop, this episode visualized the rapid urbanization of Daliang by first presenting, as a point of contrast, a few black-and-white images of the past depicting the former landscape dominated by the omnipresence of mulberry cultivation, silk production, rice agriculture, and large fishponds, and dotted with numerous water buffaloes. These nostalgic pictures were quickly replaced by colorful scenes from modern times—glass-shelled skyscrapers and fast-moving production lines for a wide variety of small electronic appliances, symbolizing the soaring growth and successful transition of Shunde from an agricultural base to one of the richest, most industrialized cities in southeastern China. To ensure that viewers understood that the disappearance of water buffaloes in Daliang was an unavoidable consequence of the modern development of Shunde, the narrator explained that the government had banned the raising of water buffaloes in Daliang city owing to the pollution these animals created in the rivers. After this brief introduction, Auntie Huan, an "authentic" cheese maker from Jinbang village, came on camera to tell her forty-year cheese-making story. Jinbang village is known as the birthplace of Daliang's water buffalo cheese (*niuru*), which at the time of the program's broadcast was close to disappearing. Dressed in a loose, deep-blue

Chinese *qipao*-styled shirt, which she always wears while working in her water-buffalo-cheese workshop, Auntie Huan shared her hardship:

> I have been making *niuru* for over 40 years. I am an authentic cheese maker from Jinbang village, as I have made cheese since I was 16 years old. Nowadays, there are many "fake" cheeses made by people in the northern, rural, mountainous areas and sent to Jinbang village for sale.
>
> Cheese making is harsh. There is a maxim in Jinbang village: *If you have a daughter, do not marry into Jinbang village. Otherwise, her pair of sandals will be covered with cow dung and urine.*
>
> Nobody wants to make cheese these days; neither do my son and daughter. Most young people only drink cow milk and do not know about our Chinese water buffalo cheese. That is why there are so many reporters who want to interview me. I was on a French culinary TV program a few months ago, and next week I will have another interview.

This nostalgic TV program points to one of the two phenomena I will explore in this chapter—the decrease in production and consumption of Jinbang *niuru,* followed by a related phenomenon, the increase in consumption of Western cow milk. I use the production of traditional water buffalo milk and modern cow milk in China as a lens to examine the global and local factors underlying the adoption of new foods in China and the moral and social implications of these consumption decisions. To do this, I have divided my analysis in this chapter into two parts. First, I look into how the production of traditional water buffalo milk was transformed under the system of people's communes and how the industry has struggled to survive within the modernizing vision of the local government. In the second part of this chapter, I examine how the different forces of globalization have affected the production and consumption of cow milk and milk drinks in China.

Building on the idea that food marketing and food regulations under the new food regime in China are not merely empirical but also ethical, I argue that the marketing activities that boosted the sales of the milk companies created, in Pierre Bourdieu's sense, a new kind of "taste" for milk. Bourdieu, in his study of cultural products in France, pointed out that "the tastes actually realized depend on the state of the system of goods offered; every change in the system of goods induces a change in tastes" (Bourdieu 1984, 231). In China, the discourses surrounding the new taste for Western cow milk expressed the social ideals of good bodies and citizenship.

Unfortunately, in the process of bringing about a "milk revolution" in China, unexpected new food safety challenges arose, along with new social hierarchies and structural constraints that limited the life chances of dairy farmers and the poor.

The Fall of Water Buffalo Cheese

One sunny afternoon after finishing the cheese-making work for the day, Auntie Lin shared with me the seldom-told story of the changes in the institutions and production processes for water buffalo milk and Western cow milk over the past five decades.[1] Lin is one of the most senior and well-respected cheese makers in Jinbang village (*Jinbangcun*), a village located in the northern part of Daliang town. She was born into a cattle-farming family, which relied on sales of beef as its major source of income and sales of water buffalo milk as a supplementary source of income. In pre-socialist Daliang, there were hardly any imported dairy cows, and almost all of the farmers in Jinbang village would raise at least one pair of water buffaloes. When Lin was young, her family's herd numbered about twenty, including eight adult buffaloes and twelve calves. The family was the basic production unit in water buffalo husbandry, with a clear division of labor. Lin, the eldest child, described the work she was assigned in the family—preparation of feeding, herding, and milking—thus:

> Every morning, I would get up at 3 o'clock. The first thing to do was to lead the cows to the river for them to bathe for half an hour. Then, I had to clean up the cowshed. At 5 o'clock in the morning, my younger brother and I would bring the cows back to the cowshed for milking. Milking requires a special skill, as the cow may not allow you to touch her. You need to massage the udders, clean them with warm water, wiping them with a soft towel until they are dry, and then stimulate the flow of milk to the teats with your hands.
>
> To prepare the fresh water buffalo milk for the schoolteachers, early every morning I would boil the milk and then immediately fill 40 sterilized bottles with it. Then, my younger brother would accompany my mother in carrying the bottles to the school. At 11 o'clock, we would receive elephant grass from our grass-cutting partner.[2] Then, we would wash the grass thoroughly before feeding it to the buffaloes. Afterwards, we would bathe the

buffaloes a second time and then bring them back at noon. We would then bathe them again at 2 in the afternoon and milk the cows at 3 o'clock. Then, at 5:30 in the afternoon, it was time for the fourth bath and another feeding. At 7 o'clock in the evening, we would bring the buffaloes back home. The buffaloes needed to take baths four times a day to help their digestion and to aid in their milking.

Lin emphasized that the supreme quality of water buffalo milk produced by her family was due to the custom diet given to their buffaloes and the intensive care provided to them by her family. She remarked:

A water buffalo is [was] a sign of wealth for a family. In those days, a single water buffalo cost almost RMB 40, a great sum of money at the time. For this reason, if one's family owned a water buffalo, they would treat it as if it were a member of the family. We fed the buffaloes well. The grass we fed them was of good quality, and we washed it well. In addition, every day we gave the buffaloes cooked rice[3] to eat, as well as a mixture of honey and egg every ten days. This would increase the richness and the taste of the milk, as well as improve the buffaloes' health. Milk production each day was around 10 *jin* (5 kilograms) per cow. In addition, we made cooling herbal tea for the buffaloes to drink when they were "hot" [referring to the Chinese humoral system described in chapter 1], especially after giving birth. The recipe for the herbal tea we prepared for them was the same as that we drank ourselves when we were "hot," composed of ingredients such as oak leaves and scutellaria root.[4]

The importance of diet in influencing the quantity of milk that cows and buffaloes produce is well supported by scholars and scientists. Cristina Grasseni, during her ethnographic study of cheese production in an Alpine community, noted that the most productive dairy cows were those given an extra dose of calcium and glucose in their diet, in addition to hay, maize, alfalfa grass, fodder, vitamins, and bicarbonate. The ratios of those ingredients, she added, were adjusted according to the season and following the advice of a nutritionist (Grasseni 2009, 113, 130). What makes the design of cow feed in China unique is the influence of Chinese medical theories.

In addition to the composition of the feed for the water buffaloes, Lin said that the breed of the water buffalo would also affect the quality of its milk. Although the milk yield from indigenous Chinese buffaloes is much lower than that from imported dairy cows, it is said to be richer in flavor and more suitable for making cheese than the milk produced by cross-bred cows. For this reason, Shunde natives typically despise cheese made from the milk of cross-bred buffaloes, though Lin says that most consumers are probably unable to distinguish between the two.[5]

Collectivization and the New Science

Auntie Lin, as well as many of my female informants with children, told me how the knowledge of indigenous water buffalo milk production was almost lost in the 1960s, owing to the modernization and collectivization of production during the period of the people's communes (1958–1983). The most obvious change was that the number of indigenous buffaloes decreased drastically from more than four hundred to just sixty following collectivization. During the period of collective ownership, there were three production teams; each had twenty to thirty buffaloes for milk production. The reasons for the drastic drop in the buffalo population are complex, although the villagers I spoke with attributed it mainly to the collectivization of water buffalo husbandry and the new science of milk production.

Lin witnessed firsthand the deleterious effects of the series of experiments carried out on animal husbandry, including changes made to the buffaloes' diet, as well as the ill effects of the implementation of a collective system for taking care of the buffaloes. Carrying out the state's vision of progress and improvement during the commune era, local party officers began conducting experiments on the cows with the objective of increasing their milk output. For example, some local officials tried broadcasting music in the cowshed during milking. However, the buffaloes would move about when the music grew louder, making the task of milking impossible. In addition to modifying the buffaloes' living environment, the local government introduced new feed recipes, which, according to Lin, seemed illogical. In one notable example, the farmers were told to give Chinese wine to the young buffaloes on their birthdays because this was how humans celebrated birthdays. Lin lamented that the small buffaloes would immediately faint after being given the wine. A third aspect of modernization during collectivization was mechanization of the milking process. At that time, machines for milking began to appear in the village. However, Lin said that the buffaloes could not become accustomed to the machines and suffered from shortened life spans consequently.

Moreover, the buffaloes' health also deteriorated owing to the task-point system adopted by the local production teams in Jinbang village. This system led to a substantial change in the human–animal relationship. One former production team leader in Jinbang village related to me how a rewards system, in which different tasks were awarded different points (which could be converted for certain material goods within a certain time period), was introduced. Grass cutters were given the highest score of "5." This task was usually assigned to the young men as they might need to stay overnight in the countryside in Panyu or Guangzhou to handle the cutting, collection, and transportation of the grass back to Daliang. In contrast, women, the elderly, and the sick were assigned the care of the buffaloes, which, according to the local leaders, was considered to be easier work. The tasks involved in the care of the buffaloes were assigned the lowest score of "1." In other words, following collectivization, the buffalo husbandry and milking processes were divided up into different tasks and then taken up by different people. This meant that there was no longer any stable human–animal relationship, and therefore no one was responsible for safeguarding the buffaloes' health. This resulted in a precipitous drop in the population of buffaloes between the 1950s and the 1970s and a noticeable change in the quality of the buffaloes' milk.

New Land Policy

In addition to the modernization and collectivization of water-buffalo-milk production, another important factor in the decline of the indigenous milk industry was the new land use policy implemented in the late 1970s. With the opening up of the economy in 1978, the local government of Shunde, like those of other coastal regions in southeastern China, began adopting policies that favored the secondary and tertiary industries rather than the agricultural industry. Following the economic directives of the local government, each district in Shunde developed its own industrial specializations. For example, Daliang came to specialize in the production of small electronic products. Rural land was acquired for the new factories that would emerge for such industrial activity, which also saw the recruitment of large numbers of laborers at low cost (Sonobe, Hu, and Otsuka 2002). By the early 1990s, most of the water buffalo farms in Daliang had already been reclaimed by the local government, which greatly discouraged buffalo farming. This change led one informant, Sun, whose family had farmed buffalo for three generations, to instead rent a place in Liandu, part of Leiliu in the northwestern part of Shunde, to raise his twenty water buffaloes and fifteen calves.[6] Located between a river and a few fishponds, the Liandu buffalo farm was owned by a middle-aged man, whom people called *tangzhu* (literally, "the master of the ponds"). Besides Sun's family, there were nineteen other buffalo farmers renting space at the site for their buffaloes, three of whom were originally from Jinbang village, like Sun. Each rental space measured around 50 square meters, and came equipped with simple facilities, including water and a daily supply of fodder.

Today, Sun, like many water buffalo dairy farmers, finds himself relegated to a low social status owing to his chosen profession. In the past, the business of supplying water buffalo milk formed a significant part of the village economy. Today, however, in popular local media the buffaloes are usually labeled as environmentally polluting, while dairy farming is portrayed as being rural, backward, and even "uncivilized." There is a widely circulated story that the production of Jinbang buffalo cheese requires "killing the small cattle to get the milk." Dairy farmers do sometimes kill male calves in order to reserve the mother's milk for sale, a practice that has been recorded in industrialized milk production operations both in China and in Western countries (Levitt 2018). However, Lin and Sun both pointed out that they have never killed their male calves. The young buffaloes would be prevented from feeding on the mother's milk after two months, instead being fed only rice congee. Those male calves could either be kept for later mating or be sold in the market for use as draught animals or as a source of veal. Sun shared with me some of the challenges he faced in running the buffalo husbandry business:

> The local government in Shunde never gives us any support for buffalo farming. On the contrary, we feel that we are being intentionally discouraged from farming by the local government. First of all, buffalo dairy farming is portrayed as a polluting, backward and rural business in Daliang. Our dairy farm was driven out of town and forced to relocate to a suburban area. In 1984, our land was requisitioned by the government with little compensation. Second, there is no environmental protection or proper urban planning for buffalo farming in Shunde. For instance, not far away from the water ponds for the buffaloes in Liandu, there is a huge factory that produces motorcycles. This factory emits a lot of contaminated water without any proper controls. My uncle and I feel frustrated by this, but we have no

way to voice our frustration. The factory owner had previously donated a huge amount of money to the local government and the government officer has never charged the factory for anything. My uncle said that the motorcycle factory is one of the biggest tax-revenue generators in the area, as well as the biggest supporter of a local charity organized by the Shunde government, so it has a big say in local government policy.

Confirming Sun's experience, Lin told me that the cheese makers and buffalo dairy farmers received no financial or policy support from the local government to promote the sustainability of the industry despite the fact that buffalo cheese was then being promoted by the local government as part of the culinary heritage of the city. At the time of my fieldwork, Sun, thirty years old, was married to a primary school teacher, with whom he had a young son. Having been stigmatized as "rural," and therefore "uncivilized," he did not want his son to follow in his footsteps.

To sum up, the decline in traditional buffalo milk and cheese production practices began during the period of the people's communes in the 1960s and was attributable, first, to the modernization and collectivization of water buffalo milk and cheese production and, later, to the new land use policy implemented in the 1980s. As part of the state's vision of modernization, new milking machines, new divisions of labor, new water buffalo husbandry methods, and new forage recipes were introduced, all with the aim of increasing the quantity and quality of the buffaloes' milk. Then, accompanying the rapid period of urbanization beginning in 1984, the indigenous buffalo farmers in Daliang, Shunde, experienced a kind of structural violence as the government pursued an incompatible industrial vison. Most buffalo farmers lost their farms owing to the new land policy, and many were forced to move their water buffaloes to the outskirts of Daliang. Even worse, the water buffalo farmers were stereotyped as "backward" by the Shunde media. In the next section, we shall look into the local and global factors driving the skyrocketing production and consumption of foreign milk products in China, as well as their moral and social implications.

The Rise of Western Cow Milk

While the production of indigenous water buffalo milk has declined, the modern, Western-style cow-milk industry has been growing in northwestern

China since the 1980s, following the first batch of economic reforms and expanding rapidly since the late 1990s, coinciding with a surge in demand for liquid milk in China for a variety of political, economic, and cultural reasons (Hu et al. 2012).

Similar to the situation of colonial Hong Kong during the late nineteenth century, Western-style dairy farms using imported dairy cows were first established in China by Europeans in the treaty ports, which were forced in the mid-nineteenth century to open to foreign trade and residence by Western powers such as Great Britain, France, Germany, and the United States (*Encyclopedia Britannica* 2017). Most of the dairy cattle used on those farms were imported directly from Europe. For this reason, the urban dairy industry was initially concentrated in the treaty ports where most of the foreigners in the country lived. By 1870, dairy-cattle breeds from Europe had been introduced into Shanghai, which had become an open port in 1842. Dairy cattle were brought to Tianjin by foreign missionaries beginning in the late nineteenth century (Ke 2009, 73). At roughly the same time, dairy cattle were introduced into Dalian by foreign residents from Japan and Russia during the Russo–Japanese War (Dalian City Dairy Products Project Office 2000).

After the establishment of the People's Republic of China in 1949, some of the large-scale dairy farms, which had previously been owned by foreign powers, were incorporated into the government structure of *junken nongchang* (military farms) and transformed into key players in the domestic dairy industry. One notable example is Bright Dairy & Food Co., Ltd. in Shanghai, which was the fourth-largest dairy firm in China in 2017 by revenue (Marketline 2017). This firm was incorporated into the state-owned Shanghai Shiyan Jingji Diyi Muchang (the precursor to Bright Dairy Group) in 1945 following the concession of the Japanese military force.

These state-owned dairy farms enjoyed steady growth in their scale of production, probably owing to the range of exclusive privileges that they enjoyed in accessing financial and other resources. First, military farms, which supplied food and resources to the national army, usually had an advantage in gaining international support and funding. For example, before 1949 over half of the dairy cows (more than a hundred) at Bright Dairy Farm were received as postwar donations from the United Nations (Ke 2009, 74). Second, some state-owned dairy farms, such as the Wandashan milk-powder company in Heilongjiang Province, were granted resources for their technological development directly by the Communist Party. Wandashan milk powder was commercialized soon after 1963, following Chairman Mao Zedong's promotion of meat and dairy consumption to support the growth of Chinese children. Third, before the 1960s, these state-owned dairy farms received a steady supply of orders from the government, including from the army and schools. The government would usually make these purchases through state-owned sugar, tobacco, and wine companies. Fourth, the state-owned dairy enterprises were able to absorb local resources and to expand their dairy-product processing capacity while establishing new milking stations with state-backed loans (Ke 2009).

Even after the introduction of market reforms, the state-owned modern cow-milk enterprises, under the auspices of the Chinese central government, enjoyed greater international and local resources, as well as guaranteed orders from the army and other important branches of the state. This particular political structure greatly facilitated the growth of state-owned dairy farms. Taking again the example of Bright Dairy Group, in 1985 the Shanghai local government approved the group's building of a cow-milk-processing factory using funding support from the United Nations World Food Programme from 1985 to 1987, with a budget of RMB 8,550,000. At the same time, Bright Dairy Group also received an interest-free loan of RMB 40 million to develop dairying on the outskirts of the city. Third, Bright Dairy Group was supported by the government with free construction materials such as steel, wood, cement, and glass. With such a high degree of state and international institutional support, it is no surprise that Bright Dairy Group's market share reached as high as 30 percent of the total fluid-milk market in China in 1996 (Ke 2009, 86).

Still, it is worth asking: If the milk supply in China had been well established by the 1980s, why did the surge in milk consumption suddenly take place in the late 1990s rather than earlier? In the upcoming sections, I shall address this question by looking into the interaction of the forces of globalization and localization from four perspectives—global flows of capital, modern food and packaging technologies, the spread of nutrition science, and the impact of marketing. I will conclude this chapter by elaborating on the interaction between these global and local forces in shaping the meanings of milk products, our ideal bodies, and health and citizenship under the neoliberal governmentality and modernizing vision of the Chinese state.

Local Government and Global Capital

The rapid growth in demand for fresh milk in China, which began in the late 1990s, was closely related to the dramatic increase in milk production and aggressive marketing activities of the dairy companies, driven by the new economic reforms. Surprisingly, until the 1990s, China's Inner Mongolia Autonomous Region (IMAR), often symbolized by a clear blue sky, lush grasslands, and scattered vegetation being consumed by grazing heifers in advertisements produced by the major milk companies, did not have any large-scale industrialized dairy plants or foreign dairy cows when the new economic policies meant to stimulate the development of the dairy industry—led by Inner Mongolia Yili Industrial Group Co., Ltd. (Yili) and China Mengniu Dairy Company Limited (Mengniu)—were implemented.

The central government's broad economic policy prioritizing continual GDP growth and its fiscal burden-sharing policy launched in 1994 were important factors in the increase in dairy production in China. The Chinese Communist Party has adopted a pragmatic economic philosophy since the economic reforms first initiated under Deng Xiaoping. Since the implementation of the fiscal burden-sharing policy, the central government leadership has set growth targets each year that include tax revenues, investment, employment, and GDP growth targets, in addition to identifying noneconomic priorities such as social stability and enforcement of the one-child policy. Local officials then sign performance contracts and promise to meet the targets set (Teets 2015; Yu 2012). For example, if central leaders have decided on an 8 percent growth rate for the year, then meeting this target will be expected of local officials. They must then develop their own detailed indicators, such as how many dairy farms to build and how many cows to raise, in order to meet the central government's goals. Failure to meet certain goals set by the central government can result in dismissal, salary reductions, or demotion of the government officers responsible. An equity investor named Winston Mok has pointed out that there is an imbalance in the alignment of resources and responsibilities for the central and local governments. Local governments currently receive little more than half of fiscal revenues, while being responsible for more than 80 percent of expenditures (Mok 2015). All of this means that, since 1994, the party has increased the political power of local government offices in economic development, but it has at the same time shifted the economic burden to them.

In order to meet the GDP targets set by the central government, the city governments of Shijiazhuang and Tangshan in Hebei Province and the provincial government of IMAR considered the dairy industry as a potential pillar industry (Xiu and Klein 2010). To strengthen their respective regional outputs, these municipal governments also made use of preferential policies to support the development of the local dairy industry, such as encouraging individual rural farmers to raise dairy cattle (Tuo 2000), and supporting leading enterprises. They also introduced milk-price and feed subsidies, such as "exchanging grain [subsidizing parity feed price] for milk" (Chongqing Municipal Dairy Industry Administration Office 2000), and offering exceptionally low tax rates to develop and attract local and foreign investment into the dairy industry (Chen, Hu, and Song 2008).

An additional and related reason for the rapid surge in dairy production in Inner Mongolia, where over 19 percent of the total industry revenue was produced in 2011 (Beckman et al. 2011), is the increasing ease of moving investment capital into and out of China following changes made by the state government to policies on the public listing of enterprises. Mengniu, for example, had total invested capital of only RMB 1.3 billion in 1999 (Peverelli 2006, 114). Then, in 2002, Morgan Stanley, CDH Investments, and China Capital Partners jointly signed an agreement with Mengniu to purchase a 32 percent share of the company. With this new influx of foreign capital, Mengniu dramatically increased its marketing expenditures from US$5.0 million in 1999 to a staggering US$263 million in 2002, which resulted in rapid expansion of the company's market share. Mengniu's strategy of "establishing the market first and then establishing the plant" enabled the company to become a household name within five years, and even to acquire a listing on the Stock Exchange of Hong Kong soon after, in June 2004.[7] In short, the decentralization of governance and a disproportionate share of the fiscal burden created new roles and expectations of local governments, resulting in an explosion of milk production in remote areas of northern China while creating new demand for cow milk.

Dairy Technology and Food Packaging

Although the Chinese state, through local governments, has been providing economic incentives for the development of dairy production in

Northwest China, the growth rate in the dairy market would not have been as high had it not been supported by modern dairy technology and new food packaging. Modern packaging technologies, namely Ultra High Temperature (UHT) sterilization and the conventional pasteurization process, not only destroy pathogenic bacteria but also allow for perishable milk to be stored at room temperature for up to eight months and easily transported long distances at low cost. In the 1990s, two of the biggest hurdles impeding the popularization of milk in China were the lack of refrigeration, especially in rural areas of the country, and the high cost of transporting perishable milk long distances. In the late 1990s, around 70 percent of the Chinese population were living in rural areas (National Bureau of Statistics of China 2018a), and only around 1 percent of the people in rural areas and 40 percent of those in urban areas had access to refrigeration (National Bureau of Statistics of China 2018b). In addition, at that time it was extremely expensive, if not impossible, to transport the surplus milk produced in northern China to the urban coastal cities, where the demand for fresh milk was concentrated.

The new milk-processing and packaging technology not only made storage of milk more convenient for consumers but also lowered the costs of production, storage, and logistics management for the dairy companies, thereby enabling them to expand into geographically distant markets. In addition to the UHT packaging technology that allowed for "fresh" milk to be transported long distances from north to south, the development of modern food science also opened up the more important possibility of altering the composition of "milk." Before the widespread adoption of industrial UHT processing, "fresh cow milk," mostly packaged in glass bottles or plastic bags, usually denoted pasteurized cow milk without additives. Today, as long as the standards for protein content and the bacterial counts in raw milk reach acceptable levels—at least 2.8 percent for protein content and no more than 2 million/milliliter for bacterial count—the composition of a box of UHT-processed fresh cow "milk drink" may include an assortment of dairy or non-dairy products, ranging from raw milk, milk powder, and milk fat to soy, vitamins, minerals, preservatives, flavorings, and coloring additives. For example, in the case of Mengniu's *weilaixing* (future star) milk for children, additional milk protein and oligosaccharides are added to the product to meet the national requirements. In other words, thanks to the expanded definition of "milk" offered by modern food science, lower-quality raw milk could be used as milk protein to meet the government requirements. The lower technological threshold enabled more farmers with less-sophisticated feeding technology and storage facilities to produce milk, thereby rapidly improving the raw-milk-production capacity of China's western and northwestern regions (Hu et al. 2012). More importantly, China's homegrown giant milk corporations could further lower their production costs as they no longer needed to rely solely on the supply of raw milk from local dairy farmers but could instead source low-cost milk powder and milk components globally.

All of this resulted in the transformation of the dairy production chain in China and a dramatic shift in power from the well-established dairy giants in Beijing and Shanghai like Bright Dairy Group, which has now fallen to fourth place in total market share, to the newly established dairy production companies in Northwest China, like the leading Mengniu and Yili groups (Marketline 2017). Moreover, the demand for fluid milk in the south of the country could not have been met without the active participation of Tetra Pak and the shift in production technology from milk bottling to UHT production.

Although Shanghai's Bright Dairy Group and Inner Mongolia's Yili Group introduced UHT milk-processing equipment from Sweden's Tetra Laval Holdings Finance SA in 1994 and 1996, respectively, it was Mengniu that most benefited from the technology (Ke 2009, 107). According to a study of the politics of the milk industry by journalist Ke Zhixiong, in 1999 the estimated equipment and production cost for aseptic packaging was RMB 25,000,000, eight times the cost of packaging pasteurized milk products (2009, 108–109). With limited financial resources, Mengniu would not have been able to afford the process had Tetra Pak not tailor-made a rental service for Mengniu to begin producing UHT fluid milk. In addition, during this period, Tetra Pak was experimenting with a new pillow-shaped design as an alternative to the classic carton-box style of packaging—Tetra Fino Aseptic, which cost less but had a shorter shelf life of just forty-five days, compared to eight months for the UHT aseptic paper pack. Tetra Pak was willing to provide two production lines for free to its new clients, and Mengniu took advantage of this offer. This facilitated the successful launch of Mengniu's special pillow-shaped packaged milk, which was sold at half the price of Yili's UHT and quickly cornered the market. This low-cost UHT milk product enabled the Mengniu Group to enhance its overall competitiveness and to expand its market share exponentially. UHT milk then became widely available in the markets of China's medium-sized and large cities. According to data from the China Association of the Dairy Products Industry, the output of UHT milk increased remarkably from just 2 million tons in 1999 to 48 million tons in 2004. At the same time, the share of UHT milk as a percentage of fluid milk output increased from just 20 percent in 1999 to nearly 60 percent in 2004, indicating the strategic role of food packaging in the surge in milk production and consumption in China (Sun and Zhang 2005).

Nutrition Science and Public Health

The increased supply of low-cost cow milk alone would not have automatically translated into market demand unless consumers felt that those milk products were addressing a certain need. The growth in milk consumption in the late 1990s and early 2000s coincided with the proliferation of knowledge of nutrition science among pediatricians, doctors, nurses, health workers, and officers in the government's public health departments, who in turn rapidly assimilated new ideas of health and what constitutes a good diet, motivated by a combination of moral, commercial, and nation-building concerns. Dr. Cheng, an experienced pediatrician who once held a senior position in the Hong Kong Pediatric Society, told me that there was a significant change in the dietary guidelines set by the Chinese Nutrition Society in the early 2000s—the incorporation of milk products. She told me that the change was a result of increased contact between Chinese doctors and nutritionists at international conferences, as well as the pressing national concern of modernizing the health of the population. The new dietary guidelines are essentially similar to the pyramid-like hierarchical dietary model first published in the United States in the 1970s. According to the latest dietary guidelines published by the Chinese Nutrition Society in 2011, there are health risks associated with breastfeeding and the traditional Chinese diet. Cow milk is recommended as a daily drink for all and is considered especially good for young children, teenagers, and the elderly.

This set of dietary guidelines, which supports the purported benefits of cow milk, is very much the result of the lobbying efforts of both local and international milk corporations, which have invested huge sums of money into producing what appears as value-free scientific knowledge through research into the characteristics and effects of formula milk and breast milk. With control of the modes of production and the assimilation of scientific knowledge through their sponsorship of scientific research and conferences, both the milk corporations and the state benefit from higher industry profits, directly in the case of the milk corporations, and indirectly in the case of the state, which is able to enjoy higher incomes from state-owned dairy farms and higher profit taxes while simultaneously achieving its vision of building a strong national body by creating "quality" people equipped to succeed in the global economy (Greenhalgh and Winckler 2005, 280).

Innovation of Chinese Medical Heritage, Beauty Capital, and Social Class

The rapid growth of milk consumption in China was not due merely to the rise of Western science, the desire to support children's growth, and the government's endorsement. Another crucial reason for the creation of the new dairy market in China has been the development of products based on Chinese traditional dietary beliefs, syncretized with imported Western nutrition science, and coupled with powerful marketing messages that offer consumers the hope of solving their most pressing health and social problems. Although many Chinese parents consider cow milk and dairy products to be Western foods that support the growth of children's bodies, women also buy milk products based on Chinese medical principles, believing that those products will enhance their beauty and health capital and help them achieve their goals and modern identity in contemporary China.[8]

For example, Nanyan, a secondary school teacher in her late twenties, brought a pack of Mengniu cow milk with black beans and cereals, together with a slice of pizza, to school as her breakfast. She explained to me how she typically arranged her meals:

> In grandma and mother's generation, people in Shunde usually had very simple foods for breakfast—plain white rice congee, oily *youtiao* [a Chinese crispy fried breadstick], accompanied by a few thin slices of salty *niuru*. However, nowadays, we have so many better choices. Also, young people like me who need to rush to work don't have time for that. This morning, I steamed two ears of corn at home before heading to work. I will eat them during lunchtime together with a package of herbal yogurt drink. As summer is coming, I want to look slim. I believe in the slimming effect of black beans and yogurt.

Hua Wen, in her study of cosmetic surgery in China, notes that in highly competitive, service-oriented urban cities, having a pleasing, youthful appearance has almost become a basic criterion for women to secure high-paying employment and to acquire a high social status (Wen 2013). According to research conducted by the Boston Consulting Group in 2014, many well-educated urbanites in China seeking ways of gaining beauty and health capital prefer to buy products developed based on traditional Chinese medical principles. Their study found that traditional Chinese medicine is especially appealing to more sophisticated consumers, being preferred by 55 percent of buyers in large cities, compared with just 35 percent in smaller cities. This is largely because more knowledgeable consumers have concerns about the side effects of Western over-the-counter products. In contrast, relatively less sophisticated consumers believe that Western medical products, which are readily available in retail stores, are more effective than similar traditional Chinese medical remedies and easier to consume (Wu et al. 2014).

The type of herbal yogurt drink or herbal milk drink mentioned by Nanyan is a good example illustrating how Chinese medical principles can be successfully used to develop new dairy products, which women consume in the hopes of enhancing their beauty and accruing other social benefits. In 2007 Hebei's Junlebao Dairy Group pioneered a new, flavored yogurt drink incorporating principles from traditional Chinese medicine—yogurt with red dates. As outlined in chapter 1, based on traditional Chinese health beliefs, foods can be categorized into "hot" and "cold" categories derived from the theory of yin-yang and the doctrine of the Five Phases (Porkert 1974; Unschuld 2010). Although Western cow milk is widely considered to be a nutritious food because it is rich in protein and calcium, it is categorized as a "cold" food under the Chinese humoral system and is thus not considered good for health if taken directly. The coldness of cow milk can be neutralized by warming it up. Or, it can be balanced by eating *bu* (hot but replenishing) foods, such as red dates and peanuts, both of which are traditionally regarded as "blood-boosting" and "hot" ingredients. Owing to the success of the red-date yogurt drink, other red-colored or *bu* ingredients, such as wolfberries (*Fructus lycii*, sometimes called "goji berries" following the Japanese pronunciation), lotus seeds (*Nelumbinis nuciferae*) and *ejiao* (阿膠, also known by the Latin name *Colla corii asini*),[9] have also been used to develop new yogurt products.

Junlebao's application of traditional Chinese medicine concepts to Western yogurt drinks proved a hit in the dairy products market and inspired other companies to explore ways of incorporating popular Chinese traditional medical concepts into their own Western dairy products and related marketing. From a business perspective, one of the advantages of applying traditional Chinese medicine principles to the development of milk products is that it can create different meanings and functions for more granular customer segments, based not only on demographic data such as age, gender, occupation, and psychographic information, like lifestyle, but also based on individuals' self-perceived hot-cold bodily propensities. In 2008, Bright Dairy Group developed its own line of Chinese herbal yogurt drinks based on the well-known classic of Chinese medicine, the *Compendium of Materia Medica*. The three new product lines released under an umbrella moniker—"Qin Liang" ("cooling"), "Run Yan" ("beautifying"), and "Yang Yuan" ("nourishing the health foundation")—are tailored for different bodily propensities. Mangosteen, lily, and chrysanthemum are added to the Qin Liang yogurt line to help "cool" the "hot" bodies of most young people, as manifested in frequent pimples on the face and sore throats. Red dates, wolfberries, and mulberries are all added to the Run Yan "beautifying" yogurt line targeting women, who are believed generally to have "cool" bodies. These ingredients are high in antioxidants and believed to be especially good at boosting blood circulation, which is deemed essential for keeping young and staying beautiful. Lastly, poria (a type of fungus), barley, and bergamot are added to the Yang Yuan yogurt drink to give it a rejuvenating function, purportedly making it especially suitable for the weak bodies of the elderly. More generally, the individual ingredients of the Yang Yuan yogurt drinks are each believed to have specific health effects—rejuvenating the body, enhancing sleep, and strengthening mental functioning, respectively. This marketing strategy, which communicates the diversified functions and meanings of Western yogurt drinks based on Chinese medical beliefs, was so successful that sales of the line were three times higher than is typical for a newly launched product (*China Business News* 2008).

In addition to promising to enhance female consumers' beauty capital by "boosting the blood," dairy companies have tried to capitalize on the global sentiments that "slim is beautiful" and "fitness is healthy." With these trends in mind, many of the milk industry giants have developed new series of on-the-go, low-calorie, appetite-satisfying, meal-replacement dairy products based on traditional Chinese medicine principles. For example, Mengniu developed a new milk-with-grains series, based on the doctrine of the Five Phases, that can be consumed as a meal substitute and was marketed as having beauty-enhancing and slimming effects. The Five Phases, namely water, fire, metal, wood, and earth, are considered to be the most essential necessities in the human environment. The five colors of food (green, red, yellow, white, and black) are thought to correspond one-to-one to the five phases (green=wood, red=fire, yellow=earth, white=metal, and black=water) and are symbolically associated with the five internal organs (liver, heart, spleen, lung, and kidney). Based on its reinterpretation of the doctrine of the Five Phases and Five Colors, Mengniu's cow-milk products incorporating the Chinese Five-Color principles include a red-color series—featuring cow milk with red rice, red beans, and millet (which is believed to boost the blood)—and a black-color series—featuring cow milk with black grains, black beans, black flour, black sesame, and millet (which is believed to have a slimming effect). This five-color series of cow-milk drinks has been so successful that it led a major competitor, Hong Kong–based Vitasoy, to develop similar products, such as cow milk and soy milk with black beans.

The core message in the advertisements for herbal milk and yogurt drinks is their capacity to help consumers, both men and women, to achieve an ideal bodily image—slender, beautiful (or handsome), healthy, and youthful-looking—while at the same time expressing and shaping the notions of what an ideal modern Chinese person should be. Two cases are instructive to demonstrate how an ideal modern person should manage his or her body—Mengniu's herbal milk product called "Xinyangdao" (a fluid milk specially formulated for lactose-intolerant drinkers, to which red dates, *ejiao,* and wolfberries have been added), and a yogurt drink called "Go *Chang.*" In a famous 60-second TV commercial for Mengniu's *Xinyangdao* (2012) shot in Hainan, the viewer is shown the beautiful, well-known actress Zhang Ziyi (of the *Crouching Tiger, Hidden Dragon* and *Memoirs of a Geisha* fame in the West) dressed in an elegant, long white dress with a silky, red scarf, symbolizing the whiteness of the milk and the redness of the red dates and wolfberries. While immersing herself in the comforting silvery scenery of the beach at Xianshuiwan, Zhang explains her thoughts on her body, her work, and the secret to living a good life: "No matter whether at work or in my personal life, I want to do my best. However, this desire stresses my body.

Therefore, I need to nourish my qi and my body every day by consuming the right foods [i.e., milk]."

Zhang's monologue in the advertisement, together with a few flashback images of her work as an actress and model, not only suggests the nourishing function of the milk product being advertised, but also the image of an ideal women in contemporary China—smart, attractive, and resourceful, yet in need of her own space and time. The implication is also that modern women should reward themselves (J. Wang 2008, 78). The advertisement also conveys the message that it is an individual's responsibility to work hard—by consuming the advertised milk product, in this case—to stay young-looking, beautiful, and successful.

In contemporary China, the obligation to be slim, good-looking, and healthy applies not only to women but also to men. We see this in Mengniu's advertisement for its "Go *Chang* (畅)" yogurt beverage in 2018. A young, healthy-looking Chinese man, the popular singer Li Yifeng, is shown accompanying a clumsy, obese man in facing all of the embarrassments caused by his body in his daily life (such as passing through a narrow subway entrance gate and down the slide in a swimming pool). The short, eye-catching name of the product, a combination of English and Chinese words (English "go" and Mandarin "*chang*"), creates a pun while successfully capturing the meaning of the word "*chang*," which is visually similar to the Chinese word for "intestines" (differing only in tone) and refers to something going smoothly and unimpeded, that is, without blockage. Metaphorically, the name implies a level of healthiness obtained through the intestines not being blocked. Thus, the implication of the advertisement is that the solution to achieving one's goals in life without being blocked is to take "Go畅" to "clean out" the intestines regularly, especially after consuming a heavy meal.

In mainland China, the appearance in the late 1990s of an ethos celebrating self-reliance and independently achieving health, success, and happiness through consumption coincided with rising medical costs and an increase in the number of so-called lifestyle diseases afflicting young people (Wu et al. 2014). Following the collapse of the well-established cooperative medical system for rural areas in the late 1970s and the closure of many factories that had been unable to survive the series of economic reforms throughout the 1980s and 1990s, by 1999 only 49 percent of urban Chinese and 7 percent of rural Chinese had health insurance (Sun, Gregersen, and Yuan 2017). Many people simply could not afford to fall sick.

At the same time, an increasing number of men and women in affluent communities in China began experiencing lifestyle diseases. In 2014, fully 30 percent of respondents to a survey, aged 18 to 24, reported suffering from various lifestyle ailments (Wu et al. 2014). Common complaints included insomnia, fatigue, obesity, and frequent illness. Fully 73 percent of those respondents said they would be willing to trade up and pay a premium for products deemed healthier, 12 percent higher than the global average.

Furthermore, by building a socially responsible and patriotic image for itself through its support of government projects and various charitable causes, Mengniu has simultaneously sought to build up a socio-psychological tie with its customers by leveraging nationalist sentiment and offering hope to the Chinese people for the prosperous future of China at large. In support of the daily milk-drinking program proposed by then Premier Wen Jiabao, Mengniu sponsored 500 primary schools and 60,000 students in poor areas with a daily supply of drinking milk for one year in 2006. A few years earlier, in 2003, Mengniu had also contributed RMB 12 million for an anti-SARS campaign.

One of my informants from Shunde told me that when he thought of milk, he would think of Mengniu and the various charitable activities that Mengniu sponsored:

> I can still remember when, in 2006, our Premier [Wen Jiabao] announced that he wished for every student to be able to drink one *jin* [500 grams] of milk per day. Mengniu was the first dairy company to take action and immediately sponsored five hundred schools with free milk. At the time, I was really moved.

To strengthen the link between patriotic feeling and consumption of cow milk, the giant milk companies integrated their marketing activities with the most important national events or achievements. Yili has been one of the key sponsors for the Olympic Games in China since 2005 and has sponsored several Chinese athletes and Olympic competition winners, going so far as to hire the 110-meter-hurdles record breaker Liu Xiang as its brand spokesperson. Similarly, Mengniu created a series of advertisements in celebration of the successful return of the Shenzhou 5 spacecraft—the first successful human spaceflight mission of the Chinese space program, launched in 2003—boosting sales of its own products and indirectly contributing to China's image of technical advancement and national prestige. By adding to the national narrative and establishing themselves as socially responsible, patriotic, and prestigious companies through their support of major government initiatives, Yili and Mengniu have successfully built up brand personas as "caring and credible fathers" empowering their customers to become responsible citizens through their consumption decisions.[10]

In short, the sudden taste for Western cow milk in China cannot be explained merely by the surge in milk production in northern China, and new milk packaging technology, but rather by a broader set of interlocking actors in the pharmaceutical nexus: the medical institutions and doctors who have actively promoted Western nutrition science in China; the milk and pharmaceutical companies that successfully marketed their milk products by giving hope to customers of managing their health and building ideal bodies; and skillfully offering the right product designs syncretizing traditional Chinese medical beliefs and Western nutrition science. Drinking cow milk containing ingredients with medicinal properties according to traditional Chinese medicine and eating Western-style bread as the most popular breakfast food for young, educated, middle-class people in China reveal a new identity built upon lifestyle and consumption, distinguishing them from the previous generation and less-sophisticated social groups. Putting it in the language of Jean Baudrillard's approach to consumption (Bocock 1993, 67), it is a process in which the cow-milk purchaser "is actively engaged in trying to create and maintain a sense of identity" through the display of cow-milk-product consumption.

Although the giant milk companies in China lower the price of Western cow milk, making it more accessible to the masses, the dramatic shift of cow-milk production from family farms to mega factory farms raises ethical questions: in particular, what has been the impact on food safety in China of the economic pragmatism of the Chinese Communist Party and the growing importance of the mega dairies to their respective local economies? This is an important question that I will address shortly.

Global Capital, the State Vision, and Food Safety Crises

As discussed above, one of the reasons for the sudden surge in the consumption of fluid milk in China was the rapid expansion in the scale of milk production in northern China, supported by a flood of investment from both Chinese and international investors (including international dairy companies). This process has continued since the listing of Mengniu and Yili on stock exchanges at the start of the twenty-first century. Notably, in 2009 the Chinese state-owned food-processing firm COFCO and private-equity firm Hopu Investment Management Co. teamed up to invest about US$780 million for a 20 percent stake in China Mengniu Dairy Co., Ltd. Investment by foreign dairy companies has also been important in stimulating the growth of local dairy farms. As reported by journalist Gwynn Guilford, foreign dairy companies were treated with a series of carrot-and-stick incentives to help the Chinese dairy companies develop their own business if they wished to stay in the market (2013). In 2013, it was reported in a *Bloomberg Businessweek* article that Nestlé was "collaborating with local governments, banks and investors to accelerate the consolidation of China's dairy farms," while Danone bought a 4 percent stake in Mengniu in 2013 to improve Mengniu's infant-formula production processes (Guilford 2013). At the time of writing, many foreign dairy companies hold significant equity stakes in China's major dairy companies. For example, the Danish-Swedish dairy group Arla now holds a 31.43 percent stake in China Mengniu Dairy, while Fonterra, which had initially entered into a joint venture with the Sanlu Dairy group before Sanlu went bankrupt in 2008 in the aftermath of the melamine-tainted milk crisis, entered into a new, "game-changing" deal in 2014 when it invested US$615 million in Beingmate, one of the leading formula-milk manufacturers in China (*New Zealand Herald* 2017).

The development of enormous milk factories in northern China, driven by the combined forces of modern state building, China's GDP-centric political system, and the globalization of food, has not been without regulatory and food safety problems. Since the economic performance of the giant milk corporations in the north has such a large impact on the GDP performance of their respective provinces, local government officials in those regions have an enormous incentive to establish and implement rules and regulations favoring the dairy business. This is the major reason why most of the big dairy corporations, including Sanlu, Yili, Nestlé, and Wahaha, have been invited to draft the standards guidelines for milk powder, butter, cheese, condensed milk, and milk beverages, resulting in China having lower dairy product standards than the international norm (Ke 2009, 34; *South China Morning Post* 2010).

Yet, it would be an oversimplification to conclude that the state–corporate alliance led to corruption and food-safety problems. In fact, in the past decades, safeguarding the food-safety system has been one of the top priorities of the Chinese government in attempting to maintain a "harmonious society" (*hexie shehui*)—a vision laid down by ex-President Hu Jintao for the country's future socioeconomic development (Chan 2009). The first notable effort to ensure the safety and quality of the country's food supply was put forth in 1992, when the Chinese government established the China Green Food Development Center, which was tasked with overseeing the implementation of innovations in food production and began issuing "Green Food" certificates for qualified products following stricter standards on pesticide, fertilizer, and other additive use than their conventional counterparts. In the early 2000s the Chinese government also launched two state-approved quality standards for products and brands—the "*Zhongguo mingpai*" ("Chinese famous brand")[11] appellation and "*guojia mianjian*" certification ("national products exempt from inspection"). The large dairy corporations Sanlu, Mengniu, and Yili were the first in the sector to be accredited by the Chinese government as "Chinese famous brands." These companies were also accredited as "*guojia mianjian*," which granted them privileged exemption from regular inspections by the government, based on the assumption that these mega dairies could be trusted to self-regulate. The objectives of these state accreditations were twofold: to promote the image of made-in-China products to local and international markets; and to lower the operating costs for these corporations so as to support their rapid growth. However, a food-safety system that relies on food companies to self-monitor is risky. This case illustrates an example of failure due to what the political analyst and historian Thomas Frank has called "extreme capitalism," which puts profit making and expansion ahead of sustainability—in this case, of the dairy farmers' livelihoods, the environment, and the health of consumers—and is being practiced around the world (2000). The official accreditations enjoyed by these dairy giants enabled their substandard dairy products to go to market without being inspected, paving the way for the subsequent food-safety crises.

The most salient example showing how the national brand-accreditation system and inspection-exemption system failed is the now well-documented Sanlu melamine-tainted milk crisis, which killed four babies and affected some 54,000 children, who developed kidney stones and became sick

(Stevenson and agencies 2008). Melamine, a nitrogen-rich industrial additive used to make plastics, fertilizers, and concrete, was illegally added to the watered-down milk to increase its apparent protein content since nitrogen content often is used to estimate protein levels (BBC 2010; World Health Organization 2019b). Melamine is known to be toxic and can cause kidney stones and even kidney failure (BBC 2010; Bristow 2008).

This case actually had its roots in an earlier, though less-well-publicized, scandal. In 2004, when forty-five types of fake formula were found on sale in Fuyang City, Anhui—resulting in the death of at least thirteen children—the national government reacted by telling people to only buy formula milk from one of the thirty state-approved brands, a list that included Sanlu, Mengniu, and Yili (BBC News 2004). Yet, during the melamine-tainted milk crisis of 2008, it was revealed that not only products from Sanlu but also those from Mengniu, another large state-accredited milk company, and some other state-approved dairy firms contained the toxic chemical (BBC 2010; Bristow 2008).

Fears escalated when it was revealed that virtually all Chinese-produced dairy products, including ordinary milk, ice cream, and yogurt, contained melamine. Countries around the world announced bans on imports of products that contained Chinese milk, including bakery products and candies (Xiu and Klein 2010). Panic spread further when news reports indicated that Sanlu Company officials had known about the problem for months and possibly as far back as December 2007, without taking any corrective actions (*China Daily* 2008; Wang 2009). Worse still, on October 31, 2008, Chinese state media admitted that melamine was being routinely added to Chinese-produced animal feed.

Trust in the Chinese government to strengthen food-safety regulations collapsed in 2010 when people later learned that, rather than tightening the standards on milk production after the Sanlu scandal, it had instead lowered the standard for raw milk. In the revised 2010 national standards for the dairy industry, the required protein content for raw milk was lowered from 2.95 percent (the 1986 standard) to 2.8 percent, far below the international standard (34 percent m/m) (FAO and WHO 2011). In addition, the allowable quantity of bacteria was increased fourfold, from 0.5 million/mL to 2 million/mL. This combined lowering of the standard for raw milk favored the milk corporations in the north, as most had outsourced dairy-cattle husbandry to small, third-party dairy farmers who sometimes had problems meeting the earlier, more-stringent requirements.

Ironically, the revision in the standard had been initiated by the milk giants in the north as a way of addressing the food-safety problems presented by melamine-tainting during the Sanlu scandal. The argument of the northern milk manufacturers was that if the standard for the raw milk were lower, there would be no need to add melamine or other additives to the low-quality milk to boost its apparent protein content. This argument and standard were highly criticized by some of the milk corporations based in urban areas such as Bright Dairy Group, which exercised better control over the quality of its raw milk. China is not unique in this respect. As nutrition policy advisor Marion Nestle (no relation to the Swiss corporation) reminds us, milk corporations have long exercised their lobbying power to influence the rules and regulations concerning their industry in the United States (Nestle 2002, 81).

Although the globalization of food and capital have made Western cow milk more affordable and accessible for many in China, there is a growing distrust among upper-class and middle-class Chinese toward locally branded milk as people have learned from experience that the serious food-safety problems of these "famous brands" have not been resolved. In 2012, Inner Mongolia Yili Industrial Group found elevated levels of toxic mercury in its infant formula, while health officials in the southern metropolis of Guangzhou discovered milk products containing excessive amounts of cancer-causing aflatoxin, despite earlier official pledges by the government to clean up the industry (McDonald 2012). Following this series of food crises, the Chinese government has lost credibility regarding its capacity to guarantee food safety in the eyes of many Chinese people (Huang 2016; Yu 2015).

A Modern, Healthy Middle-Class and the Rural, Unlucky "Other"

While the conventional public health reading of the shift away from the classic eating pattern in China—consumption predominantly of cereals and low-fat mixed dishes—toward increasing consumption of animal-food products, which is often seen as a kind of natural "evolution" owing to economic progress and Westernization of people's lifestyles (Du et al. 2002; B. Ng 2017), I would like to propose that this dramatic dietary change is instead a result of the success of the new milk regime, formed by the alliance between corporations and the Chinese national state.

The reason for this is that the establishment of a new milk regime is part of the strategic political agenda of the Chinese Communist Party. As Charles Parton, a foreign affairs advisor on China to the UK House of Commons and an associate fellow of the Royal United Services Institute, rightly notes, "The legitimacy of the party is based on several pillars, but the first is economic. It's the promise that the party will make you better off than you were before." Parton continued, "Meat used to be an occasional luxury; dairy was mostly not available, so if you can now afford both meat and milk regularly, you feel wealthier" (Lawrence 2019). That is to say, the rise of Western cow milk and the decline of traditional water buffalo milk was not simply a natural evolutionary process accompanying modernization, but rather a triumph of modern food production processes, driven by the market and the modernizing state, in creating new hopes for the citizens of China, and especially women, to solve modern problems and to establish new social boundaries *within* the vision of the modern state.

The dramatic increase in the scale of Western cow milk production in modern China raises obvious ethical questions: Is there a new, unequal distribution of power and risk between the rich and the poor, and between the dairy corporations and the small dairy farmers? The popular discourse on the traditional water-buffalo-milk-and-cheese culture in state-censored media seeks to describe the industry's decline as a natural and unavoidable part of modernization serving a social good, thereby obscuring the structural disadvantages faced by the traditional industry owing to its incompatibility with the state's own modernizing vision. Similarly, narratives on the decreasing number of cheese makers generally focus on their rural and backward lifestyles while concealing the structural factors that hinder cheese makers in Jinbang village, who, much like the water buffalo farmers, lack the cultural, social, and financial capital to create a "sign value" and "symbolic value," in Baudrillard's sense, by marketing their products with a view to increase their price, expand their product lines, and draw on government resources to establish those products as a type of cultural "heritage" (Baudrillard [1970] 1998).[12]

Perhaps worst of all, some cheese makers use a strategy of "self-orientalism" or self-exoticization to attract tourists, further normalizing their "otherness" in the minds of modern consumers and their low position in the social hierarchy owing to their perceived backwardness and rural identity (Mak 2014). In Daliang, water buffalo cheese is now treated as a type of disappearing, out-of-fashion food for those seeking a nostalgic experience in popular narratives, rather than as an art form like *Parmigiano Reggiano*, which brings prestige and income to its home region in Italy and for which consumers from around the world are willing to pay a huge sum for just a small slice (Chen 2015). In the present case, the unequal treatment that the water buffalo cheese makers and farmers face in sustaining their business, I would say, is a kind of state-supported structural violence of the kind described by anthropologist João Biehl (2013), which has led to the "bureaucratically and relationally sanctioned" abandonment of the cheese makers (20).

In addition to the marginalization of the Shunde cheese makers and water buffalo farmers by the modernizing project of the state, there is also a new, unequal distribution of power and risk between large dairy corporations and the small dairy farmers. The Communist Party's five-year plans, beginning in the late 1990s, have introduced a raft of supports for dairy businesses. The state provided loans to farm companies to buy cows, gave processing companies tax breaks, and issued tens of millions in national debt funds to improve breeding stock and milking and packaging facilities. The rapid growth of the dairy industry in Inner Mongolia was further facilitated by the practices of the fragmented and flexible supply chain. Traditionally, small dairy farmers in China would have to spend almost all of their financial resources on running their dairy farms, while their family members would be deployed to work on milk processing. Today, the giant milk corporations like Mengniu and Yili have succeeded in building dairy empires by directing their resources primarily into marketing, data management, and information flows while outsourcing the high-risk and labor-intensive core tasks, such as dairy cow husbandry, to small-scale dairy farmers. Many of the giant milk corporations, as in the case of Sanlu—which was the largest milk-powder manufacturing corporation in China before its bankruptcy—even outsourced the tasks of inspection, collection of the milk supply, and price bargaining to brokers, who established the company's milk stations and usually earned a profit margin of 50 percent (Zhang et al. 2009, 10).

Under the new milk regime, the lower classes are often exposed to higher levels of food-safety risk and face greater uncertainty in their overall life chances. First, the poor and working-class consumers, who have internalized the idea that milk is a staple, are structurally constrained in their food choices. For instance, most of Sanlu's customers were members of the lower classes and unable to afford foreign brands of formula milk and therefore relied on Chinese brands.

Second, the dairy farmers themselves, who are also typically members of the lower classes, are forced to bear a higher livelihood risk and might even be forced out of business owing to the structural disadvantages they face. Following the transformation in the supply chains of dairy products, small dairy farmers could no longer rely on the customers at the neighborhood market, but would instead have to earn their living by supplying milk to the dairy-collection stations (or dairy factories) that collected milk for the giant dairy companies such as Sanlu, Mengniu, and Yili. Unlike in the United States, where the price of milk paid to farms has been regulated since the 1930s (Masson and DeBrock 1980), the price of raw milk in China is almost entirely determined by supply and demand. Since the dairy corporations stimulated sales and expanded the markets for their milk products by selling them at extremely low prices (e.g., Mengniu won its first market by offering its ice cream bricks at half the price offered by its key competitor Yili), they needed to force down the price of raw milk they paid the dairy farmers while still meeting the government's quality standard.

As Xiu Changbai and K. K. Klein have noted, small dairy farmers are simply "price takers" with no power to affect the terms of sale or matters such as quality inspections (Xiu and Klein 2010). They were obliged by the local Chinese government to sell their milk only to a specified processing company, which diminished their bargaining power. Exacerbating their situation, many small dairy farmers purchased their cows with financing assistance from the giant milk processors, which generally dictated the terms of the loans, including the interest rate and the payback period. This is a very competitive strategy for forcing the small dairy farmers to accept the low purchase price and for enabling the giant milk processors to sell the milk products at incredibly competitive prices in the lucrative milk market (Barboza 2008).

With no control over price, quality inspection, or other conditions of sale, a reduction of average costs has been the principal way for small farmers to maintain profits. One rarely noted fact is that it was very easy for anyone to purchase melamine and learn how to add it to milk. A survey in Helinger County of Inner Mongolia, where the large Mengniu Dairy

Processing Company is based, found that melamine was openly sold in some of the local drug markets. Instructions for its use were printed on the bottles, with clear directions on the proportions of water and melamine to mix together to raise the protein content of milk, the basis on which the small dairy farmers were paid (Yan and Xiu 2009).

Increasing global fodder prices also pose a significant threat to local Chinese dairy farmers, forcing them to take up improper dairying practices. When fodder prices soared, local Chinese farmers would have no choice but to respond by feeding the dairy cows poorly in most cases. The resulting cow milk might not be fit for sale to the milk-collection stations as the protein could not meet the national standard. Thus, faced with rising fodder prices in the mid-2000s, the business model of the small dairy farmers broke down, resulting in many of them resorting to slaughtering their dairy cattle and declaring bankruptcy (Xinhua News Agency 2015). Without sufficient help from the local government or the giant milk companies, adding melamine to the diluted milk to maintain sales emerged as the only viable alternative for survival that the dairy farmers were aware of.

China's small dairy farmers were further marginalized after the melamine-tainted milk scandal. To rebuild confidence in Chinese products, the state has accelerated investment in large-scale farms. Before the scandal, 70 percent of dairy farmers in China had herds of 20 or fewer cows. Six years after the scandal, the number of small herds had dropped to 43 percent, and industrial units with more than 1,000 head of cattle accounted for nearly 20 percent of the dairy farms. The most significant change was that the state imposed tough licensing on farmers, forcing many with smaller herds out of dairy production altogether (Lawrence 2019).

As this chapter has shown, the globalization of food and capital, supported by the modernizing Chinese state, created a new food regime in China. The rise of enormous dairy companies, the massive uptick in cow milk production, and aggressive marketing in China resulted in a dramatic change in milk-consumption behavior, from treating it as a *bupin* ("nourishing product") for upper-class people to a daily drink or snack accessible for many. At the same time, this change created new problems. First, it created new food-safety problems and structural constraints on the life chances of the poor and the dairy farmers, who are often stereotyped as unlucky "others." Second, the marketing of cow milk in China gave rise to two illnesses—the insufficient milk syndrome and picky-eating mental disorder—which we will discuss in the next chapters.

4 | Bottle-Feeding as Love, Success, and Citizenship

> Thanks to the big customers from China, all of Mead John-
> son's *Stage One* formula milk is priced 20 percent higher
> than usual. Even if you can pay the price, it is ALL out of
> stock! Hong Kong babies need to feed on shit! Will the
> Hong Kong government only intervene when our babies
> are dying?
>
> Tiffany, Baby-kingdom.com 2011

Tiffany, the mother of a six-month-old baby, posted this comment on one of the most popular parenting websites in Hong Kong, expressing her frustration and anxiety at trying to obtain a can of a coveted imported formula milk brand.[1] This particular brand of formula milk was viewed by Tiffany as a necessity for her baby. Tiffany's feeling that the wealthy shoppers from mainland China posed a threat to the livelihood and well-being of her baby and her family members in Hong Kong is hardly unusual. As mentioned in the introductory chapter, in 2013, a group of educated, technologically savvy, middle-class Hong Kong netizens became so agitated by the formula milk shortages in the territory that they submitted a petition on the White House website titled "Baby Hunger Outbreak in Hong Kong, International Aid Requested," asking the United States to intervene on their behalf. Five months later, this "right-to-formula" movement was further picked up by famed Chinese contemporary artist and dissident Ai Weiwei, who used 1,815 cans of the seven most popular milk brands in Hong Kong to form a gigantic map of China. This stunning formula-milk map took up most of the gallery floor space at the Para Site exhibition in Hong Kong. One commenter described this hyperbolic and subversive "Baby Formula" installation art piece as a way to "explore Hong Kong's identity and anti-Mainland [Chinese] sentiment" (Chow 2013).

The New Morality of Bottle-Feeding

This "right-to-formula" movement and art representation not only highlight the anxieties of parents in modern society over the food supply and the growing Hong Kong–mainland China conflicts, but also the fact that bottle-feeding has become the norm in infant feeding—a new ritual that has only developed in Chinese societies in the past fifty years.

Bottle-feeding was not only unpopular in the past in China but was even considered immoral in the 1920s. Unlike the situation today, where bottle-feeding is the preferred feeding approach of a majority of new mothers, mothers in 1920s China were blamed for being selfish if they fed their babies with milk substitutes to maintain their figures or to avoid being confined to the chore of breastfeeding (Li and Hua 1925; Lo 2009). The pro-breastfeeding elite, which in China mostly comprised authors writing on home economics, employed various scientific findings to advocate against bottle-feeding. Their arguments were generally based on the following three points. First, the composition of cow milk is tailored for calves, not human beings. Second, related to the first point, the proteins in cow milk are less easily digested by babies than human breast milk and thus inferior in quality. Third, the risk of milk contamination during preparation, owing to the compromised hygiene of the cowshed, was high (Lo 2009). In short, "breast was best."

Given this historical opposition to bottle-feeding and the unique non-dairy cultural background of Hong Kong and Chinese societies, it is surprising that Hong Kong has one of the lowest rates of breastfeeding in the developed world (Callen and Pinelli 2004; Foo et al. 2005; Government of Hong Kong SAR 2013a). In 2017, only 27 percent of babies were exclusively breastfed after the age of 6 months (Government of Hong Kong SAR 2017a).[2] In mainland China, too, the breastfeeding rate declined, by one quarter, to just 20.8 percent over the five-year period leading up to 2013 (Liu 2013). In contrast, in New York City, fully 58 percent of infants born in 2011 were breastfeeding at 6 months of age (New York City Department of Health and Mental Hygiene 2015).

Understanding why mothers choose not to breastfeed is a big concern for public health officials and local officials, as encouraging mothers to breastfeed offers the possibility of improving the health of infants (Gottschang 2007, 67). Promoting the benefits of breastfeeding and providing professional support to mothers with newborn babies has been one of the major roles of the Health Department of the Hong Kong and PRC governments since the 1970s. Current studies of infant feeding in Hong Kong and China show that the two most important factors in mothers choosing to bottle-feed are: the mothers' perception of having "insufficient milk" and the need to return to work (Tarrant et al. 2010; Xu et al. 2009).[3] Also, the prevalence of breastfeeding is lowest among members of the middle class, while in the United States it is members of the lower socioeconomic classes that have the lowest rates of breastfeeding. Why do most urban Chinese women suffer from the aforementioned "insufficient milk syndrome"? What are the conflicts they face between work and breastfeeding? Why is it members of the middle class in Hong Kong breastfeed the least? Unfortunately, thus far, there has been scant research documenting how different infant-feeding discourses operate on different social classes in the context of the media-saturated, rapidly changing post-colonial and post-Mao neoliberal societies of Hong Kong and mainland China, respectively, which share a gendered division of responsibility that falls unequally on the shoulders of men and women.

Mothers as Workers and Health Gatekeepers

Sharon Hays, in her study of motherhood among different social classes in the United States, observed that working mothers today confront not only conflicting demands on their time and energy but also conflicting ideas about how they are to behave: they must be nurturing and unselfish while engaged in child-rearing but competitive and ambitious at work (Hays 1996). As more and more women enter the workplace, it would seem reasonable for a society to make mothering a simpler and more efficient task. Instead, many working mothers are affected by the ideology of "intensive mothering"—an ideology that holds the individual mother primarily responsible for child-rearing and dictates that the process should be child-centered, expert-guided, emotionally absorbing, labor-intensive, and expensive. As Hays explained, the imposition of unrealistic and unremunerated obligations and commitments on mothering is an attempt to deal with our deep uneasiness about self-interest promoted by the world of the rationalized market (Hays 1996, 97).

The revival in the popularity of breastfeeding in Western societies in recent years can be explained by this ideology of intensive mothering, in which "good mothers" are solely responsible for meeting all of their children's needs and for taking measures to minimize the potential risks posed to their children by food and feeding-related consumer items (Afflerback et al. 2013; Avishai 2007; Hays 1996; Lee 2007, 2008; Murphy 2000; Stearns 2009). Motherhood, as many studies have suggested, is being reformulated in such a way that mothers have become veritable "risk managers" (Furedi 2002; Lee 2008). As a consequence, breastfeeding mothers in contemporary Western societies have come to be respected as "good mothers," while those who bottle-feed are labeled "bad mothers."

At first glance, the milk craze in China seems to contradict the recent trend of breastfeeding and intensive mothering in modern Western societies. Yet, I argue that formula milk is used by Chinese mothers as a technology to deal with the contradictory demands of work and family under the ideology of intensive mothering in order to minimize the food-safety, social, and environmental risks that their children face (Knaak 2010; Lee 2008; Murphy 2000). I begin by exploring a few narratives of middle-class mothers in Hong Kong and migrant mothers in China to explore how formula can be used as a technology to help them achieve social ideals.

Successful Career Women and the "Insufficient Milk Syndrome"

In Hong Kong, most of the middle-class mothers I interviewed, who were in their thirties or early forties and mostly employed in managerial positions, told me that breast milk is best. The problem is that they do not think they personally can produce sufficient milk to meet their babies' needs. Nicole Lai is a 32-year-old senior journalist who works at one of the top-selling print media agencies in Hong Kong. As we will see below, Nicole tried to decrease her workload before giving birth to improve the health of her unborn fetus, as well as to improve her baby's health after childbirth through breastfeeding. However, she began bottle-feeding her daughter just two weeks after giving birth because she perceived herself as having insufficient milk.

> Once I learned I was pregnant, I decided I would breastfeed. I had read a lot about the benefits of breastfeeding, such as better nutrition. One key thing to successful breastfeeding, which I learnt from parenting magazines and websites, is that I should not be stressed out. So I decided to change jobs. I used to work in the daily newspaper department, which has tight deadlines and long working hours. Our work had also become more intense following the launch of our online news website. Video and instant news now have to be uploaded almost immediately from the news collection. So, I requested to change my position from the daily newspaper department to the weekly magazine department six months before giving birth.
>
> However, it was a big blow for me when I wasn't able to produce enough breast milk to feed my daughter. She kept crying every time after a short suckling in the first few days. I also couldn't produce any milk after she had finished suckling. I was shocked, depressed and totally unprepared to handle this. I didn't even have a can of formula milk or baby bottles at home, you know. What's wrong with me, I thought. Should every mother be able to breastfeed?

Nicole is not unique in identifying her work as one of the most important factors in her lacking sufficient milk and thus having to cease breastfeeding. All twenty of the mothers I interviewed had tried to breastfeed their babies, and all but one had quickly switched from breastfeeding to formula feeding upon their return to work. Many of these women told me that they did not even think that pumping milk in the office was an option, saying things like "I have never heard of anyone pumping milk in the office." Those few who did consider this possibility also ultimately chose to bottle-feed. The most frequently stated reasons included a lack of nursing space and storage facilities for the pumped milk and a lack of nursing breaks. Some told me, "I simply cannot stand pumping milk in the toilet during rush hour" and "I don't think I can digest my meal if I eat and pump milk at the same time in the tight one-hour lunchtime." Although many mothers had a sense of guilt at not having sufficient milk, most justify breastfeeding as something they had to give up for the sake of their successful careers.

In addition to stress from work, the cultural norm of having to slim down to return to work in the fittest condition possible is another important reason for the switch to bottle-feeding. Most of my informants related to the image of the beautiful, successful career woman, with kids enrolled in a reputable English-language school, rather than that of a self-sacrificing, breastfeeding stay-at-home mother. The famous singer Kelly Chan, who at the age of 36 was able to slim down in five days and return to work just a week after giving birth, represents their ideal of a new mother (*Apple Daily* 2009). Pauline Lai, a 32-year-old entrepreneur, stressed the importance of slimming down before returning to work. She articulated why she stopped breastfeeding after two weeks because of a dilemma she would face: "A friend suggested that I eat a club sandwich before bed so that I would have more breast milk to feed my baby the next day. This frightened me. God! How can I lose weight and get my body shape back before I return to work?" To return to work *in shape* soon after delivery is the new, celebrated spirit of a model worker, as popularized through the digital and mass media. This restoration of the prenatal body shape is not perceived as natural, but rather something that must be actively cultivated by the persistent, disciplined, and hardworking self, all of which are also traits highly valued in the capitalist labor market. Thus, the celebrity mothers that serve as role models are reported to follow strict dietary rules and exercise schedules in both the prenatal and post-natal periods (Shih 2016).

In addition to the "insufficient milk syndrome" and active dietary control to slim down, a third reason for bottle-feeding is the symbolic association between formula milk and academic excellence. Pauline Lai shared with me her view that the most important thing for a mother today is to make sure that her son or daughter can get into a good English-language school. "This is almost the only thing that parents and even grandparents talk about in dim sum restaurants and on Facebook," she explained. Mothers in middle-class families that I talked to were well versed in the names of chemical compounds related to nutrition that appeared as ingredients in formula milk, in particular the Omega-3 fatty acid DHA, which was believed to enhance children's cognitive development. For this reason, beginning in the early 2000s, formula milk began to be consumed not only by babies and children, but also by many expectant mothers. Many of my informants told me that they only began drinking milk during their pregnancies, and many said that they drank DHA-enriched formula milk marketed for pregnant women, believing that their diets during pregnancy would directly affect the physical and intellectual development of the fetuses growing inside their bodies. The advice given by professionals, such as doctors and nutritionists, and the new scientific knowledge gained from newspapers, magazines, and social media are the key reasons for this new practice of milk consumption. One of my informants, Elaine Law, a 40-year-old banker and the mother of a four-year-old, shared her dietary behavior during pregnancy and the reasons underlying it as follows:

> I learnt from *Time* magazine online that the nine months of pregnancy are the most critical time for the child's brain and bodily development. At that time, my doctor also recommended a DHA-enriched formula milk to me, and I knew that DHA is particularly important for brain development. So, to ensure a good start for our baby, I drank the formula milk for a month even though it tasted horrible.

Elaine told me that she also ate traditional *bupin* ("nourishing product"), such as *yinwo* (edible bird's nest) soup, which was recommended by her mother. Elaine is not unique in altering her diet—consuming both Western formula milk and traditional Chinese *bupin* in her case—during her pregnancy in order to produce a smart and healthy baby. In fact, most of the middle-class mothers I interviewed told me that they had thoroughly studied the ingredients and benefits of the formula milk for expectant mothers and for infants before making what they considered to be smart and rational choices.[4]

Perhaps surprisingly, the symbolic link between formula milk, DHA, and the brain's development is a recent one. In the early 2000s, following the SARS epidemic, many pharmaceutical companies began promoting their products as a means of boosting the immune system. One of those products was Mead Johnson's Enfapro A+2 formula milk. However, in the early 2010s, Mead Johnson, understanding the strong desire of Hong Kong parents to enrich their young children's academic performance, instead began highlighting the benefits of its heavily DHA-enriched formula in enhancing children's brain capacity. For example, Mead Johnson had two key advertising messages in a series of TV ads: "With health and good brain development, babies and children can achieve academic excellence," and "The highest DHA among all brands in HK." In the campaign launched in 2011, the slogan Mead Johnson chose to adopt for its newest formula milk, branded Enfapro A+, was "Be healthy and smart, excel over others through intelligence and creative learning." This positioning of "winning" above other children through being smart, healthy, and creative was so well received by consumers that Mead Johnson's Enfapro A+ quickly became the number-one-selling brand in Hong Kong.

The rise of DHA as a nearly magical nutritional supplement trusted by parents to solve the complicated education problems in Hong Kong through engineering their children's cognitive abilities is closely related to the rapid political and social changes since the 1997 handover. The decline in Hong Kong's regional competitiveness following its reunification with mainland China has created substantial social discontent (Chan 2010; Choi 2005).[5] What made the parents worried further was the implementation of neoliberal policies, such as privatizing primary and secondary schools, and withholding a commitment to compulsory schooling. To safeguard their children's future economic and cultural capital, Hong Kong parents queued overnight at several kindergartens for coveted slots (Chan and Kao 2013), arranged for their children to attend preschool mock-interview training sessions, enrolled their children in piano lessons and sports, and took their children on international trips (i.e., to suggest a degree of "internationalization"), all of which can be added to aspiring students' resumes (*Singtao Daily* 2015). Social geographer Cindi Katz has called these strategies, which are also used by like-minded, well-resourced parents in New York City and other major international cities, "parental involution"—the "saturation of parental, social, and economic resources in particular children" (2008, 12).

As we have seen, the choice of bottle-feeding by working women is an attempt to achieve the four seemingly contradictory goals of successful modern motherhood—to provide excellent nutrition to their infants while maintaining strict bodily control to slim down to their pre-pregnancy size; and to invest time and energy to prepare their children for the "kindergarten battle" despite those mothers' long working hours and high pressure to perform at work. As witnessed in the cases of Nicole, Pauline, and many of my other informants, the high incidence of insufficient milk syndrome, the top reason given for resorting to bottle-feeding, is related to mothers' perceived work stress. Their hardworking ethos and anxiety over their body shape stem from their job insecurity and the financial pressures created by the privatized education system. Contractual, part-time, and temporary jobs have replaced more stable, tenured jobs to become the new normal in Hong Kong since the start of the twenty-first century.

The growing trend toward short-termism and periodicity in employment, which affect the choice of infant feeding, is of course not unique to Hong Kong. Rather, the shift from a clear, fixed long-termism to a more harried short-termism, as pointed out by Elliott and Lemert, is part of a broader global trend, driven by the dynamism of technological innovation, the power of multinational corporations to export industrial production to low-wage locales around the globe, and the restructuring of investment in the West away from manufacturing toward the finance, service, and communications sectors (2009a, 2009b). This new global, neoliberal economy has meant major changes in the ways people experience time, how they live their lives, how they approach their work, as well as how they position themselves within the employment marketplace.

In this culture of short-termism, Chinese mothers desperately attempt to improve, transform, reinvent, and refashion their bodies and themselves as slimmer, more efficient, inventive, and self-actualizing versions of themselves, while delegating the job of nourishing their children to the DHA-enriched formula milk that they believe can create a healthier and smarter baby. Moreover, the culture of slimness, which exists in both work and private spaces, is common not only in Hong Kong, but around the world. It is driven by the forces of globalization and capitalism, especially as those forces concern the modern job market requirements for women (Becker 2004), where a career ceiling for women still persists in the male-dominated job market (Lee 1999), and unstable marital relationships (Tam 1996). In addition to seeking to nurture their babies and toddlers to be taller, smarter, and more cosmopolitan, women in China are consistently reminded by thousands of advertisements and media messages to equip and to reward themselves by following the proper rituals of "healthy" consumption, so as to be competitive in the battlefields of love and work, while performing their social roles as ideal mothers and educated citizens.

Mobile Mothers and Formula Milk as Gifts

While many upper- and middle-class mothers in China routinely buy the pricey imported formula milk from top-selling brands without a second thought, most migrant workers and other working-class people in China simply cannot afford to do so. Yet, many migrant workers have strategies for balancing their perceived obligation to provide formula milk against their other expenditures. Many of the mothers I interviewed who had migrated to Shunde to work explained how they categorized formula milk as a *bupin*, which would have a positive effect on the health of their children even when consumed occasionally rather than as a daily part of their diets. In the traditional Chinese humoral system, *bupin* cannot be taken on a daily basis; otherwise, the body may become too "hot." Here is how Hua-ying, a rural migrant from Guangxi now working at a Western-style res-taurant in Daliang as a waitress, uses the local premium brand as a *bupin* for her three-year-old son:

> Last winter when I returned home, my heart broke when I discovered that my poor son was thin and his hands were always cold. I fed him an expen-sive formula milk, BIOSTIME, which is known for being nutritious and can help children to gain weight.[6] I knew from the advertisement for it that it is composed of cow milk and various types of vitamins and minerals from vegetables. After taking two cans of BIOSTIME over two months, he gained weight and became energetic again. The powder costs RMB 150 per can and lasted about a month, as I fed him only once a day instead of three times a day according to the formula milk instruction. In addition to BIOS-TIME, sometimes, I would give him a bottle of Yakult after dinner. Yakult has probiotics that are good for health, for digestion and for stimulating his appetite.[7]

The idea of using a modern, Western food as a *bupin* in a Chinese sense is not just limited to the folk beliefs of a few working-class people; it can also be seen in the daily medical prescriptions prepared by professional doctors in Shunde.[8] For example, Xiaohong, a migrant working as a wait-ress at a locally renowned Chinese restaurant, told me that a local doctor had asked her to give her son calcium injections for *bu* (nourishment). At the time of the prescription, her son was a year and three months old, and had been feeding on Mead Johnson Enfapro since discontinuing breast-feeding at one month of age. Xiaohong was proud of her son for being taller than average for his age. The doctor told her that her son had reached the average height of a one-year-old boy when he was only ten months old and the height of a one-and-a-half-year-old when he was only one year old. To further support his outstanding growth, the doctor recommended that Xiaohong's son be given calcium injections and oral calcium supplements. In addition, the doctor strongly advised that Xiaohong feed her son highly nutritious foods to keep up with his rapidly growing body's needs. She then bought five types of expensive nutritional supplements for her son from Amway, including Nutrilite protein powder.[9]

As gifts, the milk powder and calcium supplements given by the mothers to their children are not merely a tasty commodity to boost the children's health but, following Mauss, can be understood to be a part of the mother's spiritual essence that has to be repaid ([1954] 2011). Huaying and Xiaohong are two of the more than 480,000 migrant workers who have moved away from rural areas to work in Shunde (National Bureau of Statistics of China 2018). Like many of the other female workers who take up any of the numerous opportunities for low-paid service-sector jobs in urban areas, these two women now live far away from the villages where their babies are growing up. As such, local brands of formula milk have become a crucial technology facilitating their mobility and the delegation of their nursing and child-rearing tasks to their parents, in-laws, or other caretakers.

For this reason, these migrant-worker mothers, during their annual visits to their hometowns, usually bring home imported brands of formula milk, which as a symbol of class, health, modernity, and wealth, could give them a chance to earn the respect of their relatives and friends. This pattern of consumption contrasts somewhat with those observed elsewhere. While in Ivana Bajic-Hajdukovic's study of Serbian mothers, the gifts of locally branded *kajmak* (a very fatty cheese spread), *prsuta* (smoked air-dried ham), or homemade sweets sent by mothers to their children and grandchildren were meant to remind the latter of the authentic taste of the past and of home (2013), the migrant mothers in Shunde have been sending a taste of the "future" and "Western-ness" to their children in the villages, hoping to enable their smooth transition into a better, more modern world.

Studies of migrant workers around the world illustrate that migrant mothers adopt several strategies to express their love to their families and to negotiate their absences from home by redefining motherhood. Transnational and gender studies perspectives on ideas of motherhood common among migrant women have illustrated alternative means for providing nurture such as sending remittances and gifts, making telephone calls, and turning to their extended families to care for their children. In the case of the migrant workers in Shunde, the provision of imported formula milk, or high-end brands of local formula milk with Western names, in lieu of breast milk can be seen as an example of what Rhacel Salazar Parreñas has termed "commodification of love," which appears to be one of the dominant characteristics of transnational mothering (2001). One cardinal difference between transnational mothering and fathering is that migrant mothers are not only obliged to send remittances home but face additional pressures. For transnational fathering, bringing money home is already an accepted way of performing the role of a good father and expressing their masculinity (Thai 2006). In contrast, migrant mothers live under a double burden and face constant pressure to conform to the image of a "good mother." Hence, sending formula milk home becomes a gendered activity: even when migrant-worker mothers are away from home, they are expected to perform emotional and care labor for their families and to maintain intimate emotional relationships, particularly with their children (Alicea 1997; Dreby 2006). The cases of Huaying and Xiaohong illustrate how such women adopt creative strategies to satisfy conventional expectations by re-categorizing formula milk as a *bupin*, to be consumed at a lower, more affordable cost. Sending formula milk as a gift to their children thereby establishes a reciprocal relationship, which they envision their children will one day repay.

Fathers as Breadwinners and Life Protectors

In traditional Chinese society, a father's love for his children is expressed through his social roles as the breadwinner and protector of the family and lineage—an inseparable part of his masculinity. Chinese scholars stress that the "father had obligations far beyond that of providing food and clothing and shelter for his [children]. He also had to provide, especially in the case of his sons, sufficient funds to obtain a wife and receive an inheritance" (Levy 1968, 169). Although most fathers felt a deep sentiment toward their children (Li 1969; Solomon 1971), the articulation of that sentiment was strained by their traditional parenting role and its accompanying expectations (Levy 1968).

"Earning Milk Powder Money" and Postmodern Masculinity

In contemporary studies of fatherhood in Hong Kong and mainland China, the idea of masculinity held by fathers is closely linked to economic power (Liong 2017; Yang 2010). The ideology that men should be breadwinners remains strong (Choi and Ting 2009; Gender Research Centre 2012). Jason, a thirty-five-year-old architect and a father of two, shared with me his experience of *zhuan naifen qian* (literally, "earning money for milk powder"): "When I returned to Hong Kong from Beijing and was looking for a job in 2012, I had more time to spend with Angel, my oldest daughter. I brought her to kindergarten before I attended interviews. I felt so nervous at that time because I needed to 'earn money for milk powder.'"

Jason was not alone in using the idiom of "earning money for milk powder" to denote the importance of making an economic contribution to being a good father. "Earning money to buy milk powder" has long been a popular idiom in Hong Kong, used to denote parents' economic contribution to child-rearing. Exerting one's full effort and working day and night to earn money for the family has long been glorified as a key responsibility of a responsible father, and the saying "earning money to buy milk powder" has come to be used by fathers as a justification for working long hours outside of the home.

In reports in print and digital media, the idiom "earning money to buy milk powder" has also come to be used by celebrities to explain their aggressive work ethic and sometimes their choice of undertaking risky, life-threatening, and even disgusting jobs (see, for example, *Apple Daily* 2015, 2016; *Singtao Daily* 2018). Celebrity fathers who own deluxe houses, big cars, and also take on all of the economic responsibility so that their wives can act as full-time stay-at-home mothers are revered as responsible husbands and powerful men. In more typical cases, the expression has been adopted by middle-class fathers as a socially acceptable reason to justify their lack of time spent at home, engaged in child-rearing or housework, which has the effect of shifting those responsibilities onto their female partners, who typically also have full-time work.

In recent years, however, masculinity and the father's role have evolved into a kind of postmodern masculinity that poses a challenge to the dominant patriarchal discourse (Pease 2000, 137). Not only have celebrity fathers been assumed to be the economic pillars of their families, but there have also been a growing number of media reports concerning the greater involvement of good celebrity fathers in the seemingly feminine domain of child-rearing. It is common to find adjectives like *tiexin* (understanding), *woxin* (heart-touching), and *nuannan* ("warm man") used in newspapers and online news to describe young male celebrities accompanying their wives in attending baby seminars and regular check-ups, and joining their wives in the delivery room to witness the whole birthing process. The reports also focus on the ways these fathers help out with changing diapers and bottle-feeding once their babies are born. These popular narratives on the characteristics of good fathers who are actively involved in child-rearing resonated with my female informants, who described similar virtues in an ideal husband-father. Influenced by modern parenting styles that emphasize providing more intensive attention, such as using more child-oriented negotiation methods in place of strict rules and discipline, fathers in Western societies—and increasingly in Chinese societies—are also spending more time than their fathers' generation did in playing with their children (Cowdery and Knudson-Martin 2005; Liong 2017).

In addition, there is growing influence from fathers on the choice of infant-feeding methods. Some of the mothers I interviewed told me that they had given up breastfeeding at their husband's request based on the latter's understanding of health and science. One father I interviewed, Gilbert Law, a 44-year-old civil servant, described how he had successfully convinced his wife to switch to bottle-feeding:

> Our son weighed 2.4 kg at birth and needed to stay an extra week in hospital for health monitoring until he reached 2.5 kg. The hospital gave us a helpful chart showing the normal growth curve. So, when our son was three weeks old, I began measuring his weight every week. I found that my son was still below the "normal" growth curve in weight and height at the age of one month. I cannot believe that my son will be short in the future. I am 5'10" tall and my son should grow up to be as tall as I am. I think that this is probably because my wife does not have sufficient breast milk to feed my son, so he has not been growing well. I do not want to take the risk of having a son who will be shorter than I once he grows up. So, I talked to my wife every day, explaining the problem to her scientifically. She was very emotional in the beginning but finally she was convinced. We started to bottle-feed him from the time he was three months old. He is now four years old and big and strong. I feel that we made the right decision.

Gilbert's ideas about the standards for measuring growth, health, and ideal body shapes and his role in switching to the "superior" formula milk have been mediated through idioms, metaphors, medical language disseminated through pediatricians, medical institutions, parenting seminars, and global media. My findings on the importance of the husband in influencing choices on infant feeding are in line with the results of previous quantitative studies conducted in Hong Kong (Chan et al. 2000; Tarrant, Dodgson, and Choi 2004). In Tarrant and colleagues' study of breastfeeding mothers in Hong Kong, many of the respondents expressed that they had been under pressure from their husbands to cease breastfeeding because their husbands thought they did not have sufficient breast milk, especially in cases where there had been signs of a perceived health problem.

In Shunde, by contrast, although the fathers also bought imported formula to express their masculinity by performing the roles of breadwinner and protector for their offspring, their reasons for doing so are significantly different from those seen in Hong Kong. The expensive imported formula milk brands are almost double the price of locally manufactured ones and may easily eat up one-third to even one-half of the salary of a working-class father. Mr. Chen, a bus driver employed by a school in Daliang and the father of a two-year-old son, told me why he felt it was "natural" for him to spend RMB 1,500—half of his monthly salary—on imported formula milk bought in Hong Kong:

> I think that the imported formula milk is a necessity for my son. [I want to ensure] that my son doesn't have to risk drinking any milk from China. . . . I spend 50 percent of my salary on premium formula milk because this is my duty as a father. A man goes through different stages during the course of his life. Before you get married, you spend your money on things that give you pleasure. Then, to establish your own family, you save up money to buy property before marriage. Then, you spend money on formula milk for your baby. This is the life cycle. . . . In the past, just surviving was what the Chinese needed. Now, you want your next generation to have those things you didn't have. For example, we didn't have the chance to study overseas. You want your child to do what you could not. It's a kind of compensation.

Mr. Chen traversed the family cycle to explain and justify his attitude about formula milk consumption. Strikingly different from the narrative in Hong Kong, the symbolic meaning of drinking cow milk and imported formula milk in mainland China goes beyond the simple display of economic and health capital, but has also come to connote cultural and social capital. Many of the parents in Shunde whom I talked to, who were in their fifties or older, were able to recall the rationing of food during the period of the People's Communes, when milk was typically only available for senior government officials and some privileged groups well connected to the government. In other words, access to milk used to depend not only on an individual's economic resources but also on his or her background and social network.

Yet, in addition to the social and cultural capital that has long been associated with milk in mainland China, imported formula milk is also part of the cosmopolitan imagination of Mr. Chen. Mr. Chen was one of the many parents who emphasized the importance of "being international." He was employed as a driver by a reputable secondary school in Daliang, and his main responsibility was to drive the senior directors of the school and to receive important guests invited by the school. When he learned that I was from Hong Kong, he greeted me wholeheartedly, saying that he liked to make friends with people from "international" cities, like Hong Kong. "We (in Shunde) have reached the age of internationalization. We have to be modern and international, open and competitive in order to succeed." For Mr. Chen, consuming an international brand of formula milk was the first step for his son to become "international." In his opinion most products from the West were better and worth the cost. For him and others like him, such products are signs of internationalization in a modern family.

But how was Mr. Chen, who was employed as a driver, able to support his family if half of his salary went to formula milk? He told me that there were many ways to earn extra money. One anecdote might offer an example: when he learned that I was researching buffaloes and buffalo milk in Shunde, he asked me whether I would be interested in eating some high-quality veal as he could recommend a good place. I suspect that this kind of "extra service" he offered was one of his many ways of gaining additional income—earning a commission from a steak restaurant, in this case. Other informants also told me that they aggressively sought opportunities to earn more. Many of the indigenous people of Daliang received decent annual bonuses of as much as RMB 10,000 from the local government, which rented out their village properties. To summarize, formula milk for both babies and children has become a kind of necessity in modern Shunde, which has made parents, and especially fathers like Mr. Chen, feel obliged to work harder to purchase imported formula milk, even if it means hustling for business opportunities to supplement their salaries.

Cultural Capital, Food Safety, and Geopolitics of Milk

So, if premium imported formula milk, a symbol of the father's masculinity and the children's future cosmopolitan capital, can be easily bought in a nearby grocery shop, why do people from Shunde, as well as other places in China, bother to travel to Hong Kong each month to purchase imported formula milk brands?[10] Hong Kong media usually attempt to make sense of this geopolitics[11] of milk consumption with economic, political, and social explanations. The political explanation is that since December 2010 the local government of Shenzhen has allowed its four million official residents to travel to Hong Kong as a means of boosting the tourist industry. The economic explanation is that owing to the strengthening of China's national currency (the RMB) and the food-safety problems that have troubled the country in recent years, many mainland Chinese people began traveling to Hong Kong during the Chinese New Year of 2011. This influx resulted in shortages of the most popular imported formula milk brands in most parts of Hong Kong for a period of more than ten days (see, for example, *Ming Pao* 2011).

Yee, a mother of a ten-month-old baby, told me that although the manufacturers of the formula milk in Hong Kong and China are the same and the milk products look the same, she believes that the two products are different:

> My husband and I don't really want to go to Hong Kong and Macau to buy milk powder. It is a big hassle during the long national holiday when many tourists come here for shopping. Especially between last November and February of this year (2011), I couldn't find any cans of the brand that I wanted to buy in Hong Kong. But my husband has some close friends who used to work at the milk powder companies. They told us that although the milk sources for making the milk powder sent to Hong Kong and the mainland are the same, the factory divides production into different lines: one for *dalu* (China), and one for *xianggang* (Hong Kong), which has a certain set of ingredients following stricter food safety requirements. Usually, they pay more attention to the export product and leave some leeway for the local goods (there are many loopholes despite the strict regulations). All I can do is to buy the expensive milk powder imported from *xianggang*. It's not just a blind belief that the same brand of milk powder in *xianggang* is better than that in *dalu*. We have friends who have concrete information about it. Not only that, I also found the Abbott formula milk produced for *dalu* to be sweeter and it has more bubbles, totally different from the one sold in *xianggang*. But on the other hand, I have some friends whose babies are fine with the local brands of milk. So, it is not necessarily true that foreign brands are better. (Yee, aged 30, mother of a 10-month-old girl)

Performing the role of the life protector of their children by building up their expertise about milk products, several other middle-class fathers from places like Guangzhou and Ningxia whom I talked to would personally taste the different brands of formula milk to make sure they were safe before they fed them to their babies. They found firsthand that the same brand of formula milk from mainland China and Hong Kong tasted different. Quite a number of my informants were also proud of their children for preferring the taste of the imported formula milk bought in Hong Kong to that from mainland China, as they consider this preference a marker of social class. The ability to spend huge amounts of time, money, and effort on making cross-border purchases of the "authentic," "safer" imported formula milk increases the life chances of the upper and middle classes, who already have better economic and cultural capital. In recent years, a spate of food-safety scandals and crises (discussed in more detail in chapter 3) have caused consumers to lose faith in the ability of the Chinese government to properly ensure the safety of its citizens. Such scandals have affected rich and poor alike, although members of the upper and middle classes are able to leverage their greater resources to respond more effectively to food-safety threats.

While Ulrich Beck states in *Risk Society* (1992) that the rise of the social production of risks in the risk society signals that class ceases to be of relevance, the phenomenon of cross-border formula-milk purchasing among upper- and middle-class families in China reveals how the cultural and wealth differentials associated with different class memberships actually affect individuals' respective life chances in the risk society. The Sanlu melamine-tainted formula milk scandal provides an example of this. Most of the victims of the food contamination came from working-class families. With the growing production and distribution of bad food (contaminated dairy products in this case), class inequalities take on added significance: it is cultural and economic capital that both enables the advantaged to minimize their risk exposure and forces the others to face the intensified risks of the risk society.[12]

The State, the Market, and Charismatic Nutrition

The most salient difference in what infant feeding means for parents in Hong Kong and mainland China lies in their respective beliefs about the nutritional values of breast milk and the meaning of weaning. In Hong Kong parents believe breast milk is the best for babies and that, if possible, it should be consumed by babies even after the age of one. Among parents in Shunde, however, breastfeeding is commonly believed to be bad for babies starting from the time they are seven, or even four, months old. When I asked for infant-feeding advice from the mothers and grandmothers whose children or grandchildren were playing with my son in the open playground in Shunde, many were astonished to learn that I was still breastfeeding my one-year-old child and considered this to be an immoral choice on my part, as if I were not taking care of my son in a modern, scientific way. Here are some representative comments:

"Breast milk is not nutritious enough to feed babies over six months old."

"Breast milk is harmful for your one-year-old. You should stop feeding him this way. Let him drink wholesome formula milk instead!"

"What a shame that your son has not yet been weaned (*duannai*)! My grandson was weaned when he was six months old and is now feeding on fresh cow milk."

The mothering advice that these grandmothers gave me concerning breastfeeding eloquently demonstrates two interrelated, widely shared principles: first, the new concept of "weaning," and second, the obligation of parents to provide their infants with modern, industrialized cow milk. These conversations show clearly that the main reason for the popularity of formula milk was the revolutionary change in the meaning of *duannai* (literally, "to cut off from milk"). Until recently, in Chinese society, *duannai* denoted the intended action of the mother to accustom the child to foods other than breast milk (Huang 2002). However, I learned from discussion with all of my informants in mainland China, as well as some of those in Hong Kong, that the concept of *duannai* has taken on a new meaning—"to stop breastfeeding and start feeding on cow milk." In addition, there was a widely held belief among my informants that babies should not be breastfed past the age of six months and that they should instead consume formula milk as early as possible. Here is how one grandmother, Mrs. Cheung, described her experience of feeding her granddaughter:

Our granddaughter is very smart! She was weaned when she was three months old. Now, she is feeding on imported Mead Johnson A+ formula milk. She has a sophisticated palate and is only willing to drink imported formula milk. I also feed her water with honey, as it is good for encouraging the baby's bowel movements.

Underlying the narratives of these modern grandmothers is the strong belief that the nutritional value of breast milk will drop dramatically starting from the third month. That is to say, it would be improper and unscientific for a mother to continue breastfeeding her child after the three-month mark as doing so would deny a "fair start" for her son or daughter. Today, raising a smart child requires that one provide the best physical, cultural, and social conditions for the child to develop his or her full potential. In recent years, "to win at the starting line" (贏在起跑線) has become a well-known educational goal in both Hong Kong and mainland China, and the saying has been widely adopted by private tutorial schools, music training centers, toy manufacturers, travel agencies, and children's food producers in Shunde as one of the most popular advertising slogans (Yang 2012). For this reason, a new obligation has emerged: to feed one's only child with nutrient-enriched, scientifically advanced formula milk after the three-month mark as a means of nurturing a smart and creative child.

The choice of formula milk—a technology for children's bodily and cognitive enhancement—among parents in China is directly related to the politics of childhood under the one-child policy in China. As Teresa Kuan has aptly noted, the internalized moral obligation and the anxious feeling among parents to exhaustively source "scientific" ways to produce high intelligence and strong bodies is a result of the population policies in China. Through her ethnographic studies of middle-class parents in Kunming during the early 2000s and contextual analysis of popular literature on parenting, Kuan contends that "while maintaining their child's competitive edge, parents are asked to take responsibility for helping to cultivate a well-adjusted, creative future innovator who will contribute to national strength" (2015, 18). The state's one-child policy and *suzhi jiaoyu* (quality education) are two important tools for the Chinese government to upgrade the quality of the Chinese population in order to create a knowledge economy and turn China into a global superpower (Greenhalgh 2011, 21). Following this vein, milk consumption in China is not only a private but also a political act, an expression by good citizens of their progressive contribution to building up health and cosmopolitan capital for the children who will contribute to national pride and success in the future.

The nationalist desire to build a strong, healthy national populace through modernization, industrialization, science, and technology is the result of what China regards as a series of historical humiliations beginning with the Opium Wars, which resulted in the signing of the so-called unequal treaties and the concession of lands to the European imperial powers (Dreyer 1995). The first to promote modern nutrition science as a strategy to overcome the series of humiliations in China during the 1920s were probably the dairy and pharmaceutical companies themselves (Lo 2009, 164–165). For example, in 1920, an advertisement for Old Eagle-brand condensed milk in *Shen Bao,* the most influential newspaper in early twentieth-century Shanghai, illustrated that the peoples of the world could be divided into two types: non–milk drinking Chinese and the milk-drinking Europeans and Americans (Lo 2009, 168; *Shen Bao* 1929). According to the advertisements, since dairy products constituted 15 to 25 percent of the diet of Europeans and Americans, they had bigger bodies, longer life expectancy, lower child mortality rates, and even better political and education systems. The narrative on the relationship between Western medical science and strong nationhood became so popular that in 1929 the Communist Party discussed abolishing traditional medical practices in order to develop modern medicine and hygiene (Agren 1975, 41; Palmer 2007). In the post–World War II period, the globalization of Western nutrition science also affected how people perceived infant health and evaluated weaning foods.

Although many Chinese people started to be aware of the nutritional value of Western cow milk in the 1940s, the current emphasis on bottle-feeding for babies as a staple is quite recent in origin and largely attributable to the dietary guidelines set by the Hong Kong and Chinese governments. In the 1970s, nutritional deficiencies in weaning infants had been reported in many parts of China and in Hong Kong, not only owing to poverty but also cultural factors that affected dietary practices (Field and Baber 1973; Leung and Liu 1990).[13] Consequently, drinking Western cow milk every day has been recommended by the Hong Kong government since the 1970s. For China, one remarkable difference with Hong Kong is that the state-sponsored Chinese Nutrition Society has been playing an active role in normalizing bottle-feeding for babies aged as young as four months, by disseminating a set of dietary guidelines, first published in 1989. In its updated set of nutritional guidelines for Chinese citizens in 2011, the Chinese Nutrition Society highlights the vitamin K and D deficiency of breast milk and the possible fatal health consequences of consuming it for babies: "Breast milk contains less vitamin K than cow milk. So, the expectant mother must consume more food that is rich in vitamin K, such as green leafy vegetables and spring onions" (Chinese Nutrition Society 2011, 142).

Although the nutrition society supports the notion that breast milk is best for babies under the age of six months because it contains more readily digestible proteins, minerals, vitamins, essential fatty acids, antibodies, and living immune cells, which are most suitable and vital for human babies, it articulates that the quality of breast milk is uncertain, depending on the nursing mother's own diet and behavior (Chinese Nutrition Society 2011, 141–142). According to the guidelines, if a mother does not eat enough foods rich in vitamin K, then her breastfed baby may suffer from *xiexing jibing* (literally, "blood-related disease") and may even die as a consequence. In addition, the guidelines state that if the mother does not receive enough sunshine and does not take enough foods rich in vitamin D, her breast milk will be "insufficient to satisfy the baby's demand" (Chinese Nutrition Society 2011, 142).[14] As a result, the baby might suffer from rickets and improper bone development (Chinese Nutrition Society 2011, 144). In a recent study of five heavily urbanized cities in China, only about 5 percent of the participants had healthy levels of vitamin D, owing to the combination of air pollution in many cities in China and the participants' long hours of indoor work (Abkowitz 2015). That is compared to about 67 percent of the U.S. population whose Vitamin D levels were deemed sufficient in a 2011 Centers for Disease Control and Prevention report. Vitamin D is known to be crucial for building strong bones and supporting a healthy immune system (Yu et al. 2015). However, within Chinese nutrition guidelines, Vitamins D and K appear to have become, in Kimura's terms, "charismatic nutrients" that not only have scientific nutrition values but can also solve the problem of the poor health conditions of mothers, which are caused by the air pollution and long working hours accompanying China's economic rise (2013, 19). According to the same standard, however, if the babies are fed with formula milk, there will be no problems, because the Chinese government has set a minimum requirement of 22 µg of vitamin K and 200–400 IU of vitamin D per 100 grams of formula.

The set of dietary guidelines issued by the Chinese Nutrition Society stresses the importance placed on formula milk in the infant diet during the four-to-eight-month-old window. The guideline suggests that babies should transition to feeding on baby formula alongside solid food beginning at the age of six months and continuing until the baby is one year old or even longer (Chinese Nutrition Society 2011, 150). This is significantly different from the set of guidelines issued by the WHO, which encourages breastfeeding beyond the age of six months (World Health Organization 2019*a*). One of the most important premises given for the suggestion of substituting formula for breast milk in the Chinese Nutrition Society's guidelines is that when the baby reaches four months of age, a decrease in the volume and nutrition of the mother's breast milk, such as its iron content, means that milk alone is no longer able to satisfy the nutritional demands of the baby's rapid growth (Chinese Nutrition Society 2011, 151). Thus, formula milk, which is said to provide a comprehensive source of nutrition, is deemed a must for babies once they reach the age of six months. These guidelines therefore advocate for formula milk as the best food to ensure that the baby receives sufficient nutrition during weaning, while parents are advised to give children aged one to five 300–600 ml of milk produced from formula milk powder every day (Chinese Nutrition Society 2011, 165).

The Chinese Nutrition Society has even redefined the weaning period, institutionalizing bottle-feeding at the seventh month. The society's guidebook points out that the traditional term *duannai* (weaning) is misleading. Conventionally, in Chinese society, *duannai* has referred literally to cutting off the baby from milk and transitioning to semi-solid and solid foods. However, the Chinese Nutrition Society recommends that children continue feeding on formula milk up to the age of five or beyond. As such, according to the society, the term *duannai* should refer only to stopping breastfeeding, but not to stopping consumption of formula milk. Such views were also repeatedly raised by my informants in their narratives about their own infant-feeding processes.

Historically, most Chinese medical literature suggested that babies transition from consuming mother's milk to semi-solids, such as grain porridge, at around the age of two, while no milk should be given beyond five (see Kou 2015 for examples). During the Sung dynasty, babies who had not begun to consume solid food by the age of three would have been perceived to be spoiled, and it was believed that the spleen and stomach of such children would be damaged (Liu et al. 2012; Zhou 2012).[15] Although there were general guidelines on the time for *duannai* in China, most Chinese medical doctors agreed that the weaning could take place earlier, depending on the condition of the child. During the Qing dynasty, for example, Wang Mengying recommended that a strong child could be weaned from as early as one week old and instead fed milk with grains, namely porridge (Wang 1990). However, as was pointed out by Zhou Shimi, also of the Qing dynasty, some children could not be weaned at two or three years old, and if they were forced to wean, they would get sick (1990).

What kind of foods were children in premodern China fed as weaning foods? In most cases, young children transitioned to eating grain porridge before taking up solid foods. The most common type of grain porridge was made by boiling broken rice or corn with water until thick (Hsiung 1995). Mammal's milk, such as milk from pigs, sheep, and cows, was also used as a complementary or weaning food if the mother could not breastfeed or if the child fell ill. The famed Chinese medical doctor Kou Ping contended that milk from pigs is particularly good for newborn babies as it can cure tetanus and illness caused by *jingxian* (fear). In other words, the use of cow milk as a necessity for weaning is a relatively modern cultural construction as Chinese babies had transitioned smoothly from consuming breast milk to semi-solid foods without consuming any milk for thousands of years.

Modern Chinese dietary guidelines, which support particular health beliefs and the benefits of cow milk, are very much a result of the lobbying efforts of both local and international milk corporations, which invest huge sums into producing scientific knowledge through research on formula milk and breast milk (Mak 2017; Nestle 2018). Dairy companies producing infant formula dramatically expanded their markets during the post–World War II baby boom, as the rate of breastfeeding halved in America between 1946 and 1956, dropping to just 25 percent at hospital discharge in 1967 (Minchin 1985, 216). In the 1960s, birthrates in industrialized countries began dropping rapidly, bringing bad news to the pharmaceutical companies, while sales in developing countries began to increase. Then, facing challenges such as boycotts in response to the use of misleading marketing to convince mothers to substitute formula milk for breastfeeding in Southeast Asia, Nestlé and some other major multinational corporations instead attempted to break into markets with looser regulations concerning formula-milk advertising, such as mainland China and Hong Kong (Gottschang 2007; Nestlé 2002, 145–146; Van Esterik 1989, 1997, 2008).

In recent years, it has been found that most medical researchers are sponsored by corporations (Angell 2008; Relman 2008). For example, in the United States, the National Dairy Council developed its own research and its own version of the dietary guidelines highlighting the importance of cow-milk consumption and made it widely available in schools (National Dairy Council 2017). This dietary guideline raises the suggested daily servings for foods in the dairy group to 3–4 per day. Dairy-industry funds have also paid for full-page advertisements in the *New York Times,* which warn that low intake of calcium is a "major health emergency" and "the best way to get calcium is through your diet. . . . [By consuming] three glasses of milk a day."[16] The Dairy Council also filed objections to several proposed features of the original draft guidelines. It argued for setting a higher standard for the foods defined as "high fat," opposed the inclusion of soy beverages in the dairy food group, objected to the suggestion that lactose-intolerant people could choose sources of calcium other than dairy foods, and called for special guidelines for children that made more liberal allowances for dietary fat—ostensibly in the name of health, but at the same time in pursuit of higher sales (Nestlé 2002, 81). Through control of the direction of medical and food-science research and influence over research knowledge and publication, both the milk corporations and the states benefited, from higher profits for the former and taxation for the latter, while the state and its citizens perceived themselves as benefiting from the creation of "quality" persons well equipped to succeed in today's global economy (Greenhalgh and Winckler 2005).

Bottle-Feeding Self and the Breastfeeding Others

Galina Lindquist's (2001) analysis of healing systems in contemporary Russia is relevant to a discussion of how people in post-colonial Hong Kong and post-Mao China construct their sense of parenthood and personhood with various material objects, persons, and events (Bakhtin 1981; Bruner 1986; Rosaldo 1984). Lindquist (2001, 18) states: "In Russia, individual health-seeking strategies may be pragmatic last resorts; but they may also be political and ideological statements of identity and of belonging to different social groups, of cultural and ideological strands and flows, as well as attitudes to past and present." The discourse and practice of pluralistic health-seeking strategies in Russia after *perestroika* and of formula-milk consumption in modern China share a recognition of the possibility of individual human agency, albeit conditioned by the power of external circumstances. Using and talking about different formula milks was precisely a way for the Chinese parents I spoke with to position themselves as members of a group of citizens who were concerned about their babies' health and future, as well as being an active strategy to ensure good health and safe eating after the Sanlu milk scandal.

Though impoverished and often unable to buy expensive imported formula milk, the Chinese working-class parents I met are able to assert their social worth in other ways. Namely, the migrant mothers index their love and care and underscore their self-respect by sending locally produced premium formula home as a *bupin* for their children. Working-class fathers try to find extra income to buy higher-quality, premium-brand formula. The upper- and middle-class parents who prefer to buy the "authentic" imported foreign-brand formula milk in Hong Kong thus assert their place in a globalizing world, taking up critiques of the Chinese state and its dairy and pharmaceutical industry and showing their greater trust in Hong Kong's political system. Under the "One Country, Two Systems" framework, human rights and freedom of speech in Hong Kong have been largely respected. Unlike in the PRC, Hong Kong still possesses a strong anti-corruption system that can better enforce food-safety regulations (Chen 2010).[17] Discourses on cross-border purchasing of formula milk interrogate the role of nutrition science and raise questions regarding the geopolitics of milk—namely, the Hong Kong government and the Chinese state's responsibilities toward their citizens regarding food safety, public health, and resource allocation.

While the larger social environment and historical circumstances certainly condition human possibilities, I hope this chapter has shown how parents on both sides of the border act out their moral agency, though not without unexpected consequences. In Hong Kong, although the popular discourse on "breast is best" prevails, there is an equivalence between the successful, hardworking career women suffering from the "insufficient milk syndrome" and the adoption of daily bottle-feeding. "Successful women can't breastfeed" has become the motto of these women. The choice of bottle-feeding by these middle-class mothers reflects their desire to offer better life chances to their children in the wake of the decline in

Hong Kong's competitiveness following the 1997 handover and against the growing competition for education and other resources between Hong Kong and mainland China. In such cases, formula milk is used as a technology to enable mothers in both Hong Kong and mainland China to survive in the increasingly fragmented and unstable job market of the digital era and to pursue their ideal lifestyles, while at the same time responding to the heightened mandate for self-disciplined labor that accompanies neoliberalism.

In China, the equation of formula milk with nutrition science, urbanity, health, and the obligations of parents was evident everywhere in a generalized bottle-feeding discourse, illustrating the fact that the guidelines of the Chinese dietary association, internalized by the mothers and grandmothers I talked to, have become a set of core health beliefs, shaping their daily practices and their moral judgments of others. This social norm of bottle-feeding also enables the migrant mothers to achieve better career and life chances as formula milk is now used to fulfill, partially if not fully, their role as provider of nourishment for their children when they are away from home.

The obsession with providing imported formula milk among fathers in Hong Kong and China draws on fundamental Chinese tenets of men's responsibility to act as breadwinners and their capacity to invest in the future of their children. Yet, vulnerability to food-safety risk in China is hierarchical, as illustrated by the Sanlu milk scandal. As Dean Curran so presciently argued, "whenever the means of life is mediated through the market, a superior relative level of wealth will exist as a social power that enables its possessor to better adapt to disasters and to always have the first claim on scarce social goods" (2013, 57). Grounded in the ethnographic context of Shunde, I have found that not only wealth but also social and cultural capital expand the safe-food-providing capability of middle-class fathers. These capabilities are in turn the building blocks of their sense of masculinity and self-esteem. By providing not only imported formula milk but also the "authentic" ones bought from Hong Kong, fathers in mainland China show off their social and cultural capital and index their social position, not purely in terms of their actual economic contribution.

The unexpected consequence of the normalization of bottle-feeding is the stigmatization of breastfeeding "Others," who, ironically, would be representatives of a more privileged group in other societies. A 2015 Weibo post containing a photo of a Chinese mother breastfeeding her baby on a crowded subway, made by a Beijing-based NGO, asked the mother not to "expose (your) sexual organs," stating "this is Beijing's subway, not . . . your village." This was not the first, and certainly will not be the last, such incident demonstrating many Chinese people's intolerance of breastfeeding mothers in public spaces (Ho 2015). In Hong Kong, too, a mother was driven out from a church for breastfeeding during Mass. In another incident, a mother rode in a taxi for thirty minutes simply because she could not find a place to breastfeed her baby in her office (Fung 2017).

These incidents not only highlight the rural/urban and social-class divides in attitudes to and choices of infant-feeding practice, but also demonstrate how the modern science of nutrition and marketing activities of milk companies affect the ways that people think about food, their bodies, and identity in contemporary China and Hong Kong. Feeding smart and eating right in the era of the risk society is both a duty equated with good citizenship and an identity that locates individuals within the social hierarchy. The association of breastfeeding with rural and "uncivilized" and "immoral" behavior—as illustrated in the Weibo breastfeeding controversy mentioned above and in countless daily interactions in restaurants, playgrounds, and markets—heightens the potency of the social stigma against certain modes of infant feeding at the intersection of class and infant feeding. The cumulative effect of these many collisions, between infant-feeding practice and social-class bias, is discrimination against breastfeeding mothers and those who buy local brands of formula milk.

The medicalization of the "insufficient milk syndrome" experienced by many middle-class working mothers, accompanied by the growing phenomenon of picky-eating mental disorder among young children, which I will discuss in the next chapter, obscure the structural problems faced by these mothers and young children—persistent gender inequality and growing insecurity in the job market and the increasing academic stress and competition rife in education. By utilizing formula milk to treat these problems, people commit themselves to a particular "body culture" and also adopt a variety of narratives surrounding science, the state, and the market. Such debates, practices, and hopes—and the ideological strands and flows they index—are crucial to the invention of post-colonial and post-Mao selves in Hong Kong and China, respectively. Food strategies, such as provision of infant formula for babies and specialized formula for picky eaters, thus reflect ways in which post-colonial and post-Mao selves are being refashioned through discourses and bodily practices that manifest ambivalent attitudes toward science, the state, and the market. The stigma against breastfeeding mothers and the fear of being unable to produce sufficient "good-quality" breast milk, generated by the formula milk discourse, benefit the formula-milk companies while threatening the well-being of breastfeeding mothers by questioning whether these mothers possess the qualities that are seen as essential to personhood and good citizenship in modern Hong Kong and mainland China.

5 | Pharmaceutical Nexus

Creating Illness and Giving Hope

One sunny day in the early winter of 2015, Kitty Wong's apartment in Sai Kung, a district in the eastern New Territories of Hong Kong, was abuzz with laughter and lively chatter. A birthday party was being held for her son, Jaden Chan, an energetic five-year-old who was busy running around with his friends. I visited Kitty's family with my son, Silex, who was a good friend and classmate of Jaden's. While the children, mostly boys, were at play, the mothers gathered around the dining table to chat.

Kitty Wong: I am a bit worried about Jaden. He is such a picky eater. He only eats bread and a small amount of meat, drinks no milk and he hates vegetables. He is not going to get enough nutrition. You can see how thin he is. He was absent from school for a day last week because of his flu. I am so worried about his schoolwork.

Catherine Lam: William is just the same. That is why I make him milk [nutrition-enriched formula cow milk from America] twice a day—at breakfast and at teatime.

Veronica Mak: Does William like it?

Catherine Lam: Very much! The milk is vanilla-flavored and it is sweet. The only problem is that he does not eat so much at his dinner after drinking a big cup of milk. However, it should be alright because a cup of this specially formulated milk contains all the nutrition a child needs in a meal.

The entire afternoon was for me a display of Kitty Wong, Catherine Lam, and other parents' self-professed "strategies" for dealing with the picky-eating and schoolwork problems endemic to Hong Kong. In numerous other conversations, we discussed how parents increasingly felt the stress of researching and preparing their young children to enter elite primary schools. Both Kitty Wong and Catherine Lam were avid readers of popular online news containing school rankings and of the parenting advice dished out by experts, who repeatedly urged parents to cultivate their children to build up the right eating and learning habits.

This chapter describes how pharmaceutical companies have attempted to market nutrient-enriched formula to children by turning "picky eating" into a kind of disease under the context of rapid social change in post-colonial Hong Kong. The ability of human beings to make safe, palatable, and nutritious food choices and to avoid potentially poisonous food or food with low nutrition levels is an evolutionarily beneficial mechanism that increases human beings' chances of survival while making life more pleasurable (Birch et al. 1998; Cashdan 1998; Wright 1991). Being picky in eating, a trait found especially among children, can be particularly useful for adapting to new environments. For example, food neophobia (intolerance of new foods), which emerges and peaks during early childhood, can protect children from consuming untested foods that might be dangerous (Addessi et al. 2005; Cashdan 1998; Wardle et al. 2003).

In recent years, this essential adaptive food selection behavior has become increasingly medicalized as a kind of "problem" or even "disease." "Picky eating" is a modern moniker that has inconsistent definitions and meanings in different countries. As Kerzner and his colleagues pointed out, perceived feeding problems encompass a broad range of behaviors, from the mild (so-called picky eating or selective eating) to severe ends of the spectrum, the so-called feeding disorders that are recognized in the psychiatric Diagnostic and Statistical Edition (DSM-V) and medical International Statistical Classification of Diseases and related Health Problems coding systems (American Psychiatric Association 2013; Bryant-Waugh et al. 2010; Kerzner et al. 2015). Various criteria for picky eating have been used by different authors. Based on the criteria used by the Great Ormond Street Hospital in the United Kingdom, "selective eating behavior" includes eating a narrow range of foods for at least two years and in which the children are unwilling to try new foods (Nicholls, Chater, and Lask 2000). Some psychologists will also include "fussy" children with poor appetites as picky eaters (Jacobi et al. 2003; Wardle et al. 2001). But, generally speaking, picky eating connotes a minor or transient problem and is not considered a medical condition (Kerzner et al. 2015).

However, in Hong Kong, parents are told by doctors and dietitians that picky-eating syndrome may create serious health and mental problems, inhibiting children's ability to learn, their physical growth, and future development, especially for young children. The picky-eating habit is said to "place Hong Kong people at greater risk for developing diabetes, heart disease, high blood pressure, joint problems and even cancer" (*China Daily* 2011; Fan 2011). Parents are advised to take this disease seriously and to seek professional help if their youngsters are picky eaters, as this may lead to listlessness, lethargy, and loss of concentration. As has been widely reported in the local mass media, almost half the parents of young children in Hong Kong believe their children to be too fussy in eating, especially concerning fruits and vegetables, and these parents are at a loss on what to do (Man 2012). Despite the importance of eating behaviors to the health of young children, there has been hardly any anthropological study of this topic in either Chinese or post-colonial societies.

To illustrate how "picky eating" became a disease, this chapter will first look into the relationship between eating behavior and the health of infants and young children in traditional Chinese societies. Second, I ask what are the impacts of the pharmaceutical nexus—the global companies, physicians, and the state—on the production of medical knowledge, illness (focusing in particular on the picky-eating syndrome), and the everyday management of health among middle-class mothers in Hong Kong (cf. Petryna and Kleinman 2006).

Appetite and Qi in Ancient China

Before beginning our investigation of how picky eating has become an illness in modern Chinese society, it will be essential for us to understand beliefs about the relationship between eating behavior and the health of young children in ancient China. Chinese nutrition therapy has a long written history, based on Chinese philosophy and concepts of cosmology and environment (Anderson 2000; Hu 1966). Food is closely related to health and is used as medicine systematically to treat illness and physical challenges (Kleinman 1976). As noted by cultural anthropologist Eugene

Anderson, as early as the eastern Zhou Dynasty (ca. 770–221 BCE), court dietitians were the highest-ranked of the court medical staff (2000).

The poor appetite of a young child, manifested by slowness in eating or eating a limited amount and variety of food, has typically been interpreted by traditional Chinese medical doctors as indicating that the child is suffering from *shi ji* (literally, eat-accumulate), which requires serious attention (Zhang 1978). *Shi ji* was treated as a kind of syndrome caused by the imbalance of one's qi. The insufficient flow of qi from a young child's delicate spleen and stomach will result in salivation, diarrhea, and a loss of appetite and weight. *Shi ji* is usually perceived as a kind of indigestion, being the result of excessive food and nutrition (Gong 1999). In contrast to the biomedical remedy of feeding nutrient-enriched formula milk when young children display poor appetites, traditional Chinese medical principles recommend adjusting the diet by decreasing or increasing the nutrition level to correspond to the individual child's bodily condition and the root cause of his or her "poor appetite."

The Pharmaceutical Nexus and the Invention of Picky-Eating Syndrome

As suggested above, to understand the popularity of nutrient-enriched formula milk and the way it is consumed, it is necessary to know how it came to be marketed and promoted through the pharmaceutical nexus. Even though cow milk had come to be seen as a sacred and essential food for ensuring the health and growth of babies and young children in colonial Hong Kong beginning in the 1970s, the consumption of nutrient-enriched formula milk to solve the problem of "picky-eating syndrome" was still rare. Here, it was the pharmaceutical companies that created the local market. They, together with doctors and government and media promotion, contributed to the modernization of the marketing of, as well as the modern consumption of, nutrient-enriched formula milk.

The sudden increase in the research budget for follow-up formula milk for babies and young children over six months old during the mid-1980s, and the expansion of product varieties and marketing activities in the 1990s would not have been possible if not for the introduction of the new *International Code of Marketing of Breastmilk Substitutes (the Code)* in 1981. The new code advocated banning all advertisements of formula milk targeting infants under six months of age. Originally, nutrient-enriched formula milk was developed and promoted for the sick and the elderly, who either need to be tube-fed or have problems in digesting normal meals (Liang 2014). For example, as stated on the product information page on Nestlé's website, "Nutren Junior formula contains 50 percent whey protein and can be used as a tube-feeding formula or oral supplement" (Nestlé Health Science 2019). The page also indicates that this formula needs to be consumed under medical supervision. In other words, this nutrient-enriched formula was designed to be used as a meal substitute mainly for patients, and its intake was to be supervised by physicians.

However, in the 2000s, in order to expand their business without much investment into product development, the big pharmaceutical companies came up with a bright idea—to expand the market for nutrition-enriched formula milk from the limited number of hospitalized tube-fed patients to the much larger population of normal, healthy children in China and Southeast Asian countries who are picky eaters. For example, Nutren Junior formula is marketed in Hong Kong as a product suitable for new-borns and children aged up to ten years old who are picky eaters. Wyeth even tailor-made a nutrient-enriched formula—"S26 PE GOLD"—for young picky eaters in the Asian market, highlighting that the formula contains all seven major categories of food that human beings need (Wyeth Nutrition 2015).

In marketing circles, it is believed that before you can sell a product, you must create want; thus, before you sell a drug, you need to create the disease (Lane 2006). My study of the marketing activities promoting nutrient-enriched formula milk also reveals that the various common eating behaviors of young children, such as a preference for a limited range of foods, a prolonged period between meal times, and refusal to eat certain kinds of food, were being promoted as some major components of picky-eating syndrome.

One of the reasons why picky eating could be promoted as a disease—a kind of abnormal mental and behavioral disorder—is the broadening of the scope for eating disorders in the Diagnostic and Statistical Manual of Mental Disorders (DSM-IV-TR 2000) (Sadock et al. 2009). A study conducted in Britain found that, using the DSM-IV criteria, half of the children with eating difficulties met the criteria for "eating disorder not otherwise classified" (EDNOS) or "could not be classified" (Nicholls, Chater, and Lask 2000). In the DSM-V published in 2013, infant eating disorder was renamed as "Avoidant/Restrictive Food Intake Disorder" (First 2014).

To maximize the market size, pharmaceutical companies sought to expand the customer base for their nutrient-enriched formula to all children who might occasionally display picky-eating behavior, instead of restricting it to customers diagnosed with avoidant/restrictive food intake disorder. By collaborating with psychologists, dietitians, and physicians, Abbott Laboratories, an American health-care company, created a new definition for a disease termed "feeding difficulties," which would have similar negative health consequences as the "Avoidant/Restrictive Food Intake Disorder" of the DSM-V. This new disease category encompasses a broadened scope of psychological responses and behaviors, such as poor appetite and slowness in eating, which most children have at times experienced. To establish a standard for testing this newly created disease, Abbott developed the Identification and Management of Feeding Difficulties for Children (IMFeD) tool in 2011 to help pediatricians accurately identify and manage children with feeding difficulties (Garg, Williams, and Satyavrat 2015; Kerzner et al. 2015).

Collaborating with Doctors: Creating Knowledge and Hope

However, the creation of disease can never be successful unless it is intensively felt by the target audience that certain kinds of behavior or bodily conditions are abnormal. One possible piece of bad news for pharmaceutical companies was a survey result showing that only 28 percent of the mothers in Hong Kong were concerned about their three- to twelve-year-old children's health. Instead, most mothers were only concerned with their children's school performance (Watsons Pharmacy 2003).

To create and support the knowledge and set of beliefs about this "new picky-eating disorder disease" and its associated health risks, pharmaceutical companies needed to collaborate with medical scientists, physicians, nurses, and health promoters for knowledge co-creation and dissemination through journal publications, conferences, and lectures. In recent years it has been found that most medical researchers are sponsored by corporations (Angell 2008; Relman 2008). We can see an example of this industry–academic collaboration in relation to picky-eating syndrome in a study of 153 picky-eating Chinese children (aged thirty months to five years old) conducted in 2010 in China and Hong Kong. This study of the eating behavior among Chinese young children was conducted by four professors from universities in China and Hong Kong, including Professor Leung Ting-fan, the Chairman of the Pediatrics Department of the Chinese University of Hong Kong, and six medical scientists from a pharmaceutical company that sponsored the research (Sheng et al. 2014).

The most significant impact of Professor Leung and Sheng's journal paper was the classification of picky eating as a disease that entails serious physical and mental health risks for both the children and their caregivers. Professor Leung and his colleagues defined a picky eater as a child, who, in caregivers' reports, "consumes a limited number of foods and/or exhibit[s] strong preferences for a limited number of foods, child is unwilling to try new foods, child eats slowly, lacks interest in eating, and/or does not eat enough" (Sheng et al. 2014), and is therefore in need of medical intervention. As explained in this medical paper, children with picky-eating behaviors may have lower intakes of total calories, protein, vitamins, minerals, and specific food groups such as vegetables and fruits. Picky-eating behaviors can become a chronic issue, lasting for more than two years in up to 40 percent of affected children, creating caregiver and family anxiety about the child's growth and development. Therefore, it is important to address picky-eating behaviors at an early age to support growth, adequate nutrient intake, and positive caregiver–child interactions that contribute to healthy development. To this extent, these medical professors have co-created knowledge with a pharmaceutical company and formally classified some of the eating behaviors as "picky-eating syndrome" in Hong Kong and China.

As has been pointed out by Marion Nestle (2002, 2018), most industry-sponsored research tends to generate favorable findings and recommendations for the industry, and it is therefore unsurprising that Professor Leung's findings recommend feeding these young picky eaters a brand-sponsored, nutrient-enriched supplement so as to provide a short-term remedy to support adequate growth. In the long term, the picky-eating behaviors should be addressed by nutrition counseling (Sheng et al. 2014). Thus, picky-eating syndrome can be read as one of the many efforts of the pharmaceutical companies to invent diseases (for example, see Moynihan and Cassels 2005) and influence dietary advice dispensed to the public, while establishing a favorable image of their products. Indeed, co-opting experts—especially medical professionals and academic experts—has been found to be an explicit corporate strategy that goes to the heart of nutrition as a profession (Nestle 2002).

Capitalizing on Risk, Competition Culture, and the Education Imperative

In an attempt to generate awareness of the picky-eating syndrome and its pressing health risk, pharmaceutical companies increased their marketing budget for nutrient-enriched formula milk from 1 percent of the formula-milk advertisement budget in 2000 to 15 percent in 2012, making up a total of over HK$405million spent on advertising (US$51,923,077) (*Ming Pao* 2014). I will focus on the advertisements of the most popular nutrient-enriched formula milk as a lens for understanding how the picky-eating "disease" has been made known to mothers.

As most Hong Kong mothers are more concerned about their young children's academic performance than their health (cf. Park et al. 2014), one common theme in advertisements for nutrient-enriched formula milk for picky eaters beginning in the early 2010s was the huge negative impact of this perceived eating disorder on children's performance in school and extracurricular activities.

In 2013, an American pharmaceutical company launched an "Are you Sure?" marketing campaign, directly spelling out the message that picky-eating syndrome could lead to poor school performance (Chan 2013). Headlined with a question, "Always sick and not able to go to school?" the advertisement featured a four-year-old girl who appeared listless and bored in front of her vegetable-filled lunchbox. This was only one of a series of print, television, and online advertisements depicting sad and tired children with related headlines, including "Eating lunch for an hour. Are you sure?" On the homepage of the formula milk website, the viewer would see a blackboard with the eye-catching chalk-white words "Picky eating shakes the foundation of children's learning." The body copy of the advertisement further explained, "Because of the lack of essential growth elements, children's learning ability will decrease, and their bodily growth and mental development will be hindered." This was followed by the big circled words "Performance lags well behind others."

As most parents in Hong Kong do not consider picky eating to be a kind of disease, one of the major tasks of such advertisements is to urge mothers to go for a test. The design of the online self-diagnosis test in

Hong Kong based on Abbott's IMFeD, which includes an expanded range of picky-eating behaviors, such as being uninterested in some foods for a certain period of time that other children of the same age like. Since the foods preferred by young children vary by culture, almost every child might meet some classification for being a picky eater and thus be assumed to be unable to acquire all of the essential nutrients. As described on the websites of two leading international pharmaceutical companies that produced the most popular formulas in Hong Kong to address picky eating, children diagnosed with picky-eating syndrome will lag behind in the development of their bones, teeth, and muscles, while their immune systems, vision, and ability to learn and to memorize information might all be compromised.

While one leading formula-milk company has used academic studies and social risk to trigger parents' anxiety and to create "awareness" of picky-eating syndrome, another nutrition company positions its nutrition-enriched formula milk as a way of enhancing young children's performance in extracurricular activities. In a 30-second TV commercial launched in 2013, we see a confident-looking seven-year-old boy wearing a swimming cap preparing for a jump, a formally dressed boy cheerfully playing chess, and a serious-looking girl practicing ballet in her pink tutu. The female narrator's voice-over, which presumes to represent a mother's thoughts, delivers the core message: "Every child is different. But one thing they all have in common is that there is room for them to develop their potential. As a mother, I choose Nutren . . . to cope with the present and to prepare for the future."

In Hong Kong, a child's good performance in leisure activities, such as playing chess, practicing ballet, and swimming, can be counted as credit toward increasing his or her chances of entry into elite primary schools. Moreover, by posting the award-winning photos of their children on social media, parents gain in social status and self-esteem through the huge number of "likes" they collect, thus reinforcing their propensity to engineer their children's bodies through food.

To summarize, certain traits and behaviors, including picky eating and shyness, which were once regarded as neutral or even desirable, have today emerged as pathologies—functions of brain chemistry, amenable to and indeed demanding pharmacological manipulation (cf. Talbot 2001). Nutrient-enriched formula milk has been promoted as the perfect food for enhancing children's competitiveness in school because it is claimed to support the immune system, while enhancing children's intelligence, learning ability, and memory. By building up an association between picky eating and poor performance in academics, sports, and competitive activities, physicians and dietitians have contributed to an increase in eating disorders, both by lowering diagnostic thresholds and by bringing consumers' attention to a problem suggested to be far greater than anyone, including the sufferers themselves, had imagined.

Influencing Government

As discussed in chapter 2, the British colonial government played a crucial role in introducing and promoting consumption of cow milk and formula milk in Hong Kong (Cameron 1986). The growing popularity of Western cow milk is closely related to the government's adoption of the biomedical approach to health measurement and dietary guidelines. The Hong Kong government, like other urban governments around the world, follows the health standards and dietary guidelines set by the World Health Organization (WHO) and the Food and Agricultural Organization (FAO). In addition, the Hong Kong government has promoted the drinking of milk since the 1970s, with a dietary recommendation of two glasses of milk (i.e., 480 ml) a day. These recommendations are meant to fulfill calcium-intake requirements based on those in China and America. The calcium requirement of 1000 mg per day cannot usually be fulfilled by a traditional, nondairy Chinese meal. Nutrition science, as Valenze explained, resulted in the transformation of milk from the "chief food for sick folks" and "innocent children" to the food for everyone in Western society (2011). With the goal of enhancing public health, the Hong Kong government distributed free formula samples to newborn babies until 2010.

Despite the government's efforts to promote milk drinking as a way of ensuring sufficient intake of minerals, especially calcium, for the Chinese, special formulas for picky eaters were not recommended. As has been stated clearly in the government's communications with the public, including on its website and the brochures and leaflets it has disseminated, "The sugar content of picky-eating formula milk is higher than that for regular formula or in fresh milk. Reliance on picky-eating formula milk will affect children's appetites for their normal milk, further worsening their problematic eating behaviors" (Government of Hong Kong SAR 2016).

To provide voluntary guidelines to regulate incorrect or misleading marketing claims on formula products that may cause adverse long-term impacts for children's health, a task force on the Hong Kong Code of Marketing of Breastmilk Substitutes was set up by the Hong Kong Department of Health ("The HK Code") in 2010 and a framework was proposed in 2015 (Government of Hong Kong SAR 2017*b*). Had the proposal passed, claims relating to reducing the risk of disease made on all sorts of baby foods, including infant formula, follow-up formula, and prepackaged foods for infants and children under thirty-six months would have been banned.

To counteract the huge potential business losses due to the proposed restriction on their marketing activities, the eight largest manufacturers of the top-selling formula-milk products—including Abbott Laboratories Limited and Nestlé Hong Kong Limited—created The Hong Kong Infant and Young Child Nutrition Association (HKIYCNA) in May 2011. To protect the interests of its members, the HKIYCNA invited reputable physicians and dietitians holding senior positions in medical associations, such as the President of the Hong Kong Nutrition Association, to take up roles as members of its compliance panel. The organization also counter-proposed a self-endorsed HKIYCNA Code of Practice, which would allow the manufacturers to continue to advertise and market their products to infants and children aged seven months and older and provide incentives to health professionals (HKIYCNA 2011).

This is neither the sole nor the first incidence of collaboration between local pediatricians and multinational pharmaceutical companies. As one venerable pediatrician told me, the pediatric nutrition institution in Hong Kong was established by the pharmaceutical companies, which sponsor pediatric nutrition research and conference trips, offer scholarships, organize free seminars and training in five-star hotels, disseminate knowledge, and promote pediatric nutrition science. Today, most Hong Kong physicians are accustomed to receiving frequent visits from the sales personnel of big pharmaceutical companies, who seek to ingratiate themselves with the physicians through gifts and other forms of support. In 2015, unsurprisingly, the Hong Kong Pediatrician Association voted not to support the government in passing the Hong Kong Marketing Code.

Science and Resistance

This discussion would be incomplete without a consideration of the impacts of these cultural representations of picky-eating syndrome upon their intended audience. Elaine Showalter, in her discussion of the feminist history of psychiatry in England from 1830 to 1980, argues that hysterical epidemics only take hold if there are a significant number of would-be patients who are willing to comply with the interpretations of their experiences in medical terms (1985). We must ask how, then, do mothers define "picky-eating" behavior and how do they perceive its associated health risks? What is the impact of physicians, dietitians, and nurses on mothers' understanding of their children's health and illness, and how does this affect mothers' choices on solutions to such perceived illness?

First, almost all of my informants benchmarked their children's body size by using the Asian Growth and Weight Chart developed in 1993 (Leung 1995), handed out by doctors in public and private hospitals. The mothers addressed and described their young children in terms such as "my 15-month-old, 10 percentile daughter." They also used words with negative connotations, such as "falling below the growth line," "always in the 3–10 percent (percentile)," to describe their children's development. Other significant statements describing their children's growth included "catching up with the growth path for full-term B (babies)," "the doctor was shocked to see the weight of my child caught up to the 'third line,'" "My four-year-old son('s) weight-to-length ratio) is still in the third percentile. He once fell out from the normal curve. I am now trying to boost him up back to the curve."

Second, half of the mothers I interviewed who gave their children nutrient-enriched formula milk for picky eating said that their decision to treat the "syndrome" using such formula was based primarily on suggestions by doctors, dietitians, and nurses. For example, Jenny, a mother of a twenty-month-old girl, discussed her decision-making process with me: "My daughter has been in the third percentile (for weight) from her third week until now. Half a year ago, a dietitian recommended that she drink Brand A or Brand B nutrient-enriched formula milk, which have higher caloric content than normal formula milk." The other half of the mothers who fed their young children the picky-eater formula said that they were not influenced by doctors or dietitians. However, they were still worried about the consequences of picky-eating behavior in spite of doctors' reassurance that their children were normal notwithstanding their low weight. One mother reflected:

> My daughter is tiny, and her weight is too low for the growth chart. Although the doctor in the public hospital said my daughter is "normal," as her mother, I worry a lot. She only eats a small amount of food. She eats her congee or soft rice slowly and sometimes refuses to eat at all. I suddenly had the thought of giving her Brand A or Brand B. I have heard that they can help young kids to put on weight.

In addition, my informants told me that there was a huge difference between the recommendations of doctors in public hospitals and private clinics. One mother of a two-year-old shared her experiences with public and private clinics:

> My daughter's weight dropped from the 25th percentile at birth to the 10th percentile by the time she was one. The doctor and nurse in the public hospital said that there was no problem. However, when I saw a private hospital doctor, he recommended that I feed my daughter with formula milk if her growth rate fell below the 10th percentile because this would affect the brain's development. This worries me.

Third, the ways in which mothers identify their children as picky eaters and the ways in which they associate this with health risk are partially, but not totally, in alignment with those suggested by recent articles in medical journals and claims by pharmaceutical companies. In line with the popular narrative, most of the mothers surveyed perceived that their young children were abnormal if they ate a limited range of food, such as only eating plain white rice or bread, or not taking in enough meat, fish, fruits, and vegetables. Many thought that their children were suffering from the picky-eating syndrome simply because they drank fewer than two cups of milk a day—the dietary recommendation put forth by the Hong Kong government. Another new finding concerns the speed of eating—mealtimes lasting over half an hour were treated as problematic by these mothers. All of the mothers I interviewed who feed their young children with nutrient-rich formula milk expressed their fears and anxiety about picky-eating behavior and its potential health risks.

However, resistance toward the medicalization of picky-eating syndrome was also reported. Doctors and nurses had informed some of the mothers I interviewed that there is no need for nutrient-enriched formula milk and that there is no health risk for infants or children in the smaller percentile of the weight-to-length growth chart so long as the other development indicators are fine. In fact, most of the mothers reported feeling ambivalent after introducing the nutrient-enriched formula milk to their children. Helen, like many of my informants, was very concerned about the physical reaction of her three-year-old son to the new formula, including an increase of sputum and constipation—two common side effects of the nutrient-enriched formula milk. She shared her experience of feeding her son using two of the most popular brands and her confusion in making the choice: "After feeding my son with P (a nutrient-enriched formula) for four days, I found that my son's feces was very hard and he started to produce a lot of sputum. I want to stop feeding him the nutrient-enriched formula, but I am scared that he might suffer from a lack of sufficient nutrition."

In addition, a small group of physicians, dietitians, and mothers advise against feeding young children the nutrient-enriched formula milk. Phoebe Lau, a mother of a five-year-old child, and herself a dietitian, says that she designs non-dairy meals for her clients because she was inspired by a book written by a respected pediatrician, *Why You Do Not Need to Drink Cow Milk* (Leung 2005). Another mother I talked to suggested that drinking the sweet nutrient-enriched formula milk would predispose children to overindulge in sweet foods. Others suggested using a more "natural" method to enhance the appetites of their children, such as enhancing the taste by adding sweet corn, or making the food more visually stimulating by, for example, cutting a carrot into the shape of an airplane or dinosaur.

Furthermore, although most mothers are well versed in the biomedical growth chart for the measurement of health, many accept the body shape of their children by using two alternative judgment models. The first is the body size of the parents. Some informants told me that they believed the small body size of their children to be natural and due to genetic causes. The second judgment model concerns the children's academic performance. As long as their children performed well in school and were able to speak well, the mothers I interviewed believed that slow growth in weight and height was not a serious issue. Carmen told me:

Every time we met with the government-appointed dietitian, she recorded and commented on the types of dishes we prepared at home. She recommended that we feed my two-year-old son with P (a nutrient-enriched formula milk). It didn't work as my son's weight did not improve significantly. She then suggested that I add a few drops of cooking oil to the rice for him. Still, my son did not gain much weight. My son is now in K1 (first year of kindergarten) with his height in the tenth percentile, while his weight is only in the third percentile. However, he is performing brilliantly in every subject except for physical exercise. I am not worried anymore.

Some of my informants who do not choose nutrient-enriched formula told me that they were influenced by some negative news, as reported in the newspapers. One newspaper article title pointed directly to the problem—that these "Picky Eater Formula Milks" are the causes, not the cures, for the perceived picky-eating disorder. As most of these picky-eater formula milks were developed for tube-fed patients and served as meal substitutes, the calories and nutrients delivered in one serving, such as protein and calcium, are equal to or even greater than the suggested US Dietary Reference Intakes (DRIs) for a meal. In other words, it is normal for children to have no appetite after drinking two glasses of vanilla-flavored, nutrient-enriched formula milk, and the picky-eating behavior could become even more serious.

Medicalization of Childhood and the Cultural Construction of Illness

Margaret Lock has observed that the medicalization of childhood in modern societies results from the interplay of political, social, cultural, and psychological factors. In her ethnographic study of Japan, Lock found that the depressing education system and rapid environmental and social changes in the postwar period led to a growing number of young children who apparently wanted to go to school but ended up staying in bed. These children were diagnosed as having a problematic "school-refusal syndrome" and needed to receive medical intervention, ranging from dietary changes to electroshock therapy (Lock and Gordon 1988, 401). Other valuable studies by anthropologists and psychologists have also pointed out that such modern illnesses of young children are cultural constructions. For example, Sami Timimi and Eric Taylor (2004) argued forcefully that attention deficit hyperactivity disorder (ADHD) is a disease invented to meet modern societal needs. ADHD "offers a decontextualized and simplistic idea that leads to all of us—parents, teachers and doctors—disengaging from our social responsibility to raise well-behaved children. . . . It supports the profit motive of the pharmaceutical industry, which has been accused of helping to create and propagate the notion of ADHD in order to expand its own markets" (Timimi and Taylor 2004, 8).

In this chapter, we have examined several interrelated concerns: the historical shift in the meaning of the "right" eating behavior, which also involves understanding the shifting standard for health measurement from a Chinese to an Anglo-American one; the biomedical emphasis and corporate sponsorship of "functional nutritionism" (Scrinis 2013); and, finally, the fundamental assumptions of pediatric pharmacology about normality, social competition, and adaptation. By now, we have seen how economic, political, cultural, and social forces have contributed to the invention of "picky-eating behavior" as a distinctive new psychological and behavioral disease that is believed to pose serious health and social risks to young children in contemporary Hong Kong.

Culturally, we witness the historical shift of the meaning of the "right" eating behavior, which also involves understanding the shifting standard for health measurement from a Chinese to an Anglo-American one. Previously, based on traditional Chinese medical beliefs, the picky-eating behavior of young children was believed to be a reflection of the imbalance of qi inside and outside the body. According to the traditional Chinese health belief system, being selective and "picky" in regard to food is essential and necessary for maintaining health, rather than being a threat to health. In recent decades, however, most mothers in Hong Kong, influenced by knowledge of Western biomedical nutrition, have paid greater attention to the weight-and-height health measurements, as well as the advice of doctors, dietitians, and nurses, and received additional information from mass and digital media on the ways to judge the healthy eating behaviors of their young children.

My findings also demonstrate that the perceived risks of picky eating are not only biological, but also social. The idea of a "picky-eating epidemic" also points to the way this experience has been defined and managed as a social problem. Picky eating has become an "unhealthy" state of mind and behavior for individuals, especially children, in contemporary Hong Kong society. Insofar as its behavioral "symptoms" imply a failure to achieve certain cultural values for the children, such as being intelligent, energetic, creative, and assertive, with a physically strong and tall body, picky eating has increasingly come to be defined as a problem, which will lead to cognitive underdevelopment, slowness in learning, passivity, physical shortness, and weakness. Thus, children can, and should, be treated with enriched formula milk to spare them from such undesirable states.

The promotion of biomedical knowledge and the adoption of modern Western cow milk or formula milk in the 1960s to 1970s was also political. By setting up the modern dietary guidelines and using cow milk to fill the "protein gap" caused by the Chinese weaning diet, the colonial government gained its legitimacy, credibility, and trust by showing its care, knowledge, and progressiveness. Despite concerns raised regarding the aggressive marketing campaigns promoting formula milk beginning in the 1990s—which may contain misleading messages affecting how people perceive health risks and choose to feed their infants and young children—the post-colonial, neoliberal government has hesitated to pass a marketing code of practice and has not banned such advertisements. By upholding the freedom of trade and markets, the government hopes to maintain the competitive advantages of the city and promote the stability of its governance (Harvey 2005; Liu 2009).

As the present study has demonstrated, the adaptive capability of human beings for selective intake of food has now come to be classified as a kind of illness. The conflict of interest between science and business is changing the moral economy of professional classification and diagnosis. In this study, our data show how the intentionality of medical perceptions is informed by the purpose of treatments rather than by the causes or phenomenology of symptoms. The very act of prescribing formula milk, which normally involves professional medical counseling and a diagnosis of relevant symptoms, resulting in the prescription of appropriate medications, has been reconceived. A top-down numbers game, combined with physicians' relative vulnerability and eagerness to receive gifts, has enabled the widespread promotion of nutrient-enriched formula milk.

Economically, the promotion of the picky-eating syndrome and nutrient-enriched formula milk has benefited international pharmaceutical companies directly and local physicians and psychologists indirectly. The successful promotion of the picky-eating syndrome and the modernization of the food and nutrition industries, as well as marketing and consumption, have also promoted the development of related enterprises aimed at providing all-around, well-balanced nutrition to young children, namely "DHA-enriched" cooking oil, "Omega-3-added" candies, "calcium-fortified" breakfast cereals, food supplements, and confectionary, cereal, and snack products.

The logical—perhaps inevitable—consequence of the biomedical turn in pediatric nutrition has been a growing consensus that traits often attributed to shorter, smaller body size, slowness in learning, poor performance in sports, and less creative and weaker performance in visual arts should be regarded as growth disorders in young children, which must be eliminated by food or drugs. This logic has to be understood against the political context of the competition rife between the young children of Hong Kong and those of southeastern China for gaining educational resources and cultural capital (Mak 2016). This logic must also be understood against the disillusionment in Hong Kong regarding the city's loss of regional competitiveness compared with other major cities in China, as well as in relation to the changing social fabric, resulting in growing anxiety among middle-class families. Although some mothers have not complied with the popular medical discourse disseminated by the pharmaceutical companies, people's expectations of the ideal bodies and capacities of young children and the moral role of formula feeding are being redefined by the marketing activities of this magical commodity.

Although they were developed from the authoritative DSM-V guidelines and the public-health principles aimed at improving the dietary health of children, the tests for identifying picky eaters and the various marketing campaigns launched by the pharmaceutical companies in promoting nutrition-enriched picky-eater formula seriously threatened the well-being of the very persons they purported to help. The focus on eating behavior as a health and moral measure produced a kind of vicious stigma for toddlers who failed to live by the rules of dietary health, as many of these "problematic" eating behaviors were considered normal and even adaptive for children in a different time and place.

Also, as has been pointed out by Dr. Huang Mingqin, a consultant doctor working in a public hospital in Hong Kong, treating picky-eating toddlers with sweetened, nutrition-enriched formula could make them pickier in their eating. Huang told a reporter,

Many pharmaceutical companies marketed the nutrition-enriched formula as a "short-cut" to resolve children's picky-eating behavior by filling in the nutrition gap. Many parents are misled and have bought this type of formula originally designed for tube-fed patients, without consulting any doctors. They come to me and say, "I have given my child picky-eating formula, why are they still so picky in eating?" How can the children eat their daily meals if they have already consumed 100 calories in their formula? (Liang 2014)

In addition to a deteriorating appetite, those picky eaters who are unfortunately lactase insufficient may suffer further from functional bowel disorders and other symptoms such as mal-digestion if they consume picky-eating formula as a daily food.

Yet, the empirical language of medical and scientific norms on eating behavior and nutrition intake was a powerful set of moral rules that were rarely questioned or even noted. The messages channeled by this medical language conveyed a lesson in the cultural expectations of a good child, a good mother, and a good citizen, giving hope to parents in protecting or even uplifting their social status through their children's academic achievement. Most strikingly, as one of the most powerful discourses on food and health in China at the start of the twenty-first century, the marketing activities for formula and dairy products capitalized on and expanded the products' market growth in pursuit of the food and dietary politics. This food and health discourse demanded that every Chinese, and especially mothers, should take seriously the mandate to "eat and feed your family right."

Conclusion

The World Food Regime, the State, and the Medicalized Individual

I n this concluding chapter, I summarize the major changes in milk consumption in Shunde and Hong Kong from 1950 to 2010 and then address three important factors underlying the emergence of the milk-craze phenomenon in China: the world food regime, the role of the state, and the medicalization of modern life. It is my contention that the attention I have paid to the "glocalization"[1] and syncretization of milk and economic medicalization[2] sets this study apart from most earlier studies of milk culture in China. I began my study by exploring how the new milk regime interacts with local milk traditions. I then argued that the British colonial state in Hong Kong and the socialist state in China have both been major forces in initiating or causing milk production and family changes over the six decades from 1950 to 2010 in their respective locales. These changes have resulted in a boost in milk production and consumption by the Chinese population, with significant health and environmental impacts. Finally, through the lens of milk consumption, I explored in depth Chinese parents' moral experiences, including how they exercise autonomy and agency in the process of medicalization—which is closely intertwined with their work, family life, and their children's education.

The New Milk Regime and the Old Milk Culture

Paradoxically, although the lactase persistence of people in China is remarkably low, today more than one-quarter of the milk in the world is consumed by the Chinese. In an influential publication by the International Food Policy Research Institute, business analyst Christopher Delgado and his colleagues coined the term "Livestock Revolution" to explain the surge in milk and meat consumption in China and other developing countries (Delgado et al. 1999). As Delgado (2003) has pointed out, "As per capita incomes rise, many developing countries are said to be on the cusp of a 'Livestock Revolution,' as the demand for milk and other animal-source foods increases." Since the "Livestock Revolution" was theorized by analogy to the earlier "Green Revolution," it has become a dominant "paradigm" in the narratives of development practitioners and policy makers engaged in livestock and related sectors. The basic tenet of this new paradigm is that the combination of population growth, rising per capita incomes, and progressive urbanization is creating unprecedented growth in the demand for foods of animal origin in developing countries, giving rise to major opportunities and threats for humankind. Influenced by this grand narrative, many scholars contend that modernization, Westernization of lifestyles, and the symbolic meaning of milk as an agent of growth are the cardinal reasons for the insatiable "thirst for milk" of the Chinese (see, for example, Wiley 2007). This book illustrates two previously unexplored factors: the post–World War II world food regime and the local milk culture in Chinese societies, both of which deserve closer attention.

The newly created global food system—characterized by the dominance of international corporations in the production of cow milk and formula milk, through their establishment of local production plants and aggressive marketing activities addressing local customers' needs—has important effects on the dietary patterns of people in China. This book shows the complexity of the processes of globalization and syncretization of food by adopting a historical and comparative perspective, supported by ethnographic data to avoid simplistic pronouncements about the food regime, or, more precisely, the new milk regime—now led by the Swiss corporation Nestlé and French corporations Lactalis and Danone (Coppes, van Battum, and Ledman 2018). As I have outlined in the introductory chapter, the globalization of food started with colonialism, and the introduction of cow milk products into Chinese societies was no exception to this trend (Friedmann 2005). During the late nineteenth century, the colonial powers began introducing Western cows into Hong Kong and the major treaty ports of China. The practice and health beliefs of replacing breast-feeding with diluted sweetened canned milk and the now heritagized milk-tea making would probably not have developed in Hong Kong if there had been no surplus production of military foods, including milk powder and canned milk, in Western countries after World War II. In addition, the postwar international food aid programs, which enabled Anglo-American countries to export milk to non-milk-drinking populations, made milk accessible to people from different social classes.

As food historian Francoise Sabban has pointed out, the desire for milk in China cannot simply be seen as a response to the country's economic reforms, or the opening up of the People's Republic of China. It has been shaped over centuries (Sabban 2014). This book demonstrates further that the modern meanings of milk and material culture have been shaped not only by centuries of Chinese indigenous milk culture and culinary traditions but also by the moral values of parenting. Recall, for example, the case mentioned in chapter 4 of the pricey formula milk with a higher dosage of docosahexaenoic acid (DHA) tailored for the Asian market. This was not the natural result of a scientific breakthrough in improving the brain performance of babies but rather a carefully crafted marketing strategy adopted by the leading pharmaceutical companies to expand their markets in Asia. While premium milk brands have lost their appeal in the West, pharmaceutical companies are keen to expand into China, Hong Kong, and the Southeast Asian market, where parents are willing to spend as much as half of their salaries to buy imported formula brands not only for their higher levels of safety but also as a symbol of social status and in order to realize their hopes for their children's future academic excellence.

Admittedly, the story of the successful glocalization of Western food in China is hardly new (see, for example, Jing 2000; Watson 1997). What makes the milk-craze case in China noteworthy is the combination of the local expressions of this historical trend and the specific ways that things have changed, rather than the outcome. The case of the milk craze demonstrates the important role of traditional local milk culture and the increasingly important role played by milk and pharmaceutical corporations in the syncretization of Western cow milk with local ingredients, both of which have been largely overlooked in previous studies of milk in China that tended to focus on Western modernity and children's growth.

Milk in China is thus an exemplar of syncretism. New milk products were developed by combining both modern and traditional cultural elements. Milk is modern in China because it encapsulates the image of Western nutrition science. Its recent popularity has been due in large part to the rise of nutritionalism, and the knowledge of nutrition science has become a marker of middle-class belonging (Scrinis 2008, 2013). At the same time, milk is also traditional in China because many industrialized "Western" cow milk products are developed and interpreted based on Chinese food traditions, specifically the Chinese humoral system. In this spirit, my ethnographic study supports the notion that modernity can be multifaceted (Eisenstadt 2000)—not necessarily denoting becoming "Western" or a departure from tradition, but possibly denoting a continuation of traditional Chinese and Asian values and identities. We have seen the different local manifestations of the single process of modernity, and how "tradition" negotiates with "modern" culture, which involves both continuity and change (Hannerz 1996, 44) and manifestation of tradition in modernity.

The Role of the State

In addition to the world food regime, I contend that the recent thirst for milk is a result of the state-sponsored dairy-industry-building project, which is part of the modernization plan for turning China into a global superpower. As Davis and Harrell correctly note, in China, "state power and policies have been the creators, not the creations, of a transformed society" (1993, 5). It is thus impossible to understand post-1979 China without taking into account the role played by the state. In the discussion of the Chinese government's role in promoting milk consumption, Andrea Wiley rightly points out two key factors. The first factor is the establishment of a joint government- and business-sponsored school-milk program. Second, the Chinese government's nationalistic rhetoric has supported the domestic milk industry, emphasizing the benefits for individuals' growth and national strength so as to "catch up" in size with Western populations (Wiley 2007). In this work, I have systematically analyzed—supported with ethnographic data—the influence of government power on the modern milk culture in China, covering the consumption not only of fluid milk but also indigenous water buffalo milk and formula milk. This government influence, I argue, covers five inter-related aspects: land reform and dairy-industry modernization, financial incentive programs, dietary guidelines, advertising regulations, and social policies.

First, the Chinese government's modernization project, in the form of new land policies, agricultural experiments, collectivization, and progressive ideology dissemination, led to a decline in the production and consumption of indigenous water buffalo milk and cheese in Shunde. From 1949 to 1978, under the rule of the new Communist Party, large-scale social experiments were carried out to boost agricultural production. These included a massive land-reform program that eliminated landlords and gave land to those who farmed it, which was followed by the reorganization of farm families into cooperatives and collectives. Unfortunately, instead of increasing the productivity of the water-buffalo-milk industry, these agricultural experiments resulted in a drastic drop in the number of water buffaloes and in milk production. In 1978, China's leaders began another set of far-reaching agricultural reforms. Townships and villages were reorganized, and the new land policy in Daliang, a sub-district of Shunde, prohibited buffalo-cow farming, pushing all of the farms to the suburbs during the 1980s.[3] More importantly, through a series of state-sponsored TV programs, images of water buffalo cheese, cheese makers, and farmers as "backward" and unsophisticated were circulated, which resulted in a change in perception of the health value of traditional buffalo cheese and a gradual decrease in demand for the traditional buffalo cheese, especially among the younger generations.

Second, the Chinese government launched a series of financial policies aimed at modernizing and expanding the dairy industry. At the provincial level, the government launched a taxation-sharing reform to motivate local governments to stimulate economic growth. At the international level, the Chinese state government kicked off a series of incentive programs to attract foreign capitalists to invest in the dairy industry in China. Foreign-invested enterprises in the agricultural sector, including in the dairy industry, were exempted from having to pay enterprise income tax and various value-added taxes (Ling and Zhou 2014). Consequently, the world-leading dairy companies, such as Aria, Danone, and Fortanne, formed joint ventures with Chinese milk-processing companies including Mengniu, Wahaha, and Sanlu. With these changes, the Chinese state has become the largest stakeholder in some of the leading dairy corporations.[4] With the huge sums of capital drawn from global investors, enterprises (such as the multinational pharmaceutical and packaging companies), and the Chinese government, milk-processing companies such as Mengniu and Yili were able to launch aggressive advertising campaigns, lowering prices and increasing the points of distribution for their milk products, which ranged from fluid milk to ice cream. Thus, these companies were able to create unprecedented demand across China.

Third, the dietary guidelines in both China and Hong Kong clearly instruct citizens to consume two to three glasses of milk each day, and therefore constitute a direct cause of the surge in milk consumption in southeastern China. The governments of both Hong Kong and mainland China have been supporting the pharmaceutical nexus in medical-knowledge creation and in the institutionalization and normalization of milk as a daily drink. Contrary to conventional wisdom that we should choose the right foods for our body according to our individual health conditions, Chinese bodies were trained and tuned to absorb Western cow milk. Those who cannot digest milk are now diagnosed as having a kind of disease called "milk allergy." Physicians sponsored by pharmaceutical companies advise that this illness needs to be "cured" by drinking one-third of a glass of milk each day and gradually increasing the portion to allow one's body to slowly adapt. "Quitting" milk has been dubbed "a pessimistic decision" by Mr. Samson Chim, Chief Dietitian at the VNS Nutrition and Health Centre (FrieslandCampina 2017). As such, lactase impersistence in Chinese society has been medicalized and made abnormal and the mutation for lactase persistence is now being encouraged and institutionalized by the modern pharmaceutical nexus.

Fourth, the relatively loose advertising regulations in Hong Kong and China for marketing activities of breastmilk substitutes have stimulated milk consumption. Recall from chapter 5 that the political struggle between the pharmaceutical companies and the Hong Kong government resulted in a delay in the implementation of the voluntary Hong Kong Code of Marketing of Formula Milk and Related Products, and Food Products for Infants & Young Children ("The HK Code"), which was finally implemented in 2016 (Government of Hong Kong SAR 2017b).[5] In addition, compared to those in other developing countries, the Hong Kong and Chinese codes are more liberal, restricting the marketing of milk formula and infant foods only for children younger than six months old, as compared to children under the age of two in the Indian code (World Health Organization 2013).[6] The cultural construction of milk as a nutritious staple would not have been possible without the state's liberal policy, which indirectly supports exaggerated, if not outright deceptive, advertising and marketing messages in which dairy companies link their product directly or indirectly with future academic and creative performance by the children consuming it. In addition, industrial sponsorship of medical research and academic activities is allowed in both Hong Kong and mainland China. In mainland China, although the advertising regulations are stricter than those in Hong Kong (Gao 2005), pharmaceutical company representatives there have, both in the past and more recently, offered financial incentives to health-care workers for promoting their products (Waldmeir 2013). In some instances, health-care workers have even provided these companies with contact information on new births for the purpose of product promotions, in violation of privacy agreements, as was reported in China some years ago (Harney 2013). Marketing messages, camouflaged in the form of educational medical knowledge offered by medical, psychological, and educational experts, are channeled through pediatricians' clinics, parenting websites, educational seminars, conferences, and schools and kindergartens supported by pharmaceutical companies. These messages help to normalize the expectations of a good mother and ideal children and create fear in parents of being unable to fulfill those expectations.

Fifth, the state's vision and policies on the family, such as on birth control and education, have unexpected consequences for milk consumption. In the final decade before the Chinese government put an end to the one-child policy in 2015, the health of the "only child" emerged as the core concern of the modern Chinese state as a way of sustaining the one-child policy, which was originally conceived as a state strategy to improve "population quality" (Jing 2000). Owing to the fierce competition among students to enter top-ranked schools and universities, formula milk has been marketed as a functional food to enhance cognitive development. More often than not, the unintended consequence of strong marketing messages has been the establishment of a new imagination concerning children's mental and physical capacities and reinforcement of the mother's role as intensive academic coach. This new ideology of motherhood and childhood turns out to be critical for the transformation of the moral experience of motherhood. The most important consequence of these marketing efforts, in the particular political and cultural context of modern China, has been the medicalization of motherhood and childhood, as manifested in the growing prevalence of the "insufficient breast milk syndrome" and the "picky-eating disorder."

Consumer Desires, Medicalization, and Social Justice

How should we think about the dramatic dietary change that has been brought about by the new milk regime and the Chinese government, and of the moral experiences of people in modern China? As discussed in the Introduction, Chinese milk consumers have been shaping the milkscape around the world. There is now growing concern regarding the surge in milk consumption in China and its huge environmental impact, including on climate change. In addition, from my perspective, another worrying global trend is the increasing commercialization of milk-based formula, led by China, Indonesia, Thailand, and Vietnam, creating an unprecedented change in feeding infants and young children (Baker et al. 2016).

By adopting a critical medical anthropological approach, I have sought in this book to understand the issues and problems of health, illness, milk consumption, and dietary change in terms of the interaction between the macro level of the political economy of milk production; the community level of popular and traditional beliefs about milk; and the micro level of illness experience, behavior, and meaning. While my historical and ethnographic study has provided information that is useful for the projects of studying food-consumption culture and dietary change, it also raises some important anthropological questions about globalization, food sovereignty, health, and well-being. Following the call of critical medical anthropologists like Merrill Singer, Kristen Hastrup, and Peter Elsass, I hope to unmask, rather than mystify, the sources of social inequity and ill health through the lens of milk consumption. As Merrill Singer maintains, critical medical anthropology is predicated on the awareness that "no anthropologist can escape involvement" (Hastrup et al. 1990, 302).

In addressing the health and nutritional problems that have resulted from the industrialization of food in Indonesia, Aya Hirata Kimura advocates for the food sovereignty movement, which supports the notion that at the core of the world food problem is not the lack of food but rather the lack of "self-defined ways [for local communities] to seek solutions to local problems" (Windfuhr and Jonsen 2005, 15; Patel 2007).[7] As Patel observes, it is a "call for a mass re-politicization of food politics, through a call for people to figure out for themselves what they want the right to food to mean in their communities" (2007, 91). Could this nontraditional food sovereignty movement create a new space for an alternative imagination and save Chinese consumers from falling into the trap set by giant milk corporations and pharmaceutical companies? Let's recall the case of the "formula milk shortage" online protest in Hong Kong. Ironically, the science of nutrition, to a certain extent, provided parents with a common language to gain food sovereignty: through online media, people voiced their self-defined food choices (imported formula in this case); consolidated their political capital through online community building; and ultimately forced the government to amend the law, restricting the trading of formula milk from Hong Kong into China.

In contrast to the traditional medical anthropological practice of describing "real people doing real things" (Ortner 1984, 144), this book puts power at the center of the milk-craze discussion, serving as a critique of the medicalization of motherhood and childhood in modernizing China. The new milk order, dominated by the market-leading dairy and pharmaceutical companies, would not necessarily have increased the demand for cow milk in China had the products of these companies been unable to fulfill the modern needs of their customers. This book documents and analyzes how these multinational corporations make use of science to shape consumer behavior. By making use of science in the fields of nutrition, psychology, and cognitive development, multinational corporations provide new rules and measurements for infant feeding practices, body and brain management strategies, and a new imagination of an ideal child. At the same time, these marketing activities modify the meanings of ideological concepts like disease, medicine, and social development.

Formula milk, like many other functional foods, is marketed as a panacea to empower middle-class mothers, who are being marginalized in the labor market and increasingly being scrutinized by society at large and obliged to rear competitive and smart children in a fast-changing society. Their perceived stress derives from the hard edge of unaccommodating workplaces and strong social pressure to regain a pre-pregnancy body shape. The difficulty of maintaining self-esteem in their career and the labor-intensive job of preparing for their babies' education are the cardinal reasons why many mothers come to believe they suffer from "insufficient milk syndrome" and switch to feeding their children formula milk. These findings, based on ethnographic study in southeastern China, support Susanne Zhang Gottschang's study in Beijing and her argument that consumers' desire for formula milk in China is related more to social relationships in an increasingly consumer-oriented social milieu (2007). What I hope to have accomplished for the first time is to document how mothers negotiate the meanings of two illnesses—the "insufficient milk syndrome" experienced by mothers and the "picky-eating illness" said to afflict young children—in dealing with their gendered burdens and identity building in the context of a fast-changing society. These illnesses, although now globalized, are unfortunately being neglected in current scholarship on Chinese society.

The "Insufficient Milk Syndrome" and Burnt-Out Mothers

The "insufficient milk syndrome" is a trans-cultural phenomenon and the number-one reason given by mothers for early termination of breastfeeding, not only in Hong Kong but also in developed and developing nations around the world (Gussler and Briesemeister 1980). In explaining the reasons for this syndrome, most scholars have pointed to bio-cultural and social reasons. For example, Gussler and Briesemeister note that the modern, non-biological breastfeeding method results in babies' frequent crying and misinterpretation by mothers that they have insufficient milk. A study of mothers in Bangladesh conducted by Zeitlyn and Rowshan (1997) illustrated the social reasons, such as how formula-milk bottles, which are associated with allopathy and science, provide a way of circumventing anxieties about female physiology and sexuality in the context of rapid urbanization. Although cracking the reason for this "lack-of-milk illness" could be a key to increasing the breastfeeding rate, studies exploring how the illness is experienced by mothers from different social classes and in different societies are still lacking.

What differentiates my study from previous works on infant feeding is that I pay special attention to the structural inequality among social classes in their self-perceived capacity to breastfeed. The unique phenomenon in Hong Kong, where middle-class mothers breastfeed the least, points to some structural and social barriers that these women face. Many middle-class, highly educated mothers in Hong Kong, though highly paid, usually have non-flexible, long working hours and time-demanding jobs. My informants from this social milieu told me that not only were they breadwinners and caretakers for their young children, they also acted as academic coaches for their children. Most of my informants believed that they had a moral obligation to provide rich cultural, social, and financial resources for their children's education through their own self-sacrifice— by working longer hours and giving up personal time.

In traditional Chinese societies, the cultural beliefs and expectations placed on mothers go beyond their biological role of nurturing children and extend to their social role in cultivating an academic propensity and enhancing the performance of their children. This is exemplified by the legendary story of the mother of the Confucian scholar Mengzi, who moved house with the family three times in order to find the most suitable place for her son to study. In this spirit, the modern hierarchy of care can be studied as a twisted version of so-called intensive mothering in Chinese societies, leading to higher social pressure on Chinese mothers and a higher tendency to adopt formula milk so that they can focus on the provision of social and educational resources to their children rather than nurse and create a physical bond with their children (Romagnoli and Wall 2012). We have seen this in the case of Pauline, who neglected breastfeeding and concentrated on training her child to enter an elite English school, as the latter is the measure by which good and successful mothers are judged in Hong Kong today.

Taking into account the gendered triple burden shouldered by Chinese mothers, I contend that present-day Chinese mothers experience more anxiety over breastfeeding owing to their idiosyncratic type of "intensive mothering," prioritizing academic coaching and devaluing the physical bond with the child, which is markedly different from the type of "intensive mothering" described in Western societies (Hays 1996). However, this does not mean that Chinese mothers passively fall into false consciousness and are fooled by marketers into internalizing the message that formula can lead directly to excellent academic performance. On the contrary, the Chinese parents I spoke to evaluated formula milk carefully and used it as a type of technology to handle their daily challenges. Many educated working mothers in Hong Kong who have to shoulder the triple burden of their three roles—as a laborer in a corporation, as a nurturer, and as an academic cultivator for their children—face a cultural contradiction concerning their "biological–moral" responsibility, that is to say, their biological responsibility is to breastfeed, while at the same time fulfilling their social expectation to be successful career women (Murphy 2000). Consequently, the "insufficient milk syndrome" becomes a modern cultural idiom for the expression of individual and collective discontent. This cultural idiom also enables burnt-out mothers to adopt formula milk as a socially acceptable way of partially resolving the cultural contradiction they face.

Unlike in Hong Kong, where breastfeeding is increasingly perceived by new mothers as a moral obligation, in Shunde, formula milk and dairy products are promoted as a staple for babies past the age of six months, as dictated by the prevailing medical knowledge and disseminated by the state through dietary guidelines and neoliberal medical institutions. So, it is no surprise that the mothers in Shunde whom I interviewed did not need to justify why they chose to bottle-feed. Instead, many of the working-class parents I spoke to, who can hardly afford the expensive, imported formula milk, need to negotiate, though not without difficulty, the prevailing norms and expectations placed on them by reinterpreting the meanings and feeding practices of formula milk.

"Picky-Eating Syndrome" and the Over-stressed Child

The culturally constructed "picky-eating disorder" is the second illness that I discussed in chapter 5 to illustrate how the medicalization of childhood creates unnecessary stress for parents and their children, leading further to social injustice. As this book has repeatedly shown, through standardization, re-categorization, and medicalization of children's eating behaviors, dairy and pharmaceutical companies have been selling picky-eating formula to parents. The ideal image of children has changed dramatically in the past forty years, from chubby, big, and healthy children to children who are strong, smart, and creative, while the image of the ideal mother has changed from that of a loving nurturer to that of a life manager who can help her children to maximize their full potential (Lo 2009). Through strategic marketing practices, dairy and drug companies have created fears among parents regarding the potential for brain-development problems to arise owing to the picky-eating behaviors of their children. Such problems are believed to be directly related to children's future academic underachievement. The increasing concern among parents about the brain and neuroscience and their connection to children's development is not unique in Hong Kong, but is part of a globalizing trend[8] (Macvarish, Lee, and Lowe 2014, 792).

By capitalizing on the global trend of "brain-based" parenting, education, and policy, as well as the latest neuro-scientific research, the dairy and drug companies have sought to medicalize children's picky-eating behavior by offering an array of picky-eating formulas as the proper solution to the newly created "illness." Nancy Scheper-Hughes and Margaret

Lock have aptly argued that the radical changes in the organization of social and public life in advanced industrial societies, including the disappearance of traditional cultural idioms for the expression of individual and collective discontent, have allowed medicine and psychiatry to assume a hegemonic role in shaping and responding to human distress. Illness somatization has become a dominant metaphor for expressing individual and social complaints (Scheper-Hughes and Lock 1987). By using the case of consumption of picky-eating formula in Hong Kong, I have attempted to de-medicalize and demystify the mental illness category of "feeding disorders" among children. I have argued that the cautious behavior of the majority of children in avoiding unfamiliar foods—an adaptive behavior— has been unduly re-categorized by the hegemonic force of the pharmaceutical nexus as a mental illness. The proliferation of mental illness categories and labels in medicine and psychiatry, resulting in ever more restricted definitions of that which is "normal," has created a sick and deviant majority, opening up a huge market for formula milk companies.

However, the growing trend of medicalization of childhood and the ideology of brain supremacy is not without critics. First, neurological intervention and enhancements rely on a biologically reductionist assumption that all behavior, interactions, and physiological functions are related to neuronal structures, obscuring the structural and social reasons underlying them. This book therefore serves as a corrective to assumptions of universal biological reductionism as a means of solving the "feeding disorder" of picky eaters. As my ethnographic study of the caretakers of picky eaters in Hong Kong shows, although the picky-eating formula has been designed to solve an individual biological problem—providing all of the dietarily necessary nutrition to compensate for potential nutrition gaps said to be due to the eating "disorder"—the underlying reasons and concerns are structural. The proliferation of the "picky-eating disorder" and the popularity of picky-eating formula since the 2010s coincided with a period when the rate of suicide among children increased and more and more children were feeling stressed out by the combined pressures of schoolwork and parental demands (N. Ng 2017; Y. Ng 2017; Tam 2018). Yet, the loss of appetite owing to demanding schoolwork and keen academic competition faced by children is being shaped and transformed by doctors and psychiatrists into the symptom of a new set of diseases called "feeding disorders." The greatest worry about picky-eating behavior, as expressed by many of the parents I interviewed, is the potential consequences for their children's capacity to handle the overwhelming schoolwork in a changing education and political environment. The narrow, neuro-scientific perspective on picky-eating behavior erases the *social,* creating an isolated subjectivity reliant on assistance (Rose 2001). To make a child smarter, healthier, more creative, more outgoing, or better able to perform mental or even physical tasks, parents are expected to provide nutritious formula to their picky-eating children, further reinforcing the cultural norm of valuing academic performance as the only virtue of children.

A second, closely related problem of the medicalization of picky-eating behavior among children is a shifting of attention and blame away from the structural problems of the educational and political systems to the body of the individual child. The promotion of cow milk formula as a technology for brain enhancement, as part of the brain-based culture of expert-led parent training, takes a cavalier approach to the scientific method and evidence, instead becoming overly deterministic about the early years of life and putting all of the blame for the difficulties faced by children on individual parental failings rather than on societal or structural problems. Consequently, the promotion of picky-eating behavior as a mental illness in Chinese society has expanded the scope of anxieties experienced by parents, strengthened the demands for "intensive parenting," and ultimately redefined the parent–child relationship in biologized and instrumental terms. By raising awareness of the cultural construction of the "insufficient milk syndrome" and "picky-eating disorder," I hope to unmask the structural roots of women and children's "ill health," thereby empowering these suffering people.

The dramatic dietary change of the Chinese from lactophobia to lactophilia that I have chronicled here is the combined result of the historical Chinese milk culture and beliefs, the period of colonial rule, the postwar world milk regime, the socialist engineering of the economy and population in mainland China, and the powerful impact of commodity production and consumerism on the communities of Hong Kong and mainland China in the post-collective era. In both places, the ruling parties—whether the British colonial government in pre-1997 Hong Kong or the Chinese party-state—have played a critical role in initiating or causing dietary changes, albeit in different ways and for different purposes. The transformation and industrialization of diet in Shunde and Hong Kong have manifested as a paradoxical process with three features: (1) The state-capitalist alliance formed by the government and the pharmaceutical nexus is the ultimate creator of medical and nutrition science, which directs how people understand and feel about their bodies. (2) The Western science of nutrition and dairy products have both became popular owing to creative syncretization. (3) In the process of marketing, women's and children's bodies are medicalized as a way of creating new needs, obscuring structural, environmental, and social stresses, constraints, and inequalities, while naturalizing the dubious redefinition of health as the individual's, and especially women's, imperative and responsibility.

Given that the socialist state remains supportive of the dairy industry and the scientistic view of infant feeding and child-rearing, so long as working mothers in urban cities continue to face the aforementioned "triple burden" and shoulder enormous levels of daily stress, milk consumption in Chinese societies, whether in the form of fluid milk or formula milk, is likely to continue to grow. The transformation of diet, therefore, appears to be a mixed blessing for people in Hong Kong and Shunde. If one views the case of the milk craze in China as one of many examples of the global trend of industrialization, as the Westernization of lifestyle owing to modernization and economic growth, or as a result of the food-safety crises that are now arising in many parts of the world, one can clearly see that there are still many more critical issues concerning food consumption, not only in China but around the world, and significant implications waiting to be explored.

Notes

Introduction

1. Based on the everyday use of the terms in Shunde and Hong Kong, I use the term "formula" and "formula milk" to denote infant formula and follow-up formula for infant and young children, but not formula for special medical purposes. Since in China and Hong Kong, most of the formula milk is in powdered form, people use the term *nai fen* (literally, "milk powder") interchangeably with the term formula, I too use *nai fen* to denote formula milk.

2. Although China's per capita milk consumption is about 36 kg/person, which is less than 1/3 of the world average and less than 1/10 compared to developed countries, the number of milk drinkers has been increasing (Inouye 2018).

3. Hong Kong–style "silk-stocking milk tea" is one of the most frequently consumed beverages among Hong Kong people. It was first served at affordable prices in *daipaidong* (street stalls) and was believed to mimic the British milk tea, which in days of old was offered exclusively in high-class hotels. Yet, this silk-stocking milk tea differs from the British milk tea in two key ways. First, instead of being prepared from a tea bag of usually a single kind of black tea, such as Darjeeling or Assam, the silk-stocking milk tea is prepared by boiling a mixture of several kinds and types of tea leaves, including Ceylon tea and Pu'erh tea, in forms ranging from whole leaves to crushed-leaf powder so as to deliver a strong and unique flavor. The process of pouring and straining the water in and out of a long white cotton filter bag containing the tea turns the bag a deep brown color, resembling silk stockings; hence this type of tea has come to be nicknamed "silk-stocking milk tea." Second, unlike the British milk tea, which is usually served with fresh milk, Hong Kong–style milk tea is made with evaporated milk or sweetened condensed milk.

4. Zhen Shihan and his colleagues categorized the traditional Chinese dietary pattern as one loaded heavily with rice, red meat, pork, poultry, (leafy) vegetables, and fish. The modern dietary pattern, they noted, was loaded heavily with wheat buns, cakes, legume products, nuts, pickled and salted vegetables, fruit, red meat, processed meats, poultry, eggs, fish, milk, and fast food (Zhen et al. 2018).

5. One such example, Andrea Wiley's *Re-imagining Milk,* demonstrates how milk was promoted in China and India with reference to its health benefits in encouraging growth (2011, 93–95). By analyzing how cow milk was promoted by milk companies using famous Chinese athletes, astronauts, and even the state through the Chinese premier, Wiley concluded that milk emerged as a "Western" food, a nationalist symbol of modern China, and a way of catching up with the West and overcoming perceived Chinese "size deficits." Economist Prabhu Pingali also has studied the impact of the Westernization of the Asian diet on the food system (2007).

6. Infant feeding is defined as the practice of feeding children under one year of age.

7. In addition to the ideology of intensive mothering, urbanization and the changing power relationships within the nuclear family also affect the perceptions of mothers regarding their breastfeeding ability and the moral implications of bottle-feeding (Zeitlyn and Rowshan 1997).

Chapter 1: Milk, Body, and Social Class in Ancient China

1. The Chinese text of the song reads "鮮蠵甘雞，和楚酪只。醢豚苦狗，膾苴蓴只。吳酸蒿蔞，不沾薄只。魂兮歸來！恣所擇只。" It was translated by Arthur Waley ([1919] 2005).

2. The *Chu Ci* is an anthology of Chinese poetry traditionally attributed mainly to Qu Yuan and Song Yu of the Warring States period (ended 221 BCE), though about half of the poems seem to have been composed several centuries later, during the Han dynasty (Hawkes 1985).

3. Wine from milk (*rujiu*) was lauded in a poem by the famous Tang poet Du Fu (Huang 2002).

4. *Huangdi Neijing* is an ancient Chinese medical text that has been treated as the fundamental doctrinal source for Chinese medicine for more than two millennia.

5. *Compendium of Materia Medica* (*Ben Cao Gang Mu*), a registered UNESCO world heritage, is the most complete and comprehensive medical book ever written in the history of traditional Chinese medicine. Compiled and written by Li Shi-zhen (1518–1593), a medical expert of the Ming dynasty (1368–1644) over a period of 27 years (UNESCO 2017). The compendium lists, analyzes, and describes all the plants, animals, minerals, and other objects that were believed to have medicinal properties. The compendium in effect epitomizes the pharmaceutical achievements and developments of East Asia before the sixteenth century. It is also more than a mere pharmaceutical text, for it includes a vast amount of information on topics as wide-ranging as biology, chemistry, geography, mineralogy, geology, history, and even mining and astronomy.

6. One important informant who discussed the practice of cheese making is Auntie Lin, who was referred to me by the officer, assistant officer of the Jinbang Community Committee Association of Chinese Party, and many indigenous residents of Jinbang, including another cheese maker, Miss Leung, as the most venerable and senior producer of buffalo milk cheese.

7. Chinese publications and food guides sponsored by the local government suggest that the production of water buffalo cheese began in the Ming dynasty (1368–1644) and has a history of more than 600 years (Feng and Ceng 2010). However, the book provides no references to support this claim.

8. "Water buffalo." *Encyclopedia Britannica.*

9. Bray (1984, 2:601) points out that a similar kind of tank irrigation method had been practiced in South China since the Han dynasty.

10. Longan is a kind of tropical fruit tree, whose name comes from the Cantonese *lungngaan,* meaning "dragon's eye."

11. I learned this verse from a cheese maker in Jinbang village during my fieldwork in 2010. This verse is well remembered by most of the cheese makers whom I met.

12. Pseudonyms are used throughout to protect the identity of my informants.

13. This procedure was recorded based on observation and interviews with six cheese makers in Jinbang village. They told me that, ten years ago, they also boiled the extra mixture, which was squeezed out from the wooden mold to make milk butter.

Chapter 2: Dairy Farm, British Milk Tea, and Soy Milk in Milk Bottles

1. As early as the seventeenth century, Hong Kong had become a popular anchoring site for trading fleets and fishermen, for the territory's deep-water harbor and the natural shelter formed by the surrounding hills protected them from strong winds and sea.

2. The use of Tetra Brik Aseptic packaging enabled Vitasoy to be sold in supermarkets because of the longer shelf life the technology offered, and because no bottle recycling was needed (Radio Television Hong Kong 2012).

3. According to Tang, the remarkable series of social reforms implemented from 1971 to 1977 was designed by the colonial government to regain the legitimacy that had been shattered by their handling of the 1966 and 1967 riots (Tang 1998, 61–86).

4. For additional discussion on why 1974 was a special year marking the change in identity of Hong Kong people from mainland Chinese to local Hong Kongers, see Wu Junxiong, Ma Jiewei, Lü Dale, eds., 2006, *Xianggang, wen hua, yan jiu* (Hong Kong: Hong Kong University Press). Wu, Ma, and Lü point out that the change was due to three dialectic forces: (1) significant structural and policy changes made by the local colonial government in response to rampant inflation and the growing resentment of the local people after the oil crisis (1973–1974), such as the establishment of the Independent Commission Against Corporation (ICAC) (1974), Consumer Council (1974), 10-year housing program, and 9-year compulsory free education; (2) the recognition of the Hong Kong football team in international competition; and (3) the growing popularity of local TV dramas.

5. Three more Chinese-owned high-end hotels, namely Nanping, Meizhou, and Daguan, were also established between 1912 and 1929.

6. As noted by Mark Swislocki, *fancaiguan* proliferated in Shanghai in the final two decades of the nineteenth century. These Western-style restaurants differed from the foreign restaurants by virtue of their Chinese ownership and clientele (Swislocki 2009, 110).

7. Mid-eighteenth-century Chinese imperial decrees restricted foreign residence to a set of Chinese-built dwellings on the banks of the Pearl River known as the "Thirteen Factories" (Mandarin *"Shisan Hang"*) (Downes and Grant 1997). The one-time resident merchant William Hunter explained: "Not the least remarkable feature of Old Canton life was the 'Factory,' as the common dwelling and common place of business of all the members, old and young, of a commercial house" (Hunter [1882] 1938).

8. Based on interviews with *daipaidong* owners, *daipaidong*s can be classified into four types: (1) congee stalls; (2) noodle stalls; (3) simple meals; and (4) café stalls. These outdoor food stalls used to be composed of a movable wagon with the food-serving unit affixed above the wheels. In front of the unit was a long bench upon which three small stools were installed. If a larger group of customers were to come, each *daipaidong* owner could open up the two permanent folding tables and eight folding chairs to serve them.

9. "Milk tea masters" are those who have been formally trained to prepare Hong Kong–style milk tea.

10. Wong is influential in the coffee and tea industry not only because he is the chair of the Association of Coffee and Tea of Hong Kong, but also because his family has been in the industry for two generations. Wong's father and relatives opened some of the earliest *cha chaan teng* in the 1950s and started what is now the biggest tea and coffee trading company in Hong Kong.

11. According to a rule of thumb in the industry, the tea should not be brewed for more than one hour. This is because the tea leaves will be over-extracted and the tea will be *fan* (become bitter and astringent). To ensure there is enough of a supply of tea, two teapots are used alternately for boiling water, pouring water into the tea to steep it, and lastly pouring the hot tea into a thick cup with the canned milk ("hitting" the tea).

12. SARS is a new communicable disease that swept through many parts of the world in 2003. It was a challenging and tragic event in the public health history of Hong Kong; 1,755 citizens were infected and 299 of them died (Smith 2006; World Health Organization 2003).

13. The origin of the "Umbrella Revolution" or the "Umbrella Movement" can be traced back to the evening of September 28, 2014, when the police fired tear gas to disperse the crowds gathered around Admiralty, the eastern extension of the central business district of Hong Kong Island. The crowds had turned out in support of students who were protesting against the Chinese central government's decision to block democrats from standing for election as the chief executive of Hong Kong in the scheduled 2017 election. This action, however, provoked even more people to come out in support of the students. This unexpected outcome developed into a 79-day Occupy Movement that the foreign media dubbed the Umbrella Revolution because the protesters used only umbrellas and wet towels to protect themselves from the pepper spray and tear gas used by the police (Kaimen 2014; Lee, So, and Leung 2015).

Chapter 3: Global Capital, Local Culture, and Food Uncertainty

1. Although water buffalo milk cheese is officially recognized as a "Famous Snack of China" (*Zhonghua ming xiaochi*), there are hardly any written records of the production of indigenous water buffalo cheese and milk products in Daliang during the pre-socialist period. For this reason, the data used in the present study concerning the decline of the water-buffalo-cheese industry was mainly collected through in-depth interviews with master cheese makers.

2. Elephant grass (*Pennisetum purpureum*), native to the African grassland, is considered to be the most suitable plant for green fodder in the subtropics. Because it can produce 8,000–15,000 kg of grass per *mu* (1/15 of a hectare), it has become an important food crop for cattle in Guangdong Province (Farrell, Simons, and Hillocks 2002).

3. The water buffaloes in Jinbang village used to feed on lower-grade, mostly broken rice, which local people called *dami* (大米), or "large-grained rice."

4. Use of scutellaria root (黄芩 *huangqin;* Latin *Radix scutellaria baicalenses*) to support the immune system has a long history in traditional Chinese medicine (Ma et al. 2002). In related research, baicalein, a major flavonoid in scutellaria, has been shown to aid cardiovascular health (Sun et al. 2002). For more information on the value of oak leaves as a forage material, see Mackie (1903).

5. Informally, local cheese makers call the cross-bred buffaloes *cha niu* (叉牛), which has a connotation of inferiority (the term is homophonous with "差牛," literally meaning "inferior cow"). Auntie Lin even considers the milk from cross-bred cattle to be "polluting" in cheese making because it is not comparable in aroma and richness to milk from indigenous Chinese water buffaloes.

6. The cost of mature water buffaloes ranged from RMB 4,000 to 15,000, while the buffalo calves would be sold for RMB 400.

7. As pointed out by Sun and Zhang, "establishing the market before production" is one of the most successful strategies of Mengniu. One example is that when Mengniu launched its first product—the Mengniu "Pure Milk" in 1999—they spent most of their capital on advertising, while their milk was supplied by a third party—a poorly run cow milk factory in Harbin (Li et al. 2012; Sun and Zhang 2005, 75).

8. According to a study conducted by Boston Consulting Group, the younger generation in China is distinctive from the older generation in being more appearance- and health-conscious (Cerini 2016; Ouyang 2018; Wu et al. 2014)

9. Wolfberries are widely believed to be able to "tonify" the liver and kidneys (increase the available energy), improve eyesight, and moisten the lungs. Lotus seeds are used as medicine to tonify the spleen, to stop diarrhea, and to stimulate a poor appetite. They are considered neutral in property and are also used to replenish the kidneys to control seminal emissions and to nourish the heart to tranquilize the mind. *Ejiao,* also known as "donkey-hide gelatin" or "ass-hide glue gelatin," is the dry glue obtained from the hide of the donkey, *Equus asinus* (Fam. *Equidae*). This gelatin is obtained by a process involving a series of steps: washing, soaking, rinsing, and stewing. The gelatin is produced mainly in Shandong, Zhejiang, and Jiangsu provinces. *Ejiao* is sweet in flavor and neutral in property, and acts on the lung, liver, and kidney channels. It is believed to be particularly good at tonifying the blood,

replenishing yin, and moistening the lungs. It is also considered to have an anti-aging effect, and a variety of clinical functions including hemostasis, fighting fatigue, suppressing tumor growth, improving immunity, and improving gynecologic diseases (Wu et al. 2007).

10. On brand persona, see Herskovitz and Crystal (2010).

11. The appellation of "Chinese famous brand" has been granted to certain mainland Chinese enterprises by China's General Administration of Quality Supervision, Inspection and Quarantine of the People's Republic of China (AQSIQ) since 2001. However, since 2008, no more applications have been accepted and the brand logo has been gradually phased out since 2012 (AQSIQ official website, http://www.aqsiq.gov .cn, accessed May 16, 2012).

12. According to Baudrillard, *symbolic value* is a value that a subject assigns to an object in relation to another subject (i.e., between a giver and receiver), while *sign value* is a value within a system of objects (e.g., a branded pen being more prestigious than another).

Chapter 4: Bottle-Feeding as Love, Success, and Citizenship

1. www.baby-kingdom.com is one of the most popular Chinese-language parenting websites. It was established in Hong Kong in 2002 and has a registered membership of over 280,000 users, representing more than 90,000 families. It has more than 400 discussion forums and the site's users contribute an average of 30,000 messages per day (Baby-kingdom.com 2018).

2. Although the rates of exclusive breastfeeding in Hong Kong for babies aged one month had increased from 14 percent in 1997 to 33.8 percent in 2017, the exclusive breastfeeding rate for the sixth postpartum month remains low.

3. A quantitative study of 1,417 mother–infant pairs conducted by Tarrant and her colleagues in Hong Kong showed that the most common reason for early weaning was "insufficient milk" (34.5 percent), followed by "returning to work" (31.4 percent), "baby is always hungry" (14.1 percent), "maternal illness" (11.7 percent), "fatigue/ stress" (10.3 percent), and "inconvenient/too time-consuming" (8.9 percent) (Tarrant et al. 2010).

4. For example, DHA is added not only to Mead Johnson infant formula but also the prenatal formula Enfamama A+ as DHA is described as the ingredient that "gives children what they need to grow a healthy brain and body" (Meadjohnson 2018).

5. For example, the media coined the term "The Great Kindergarten Scare" to refer to Hong Kong parents' anxiety over the level of competition to gain a spot in a local kindergarten for the 2014 school year. This "scare" has been attributed to the thousands of mainland Chinese parents of children born in Hong Kong who applied for kindergarten places for their children.

6. BIOSTIME is a home-grown premium brand in China that sells high-priced formula milk and milk products.

7. Yakult is a probiotic milk drink and is promoted in Hong Kong and mainland China as a healthy daily drink for children.

8. I use the term "Western, modern food" to denote a product or preparation practice of a type not indigenous to China and produced and marketed through a standardized process in accordance with health norms more common to developed, Western nations.

9. Amway is an American household products company. It distributes its products through a multi-level marketing scheme, considered by many to be a pyramid scheme. Its success in China is thought to be closely related to the excellent *guanxi* (mutually beneficial relationships) that it has built up with government officers (Bloomberg News 2013).

10. I borrow the term "cosmopolitan capital" from Don Weenink (2008). His study of parents in the Netherlands whose children attended an international school revealed that those parents viewed cosmopolitanism as a form of cultural and social capital, rather than as something arising out of a feeling of global connectedness or curiosity about the Other.

11. I use the term "geopolitics" to denote the relationship between geography and politics. Geopolitics provides a reliable guide to the global landscape using geographical descriptions, metaphors, and templates, such as "Hong Kong is the shopper's paradise" (Dodds 2007).

12. For more examples on the risk society and "distribution of bads," see Dean Curran (2013).

13. The actual extent to which nutritional deficiencies were a problem in Hong Kong and China during the 1960s and 1970s is debatable. Based on a study of 74 full-term babies in Hong Kong in 1984, pediatricians Sophie Leung and Susan Lui found that a higher protein intake than necessary was being consumed by the babies because the local Maternal and Child Health Centre (MCH) emphasized that protein, in the form of meat, must be served regularly in an edible form (minced or finely chopped), together with the full-protein formula. Moreover, Leung and Lui pointed out possible problems with the dietary guideline: "The recommended requirements for iron and calcium have been set two standard deviations above the average amount required for a healthy population. Therefore, over 90 percent of the normal population would be expected to take less than the recommended amount. For vitamin D, the recommended value was defined such that it is adequate for the majority even without any exposure to sunlight" (Leung and Lui 1990).

14. Vitamin K deficiency-related bleeding (VKDB) is much more common in infants. For more on this in the Western medical system, see Sutor et al. (1999).

15. According to traditional Chinese medicine, the "stomach," a yang organ, is responsible for "receiving" and "ripening" ingested food and fluids. It is therefore called "the sea of food and fluid." Food begins its decomposition in the stomach. The "pure" part is then sent to the "spleen." The "spleen," a yin organ, is the primary organ for digestion. The spleen extracts the pure nutritive essences of ingested food and fluids and transforms them into what will become qi ("spirit" or "air") and "blood" (Kaptchuk 2000).

16. National Fluid Milk Processor Promotion Board and National Dairy Council 1999, advertisement, *New York Times,* August 3. See also Nestlé (2002, 81).

17. On the international transparency ranking of Hong Kong and China, see Morton 2018.

Conclusion

1. I borrow the term "glocalization" from Robertson to denote the simultaneity and the co-presence of both universalizing and particularizing forces (Featherstone, Lash, and Robertson 1995)

2. I define "economic medicalization" as a type of medicalization where the motivation for the transformation is commercial profitability or, in a corporate context, achieving the objective of shareholder wealth maximization (Poitras 2012).

3. In 2013, a regulation was imposed in Daliang forbidding water buffalo husbandry. Dairy farmers were forced to move their buffaloes to other places, like Longjia in Shunde or even farther away to Panyu in Guangdong. See also chapter 3.

4. For example, the state-owned China National Oils, Foodstuffs and Cereals Corporation is the biggest shareholder of Mengniu Dairy.

5. Recall the case, discussed in chapter 5, involving how the eight largest manufacturers of the top-selling formula milk products formed "The Hong Kong Infant and Young Child Nutrition Association (HKIYCNA) in May 2011 to counter the taskforce of the Hong Kong government in implementing the HK Code.

6. Furthermore, the World Health Organization (WHO) reports that India has a functioning code implementation and monitoring mechanism, while China does not, although this assessment is unverified (WHO 2013).

7. Windfur and Jonsen (2005) contend that global hunger and malnutrition are the most serious food problems in today's world.

8. One example is the "first three years movement"—an alliance of child welfare advocates and politicians that draws on the authority of neuroscience to argue that social problems such as inequality, poverty, educational underperformance, violence, and mental illness are best addressed through "early intervention" to protect or enhance the emotional and cognitive aspects of children's brain development.

References

Abkowitz, Alyssa. 2015. "Why So Gloomy? In Sun-Deprived China, Only 5% Have Healthy Levels of Vitamin D." *Wall Street Journal,* April 23. https://blogs.wsj.com /chinarealtime/2015/04/23/why-so-gloomy-in-sun-deprived-china-only-5-have -healthy-levels-of-vitamin-d/.

Addessi E., A. T. Galloway, E. Visalberghi, and L. L. Birch. 2005. "Specific Social Influences on the Acceptance of Novel Foods in 2–5-year-old children." *Appetite* 45 (3): 264–271.

Afflerback, Sara, Shannon K. Carter, Amanda Koontz Anthony, and Liz Grauerholz. 2013. "Infant-feeding Consumerism in the Age of Intensive Mothering and Risk Society." *Journal of Consumer Culture* 13 (3): 387–405.

Agency France-Presse. 2018. "Australian Supermarkets Limit Baby Milk Formula Sales as China Demand Hits Stocks." *South China Morning Post,* May 16. https:// www.scmp.com/news/asia/australasia/article/2146351/australian-supermarkets -limit-baby-milk-formula-sales-china.

Agren, Hans. 1975. "Patterns of Tradition and Modernization in Contemporary Chinese Medicine." In *Medicine in Chinese Cultures: Comparative Studies of Health Care in Chinese and Other Societies,* edited by Arthur Kleinman, 37–51. Washington, DC: Department of Health, Education, and Welfare, Public Health Service, National Institutes of Health.

Alicea, Marixsa. 1997. "'A Chambered Nautilus': The Contradictory Nature of Puerto Rican Women's Role in the Social Construction of a Transnational Community." *Gender and Society* 11 (5): 597–626.

American Psychiatric Association. 2013. *Diagnostic and Statistical Manual of Mental Disorders.* 5th ed. Washington, DC: American Psychiatric Association.

Anderson, Eugene. 2000. "Chinese Nutritional Therapy." In *Nutritional Anthropology: Biocultural Perspectives on Food and Nutrition,* edited by Darna L. Dufour, Alan H. Goodman, and Gretel H. Pelto, 198–211. Mountain View, CA: Mayfield.

———. 2005. *Everyone Eats: Understanding Food and Culture.* New York: New York University Press.

Andres, Elizabeth M., Katherine L. Clancy, and Marcella G. Katz. 1980. "Infant Feeding Practices of Families Belonging to a Prepaid Group Practice Health Care Plan." *Pediatrics* 65:978.

Angell, Marcia. 2008. "Industry-Sponsored Clinical Research—A Broken System." *Journal of the American Medical Association* 300 (9): 1069–1071.

Appadurai, Arjun. 1996. *Modernity at Large: Cultural Dimensions of Globalization.* Minneapolis: University of Minnesota Press.

Apple Daily. 2004. "Cha Chaan Teng as the Best Design of Hong Kong." September 28. http://hk.apple.nextmedia.com/news/art/20040928/4336805.

———. 2009. "BB 30 ri duan ren nai, chenhuilin manyue su fungong." July 12, C02.

———. 2015. "Chenyinmei dan yang yi. Chenhao ji zhuan naifen qian." February 28. https://hk.entertainment.appledaily.com/entertainment/daily/article/20150228/19057612.

———. 2016. "Pai neidi zhenren sao bo lao ming, Xie tian-hua yin niao quan bei qing." January 15, C01.

Avishai, Orit. 2007. "Managing the Lactating Body: The Breastfeeding Project and Privileged Motherhood." *Qualitative Sociology* 30:135–152.

Baby-kingdom.com. 2011. "Discussion Forum." Accessed December 20, 2012. https://www.baby-kingdom.com/group.php?sgid=3986.

———. 2018. "Corporate Information." Accessed July 10, 2018. https://corp.baby-kingdom.com/community.html.

Baer, Hans. 1982. "On the Political Economy of Health." *Medical Anthropology Newsletter* 14 (1): 1–17.

Bai, Zhaohai, Michael R. F. Lee, Lin Ma, Stewart Ledgard, Oene Oenema, Gerard L. Velthof, Wenqi Ma, Mengchu Guo, Zhanqing Zhao, Sha Wei, Shengli Li, Xia Liu, Petr Havlík, Jiafa Luo, Chunsheng Hu, and Fusuo Zhang. 2018. "Global Environmental Costs of China's Thirst for Milk." *Global Change Biology* 24 (5): 2198–2211.

Bajic-Hajdukovic, Ivana. 2013. "Food, Family, and Memory: Belgrade Mothers and Their Migrant Children." *Food and Foodways* 21 (1): 46–65.

Baker, Phillip, Julie Smith, Libby Salmon, Sharon Friel, George Kent, Alessandro Iellamo, J. P. Dadhich, and Mary J. Renfrew. 2016. "Global Trends and Patterns of Commercial Milk-Based Formula Sales: Is an Unprecedented Infant and Young Child Feeding Transition Underway?" *Public Health Nutrition* 1–11. doi:10.1017/S1368980016001117.

Bakhtin, Mikhail M. 1981. *The Dialogic Imagination: Four Essays,* edited by Michael Holquist. Austin: University of Texas Press.

Barboza, David. 2008. "China's Dairy Farmers Say They Are Victims." *New York Times,* October 3. https://www.nytimes.com/2008/10/04/world/asia/04milk.html.

Barnett, H. G. 1953. *Innovation: The Basis of Cultural Change.* New York: McGraw-Hill Co.

Baudrillard, Jean. (1970) 1998. *The Consumer Society: Myths and Structures.* Thousand Oaks, CA: SAGE Publications Ltd.

BBC News. 2004. "China 'Fake Milk' Scandal Deepens." April 22. http://news.bbc
.co.uk/go/pr/fr/-/2/hi/asia-pacific/3648583.stm.

———. 2010. "China Dairy Products Found Tainted with Melamine." July 9. https://
www.bbc.com/news/10565838.

Beck, Ulrich. 1992. *Risk Society: Towards a New Modernity.* London and Newbury
Park, CA: SAGE Publications Ltd.

Becker, Annie E. 2004. "Television, Disordered Eating, and Young Women in Fiji:
Negotiating Body Image and Identity during Rapid Social Change." *Culture, Medicine and Psychiatry* 28:533–559.

Beckman, Chanda, Jianping Zhang, Susan Zhang, and Shiliang Xu. 2011. "Peoples
Republic of China—Dairy and Products Annual 2011." *GAIN Report (CH11048).*
USDA Foreign Agriculture Service. October 17. http://www.agriexchange.apeda
.gov.in/MarketReport/Reports/China_dairy_report.pdf.

Biehl, Joäo. 2013. *Vita: Life in a Zone of Social Abandonment.* Berkeley: University of
California Press.

Bielenstein, Hans. 1980. *The Bureaucracy of the Han Time.* Cambridge: Cambridge
University Press.

Biltekoff, Charlotte. 2013. *Eating Right in America: The Cultural Politics of Food and
Health.* Durham, NC: Duke University Press.

Biniaz, Vajihe. 2013. "World-wide Researches Review on the Therapeutic Effects of
Ginger." *Jentashapir Journal of Health Research* 4 (4): 333–337.

Birch, L. L., L. Gunder, K. Grimm-Thomas, and D. G. Laing. 1998. "Infants' Consumption of a New Food Enhances Acceptance of Similar Foods." *Appetite* 30 (3):
283–295.

Bloomberg News. 2013. "Amway Embraces China Using Harvard *Guanxi.*" Bloomberg Markets, September 25. https://www.bloomberg.com/news/articles/2013-09-24
/amway-embraces-china-using-harvard-guanxi.

Bocock, Robert. 1993. *Consumption.* London and New York: Routledge.

Bourdieu, Pierre. 1984. *Distinction: A Social Critique of the Judgment of Taste.* Translated by Richard Nice. London: Routledge.

Braverman, Harry. 1974. *Labor and Monopoly Capital: The Degradation of Work in the
Twentieth Century.* New York: Monthly Review Press.

Bray, Francesca. 1984. "Agriculture." In *Science and Civilisation in China,* edited by
Joseph Needham. Part II of Volume 2. Cambridge: Cambridge University Press.

Bristow, Michael. 2008. "Bitter Taste over China Baby Milk." BBC, September 17.
http://news.bbc.co.uk/2/hi/asia-pacific/7620812.stm.

Brown, Gillian R., Thomas E. Dickins, Rebecca Sear, and Kevin N. Laland. 2011. "Evolutionary Accounts of Human Behavioural Diversity." *Philosophical Transactions of
the Royal Society B: Biological Sciences* 366:313–324.

Bruner, Jerome S. 1986. *Actual Minds, Possible Worlds.* Cambridge, MA: Harvard
University Press.

Bryant-Waugh, Rachel, Laura Markham, Richard E. Kreipe, and B. Timothy Walsh.
2010. "Feeding and Eating Disorders in Childhood." *International Journal of Eating
Disorder* 43 (2): 98–111.

Burger, J., M. Kirchner, B. Bramanti, W. Haak, and M. G. Thomas. 2007. "Absence of the Lactase-Persistence-Associated Allele in Early Neolithic Europeans." *Proceedings of National Academy of Sciences of the USA* 104 (10): 3736–3741.

Caballero, Benjamin, and Barry M. Popkin. 2002. *The Nutrition Transition: Diet and Disease in the Developing World*. Amsterdam: Academic Press.

Cai Baoqiong. 1990. *Housheng yu chuangye: Weitanai wushi nian (1940–1990)*. Hong Kong: Xianggang doupin youxian gongsi.

Callen, Jennifer, and Janet Pinelli. 2004. "Incidence and Duration of Breastfeeding for Term Infants in Canada, United States, Europe, and Australia: A Literature Review." *Birth* 31 (4): 285–292.

Cameron, Nigel. 1986. *The Milky Way: The History of Dairy Farm*. Hong Kong: Dairy Farm Co. Ltd.

Carpenter, Kenneth J. 2003. "A Short History of Nutritional Science: Part 1 (1785–1885)." *The Journal of Nutrition* 133 (3): 638–645.

Cashdan, Elizabeth. 1998. "Adaptiveness of Food Learning and Food Aversions in Children." *Social Science Information* 37 (4): 613–632.

Cerini, Marianna. 2016. "How China Is Becoming the World's Largest Market for Healthy Eating." *Forbes,* March 31. https://www.forbes.com/sites/mariannacerini/2016/03/31/how-china-is-becoming-the-worlds-largest-market-for-healthy-eating/#7cb270925439.

Chan, Bernice. 2018. "Breastfeeding in China and Hong Kong: Experts Tackle Ignorance of Mothers and Doctors." *South China Morning Post,* February 26. https://www.scmp.com/lifestyle/health-beauty/article/2134709/breastfeeding-china-and-hong-kong-experts-tackle-ignorance.

Chan, Elaine. 2010. "Beyond Pedagogy: Language and Identity in Post-Colonial Hong Kong." *British Journal of Sociology Education* 23 (2): 271–285.

Chan, Gloria. 2015. "The Amahs Explores Hong Kong's 'Lion Rock Spirit.'" *South China Morning Post,* February 12. http://www.scmp.com/magazines/48hrs/article/1709383/amahs-explores-hong-kongs-lion-rock-spirit.

Chan, Jennifer. 2013. "Leo Burnett Launches First Work for Abbott Pediasure." *Marketing,* December 18. http://www.marketing-interactive.com/leo-burnett-launches-first-campaign-new-account-abbott/.

Chan, Kinman. 2009. "Harmonious Society." In *International Encyclopedia of Civil Society,* edited by Helmut K. Anheier and Stefan Toepler, 821–825. New York: Springer.

Chan, S. M., E. A. S. Nelson, Sophie S. F. Leung, and C. Y. Li. 2000. "Breastfeeding Failure in a Longitudinal Post-Partum Maternal Nutrition Study in Hong Kong." *Journal of Paediatrics and Child Health* 36:466–471.

Chan, Samuel, and Ernest Kao. 2013. "Angry Parents Protest at Mainland Chinese Children Being Given Preschool Places." *South China Morning Post,* October 7. https://www.scmp.com/news/hong-kong/article/1325980/angry-parents-want-action-preschools.

Chan, Yuen. 2014. "The New Lion Rock Spirit—How a Banner on a Hillside Redefined the Hong Kong Dream." *The World Post,* December 29. https://www.huffingtonpost.com/yuen-chan/the-new-lion-rock-spirit-_b_6345212.html.

Chang, Kwangchih, ed. 1977. *Food in Chinese Culture: Anthropological and Historical Perspectives.* New Haven, CT: Yale University Press.

Chen, Feilong. 2015. "Jinbang Old Cheese Shop, Dignity without Future." *Southern Metropolis Daily,* November 13. https://kknews.cc/news/v9yy2yl.html.

Chen, Nancy N. 2009. *Food, Medicine, and the Quest for Good Health.* New York: Columbia University Press.

Chen, Philip N. L. 2010. *Great Cities of the World.* Hong Kong: Hong Kong University Press.

Chen, Z. Kevin, Dinghuan Hu, and Hu Song. 2008. "Linking Markets to Smallholder Dairy Farmers in China." FAORAP Regional Workshop.

Cheng, Po Hung. 2003. *Early Hong Kong Eateries.* Hong Kong: Hong Kong University Museum and Art Gallery.

China Business News. 2008. "Bright Dairy Uses Chinese Herbal Yogurt to Win in the Market." February 18. http://business.sohu.com/20080218/n255203269.shtml.

China Daily. 2008. "Probe Finds Producer Knew of Toxic Milk for Months." September 22. http://www.chinadaily.com.cn/china/2008-09/22/content_7048712.htm.

———. 2011. "Ignorant Eaters?" June 16, H04.

Chinese Nutrition Society. 2011. "Zhongguo ju min shan shi zhi nan." Xizang renmin chubanshe.

Chiu, Joanna, and Amy Nip. 2013. "Hongkongers Appeal to US over Baby Formula Shortage." *South China Morning Post,* January 31. https://www.scmp.com/news/hong-kong/article/1139696/hongkongers-appeal-us-over-baby-formula-shortage.

Choi, Poking. 2005. "A Critical Evaluation of Education Reforms in Hong Kong: Counting Our Losses to Economic Globalization." *International Studies in Sociology of Education* 15 (3): 237–256.

Choi, Susanne Y. P., and Kwokfai Ting. 2009. "A Gender Perspective on Families in Hong Kong." In *Mainstreaming Gender in Hong Kong Society,* edited by Fanny M. Cheung and Eleanor Holroyd, 159–180. Hong Kong: Chinese University Press.

Chongqing Municipal Dairy Industry Administration Office. 2000. "Development of Dairy Industry in Chongqing." In *50 Years of Chinese Dairy Industry,* edited by Wang Huaibao, 37–38. Beijing: Ocean Press.

Chow, Vivienne. 2013. "Ai Weiwei's New Work Inspired by Milk Powder Debate." *South China Morning Post,* May 10. https://www.scmp.com/news/hong-kong/article/1233976/ai-weiweis-new-sculpture-inspired-hong-kong-mainland-milk-powder.

Cooper, William C., and Nathan Sivin. 1973. "Man as a Medicine: Pharmacological and Ritual Aspects of Traditional Therapy Using Drugs Derived from the Human Body." In *Chinese Science,* edited by Shigeru Nakayama and Nathan Sivin, 203–272. Cambridge, MA: MIT Press.

Copley, M., R. Berstan, S. Dudd, S. Aillaud, A. Mukherjee, V. Straker, S. Payne, and R. P. Evershed. 2005. "Processing of Milk Products in Pottery Vessels through British Prehistory." *Antiquity* 79 (306): 895–908.

Coppes, Peter Paul, Saskia van Battum, and Mary Ledman. 2018. *Global Dairy Top 20.* Rabobank Report. https://www.rabobank.com/en/press/search/2018/20180726-global-dairy-top-20-a-shuffling-of-the-deck-chairs.html.

Cosminsky, Sheila. 1975. "Changing Food and Medical Beliefs and Practices in a Guatemalan Community." *Ecology of Food and Nutrition* 4 (3): 183–191.

Cowdery, Rradi S., and Carmen Knudson-Martin. 2005. "The Construction of Motherhood: Tasks, Relational Connection, and Gender Equality." *Family Relations* 54 (3): 335–345.

Craig, Oliver E., Val J. Steele, Anders Fischer, Sönke Hartz, Søren H. Andersen, Paul Donohoe, Aikaterini Glykou, Hayley Saul, D. Martin Jones, Eva Koch, and Carl P. Heron. 2011. "Ancient Lipids Reveal Continuity in Culinary Practices across the Transition to Agriculture in Northern Europe." *Proceedings of National Academy of Sciences of the USA* 108 (44) (November 1): 17910–17915. doi.org/10.1073/pnas.1107202108.

Crosby, Alfred W. 1988. "Ecological Imperialism: The Overseas Migration of Western Europeans as a Biological Phenomenon." In *The Ends of the Earth: Perspectives on Modern Environmental History,* edited by Donald Worster. Cambridge and New York: Cambridge University Press.

Curran, Dean. 2013. "Risk Society and the Distribution of Bads: Theorizing Class in the Risk Society." *The British Journal of Sociology* 64 (1): 44–62.

Cwiertka, Katarzyna J. 2000. "From Yokohama to Amsterdam: Meidi-Ya and Dietary Change in Modern Japan." *Japanstudien* 12:45–63.

Dalian City Dairy Products Project Office. 2000. "Advances of the Dalian Dairy Industry." In *50 Years of Chinese Dairy Industry,* edited by Wang Huaibao. Beijing: Ocean Press.

Davidson, Alan. 1999. *The Oxford Companion to Food.* Oxford and Hong Kong: Oxford University Press.

Davis, Deborah, and Stevan Harrell. 1993. *Chinese Families in the Post-Mao Era.* Berkeley: University of California Press.

DBS Group Research. 2017. "China Dairy—Downstream Is Key." *DBS Asian Insight Sector Briefing 52.* DBS Group. November.

Delgado, Christopher. 2003. "Rising Consumption of Meat and Milk in Developing Countries Has Created a New Food Revolution." *Journal of Nutrition* 133 (11): 3907S–3910S.

Delgado, Christopher, Mark Rosegrant, Henning Steinfeld, Simeon Ehui, and Claude Courboi. 1999. "Livestock to 2020—The Next Food Revolution." *Food, Agriculture and the Environment.* Discussion Paper 28. International Food Policy Research Institute. https://idl-bnc-idrc.dspacedirect.org/bitstream/handle/10625/30755/121863.pdf?sequence=1.

Den Hartog, Adel P. 1986. *Diffusion of Milk as a New Food to Tropical Regions: The Example of Indonesia, 1880–1942.* Wageningen: Stichting Voeding Nederland.

DeWolf, Christopher, Izzy Ozawa, Tiffany Lam, Virginia Lau, and Zoe Li. 2017. "Hong Kong Food: 40 Dishes We Can't Live Without." CNN, July 12. https://edition.cnn.com/travel/article/hong-kong-food-dishes/index.html.

Dodds, Klaus. 2007. *Geopolitics: A Very Short Introduction.* Oxford: Oxford University Press.

Douglas, Mary. 1966. *Purity and Danger: An Analysis of the Concepts of Pollution and Taboo.* London and New York: Routledge.

———. 1986. *How Institutions Think*. Syracuse: Syracuse University Press.

Downes, Jacques M., and Frederic D. Grant. 1997. *The Golden Ghetto: The American Commercial Community at Canton and the Shaping of American Policy*. Hong Kong: Hong Kong University Press.

Dreby, Joanna. 2006. "Honor and Virtue: Mexican Parenting in the Transnational Context." *Gender and Society* 20 (1): 32–59.

Dreyer, Edward L. 1995. *China at War, 1901–1949*. London: Longman.

Du, Shufa, Bing Lu, Fengying Zhai, and Barry M. Popkin. 2002. "A New Stage of the Nutrition Transition in China." *Public Health Nutrition* 5 (1A): 169–174.

DuPuis, Melanie. 2002. *Nature's Perfect Food: How Milk Became America's Drink*. New York: New York University Press.

Eagle, Jenny. 2017. "China Will Overtake the US as the Largest Dairy Market by 2022." DairyReporter.com, August 21. https://www.dairyreporter.com/Article/2017/08/21/China-will-overtake-the-US-as-the-largest-dairy-market-by-2022.

Economist, The. 2017. "Dairy Farming Is Polluting New Zealand's Water." November 16. https://www.economist.com/asia/2017/11/16/dairy-farming-is-polluting-new-zealands-water.

Eisenstadt, Shmuel Noah. 2000. "Multiple Modernities." *Daedalus* 129 (1): 1–29.

Elliott, Anthony, and Charles Lemert. 2009a. *The New Individualism: The Emotional Costs of Globalization*. 2d ed. Milton Park, Abingdon, Oxon; New York: Routledge.

———. 2009b. "The Global New Individualist Debate." In *Identity in Question*, edited by Anthony Elliott and Paul du Gay, 37–64. London: SAGE Publications Ltd.

Elvin, Mark. 1982. "The Technology of Farming in Late-Traditional China." In *The Chinese Agricultural Economy*, edited by Randolph Barker, Radha Sinha, and Beth Rose, 13–35. Boulder, CO: Westview Press; London: Croom Helm.

Encyclopedia Britannica. 2017. "Treaty Port." https://www.britannica.com/topic/treaty-port.

———. 2019. "Beriberi." https://www.britannica.com/science/beriberi.

———. 2020. "Water buffalo." https://www.britannica.com/animal/water-buffalo.

Engels, Friedrich. 1958. *The Condition of the Working Class in England*. Oxford: B. Blackwell.

Evershed, Richard P., et al. 2008. "Earliest Date for Milk Use in the Near East and Southeastern Europe Linked to Cattle Herding." *Nature* 455:528–531.

Eyer, Diane. 1992. *Mother–Infant Bonding: A Scientific Fiction*. New Haven, CT, and London: Yale University Press.

Fan, B. 2011. "Menu of Woe for Picky Eaters." *Singtao Daily*, December 30, F05.

FAO and WHO. 2011. "Milk and Milk Products." http://www.fao.org/docrep/015/i2085e/i2085e00.pdf.

Farrell, G., S. A. Simons, and R. J. Hillocks. 2002. "Pests, Diseases, and Weeds of Napier Grass, Pennisetum Purpureum: A Review." *International Journal of Pest Management* 48 (1): 39–48.

Featherstone, Mike. 1995. *Undoing Culture: Globalization, Postmodernism and Identity*. London: SAGE Publications Ltd.

Featherstone, Mike, Scott Lash, and Roland Robertson, eds. 1995. *Global Modernities*. London, and Thousand Oaks, CA: SAGE Publications Ltd.

Feng Ye and Xiaoying Ceng, eds. 2010. *Shunde renwen duben.* Shantou: Shantou University Press.

Field, Constance Elaine, and Flora M. Baber. 1973. *Growing up in Hong Kong: A Preliminary Report on a Study of the Growth, Development and Rearing of Chinese Children in Hong Kong.* Hong Kong: Hong Kong University Press.

Fields, Gregory P. 2001. *Religious Therapeutics: Body and Health in Yoga, Āyurveda, and Tantra.* Albany: State University of New York.

First, Michael B. 2014. *DSM-5 Handbook of Differential Diagnosis.* Washington, DC: American Psychiatric Publishing, a division of the American Psychiatric Association.

Foo, L. L., S. J. S. Quek, S. A. Ng, M. T. Lim, and M. Deurenberg-Yap. 2005. "Breastfeeding Prevalence and Practices among Singaporean Chinese, Malay and Indian Mothers." *Health Promotion International* 20 (3): 229–237.

Foucault, Michel. 1973. *The Birth of the Clinic: An Archaeology of Medical Perception.* Translated by Alan Sheridan. London: Tavistock.

———. 1977. "Panopticism." In *Discipline and Punish: The Birth of the Prison.* Translated by Alan Sheridan, 195–228. New York: Vintage Books.

Frank, Thomas. 2000. *One Market under God: Extreme Capitalism, Market Populism and the End of Economic Democracy.* New York: Doubleday.

Freeman, Michael. 1977. "Sung." In *Food in Chinese Culture: Anthropological and Historical Perspectives,* edited by Kwangchih Chang, 141–192. New Haven, CT: Yale University Press.

Friedmann, Harriet. 2005. "From Colonialism to Green Capitalism: Social Movements and Emergence of Food Regimes." In *New Directions in the Sociology of Global Development* (Research in Rural Sociology and Development), edited by Frederick H. Buttel and Philip McMichael, vol. 11, 227–264. Bingley: Emerald Publishing Limited.

FrieslandCampina (Hong Kong) Limited. 2017. "World Milk Day 'Hong Kong Children Health Survey' Reveals 1 in 4 Local Children Quitted Drinking Milk as 6 Year-Old." Press Release. May 31. http://www.media-outreach.com/release.php/View/3461/World-Milk-Day-%E2%80%9CHong-Kong-Children-Health-Survey%E2%80%9D-reveals-1-in-4-local-children-quitted-drinking-milk-as-6-year-old.html.

Fuller, Frank. 2002. "Got Milk? The Rapid Rise of China's Dairy Sector and Its Future Prospects." *Food Policy* 31:201.

Fuller, Frank, John Beghin, and Scott Rozelle. 2007. "Consumption of Dairy Products in Urban China: Results from Beijing, Shanghai and Guangzhou." *The Australian Journal of Agricultural and Resource Economics* 5:459–474.

Fung, Ann. 2017. "Nursing Mothers in Hong Kong Shamed in Public." UCANEWS.com. Accessed March 21, 2017. https://www.ucanews.com/news/nursing-mothers-in-hong-kong-shamed-in-public/78636.

Furedi, Frank. 2002. *Culture of Fear.* Rev. ed. London: Continuum.

Gao, Zhihong. 2005. "Harmonious Regional Advertising Regulation?: A Comparative Examination of Government Advertising Regulation in China, Hong Kong, and Taiwan." *Journal of Advertising* 34 (3): 75–87.

Garg, Pankaj, Jennifer A. Williams, and Vinita Satyavrat. 2015. "A Pilot Study to Assess the Utility and Perceived Effectiveness of a Tool for Diagnosing Feeding Difficulties in Children." *Asia Pacific Family Medicine* 7. doi:10.1186/s12930–015–0024–5.

Gender Research Centre, Hong Kong Institute of Asia-Pacific Studies, The Chinese University of Hong Kong. 2012. *Exploratory Study on Gender Stereotyping and Its Impacts on Male Gender*. Hong Kong: Equal Opportunities Commission.

Gong X. 1999. *Gu jin yi jian*. Beijing: Huaxia chubanshe.

Gottschang, Susanne Zhang. 2007. "Maternal Bodies, Breastfeeding, and Consumer Desire in Urban China." *Medical Anthropology Quarterly* 21 (1): 64–80.

Government of Hong Kong SAR. 2013a. *80th Anniversary Family Health Service Report*. Family Health Service, Department of Health. http://www.fhs.gov.hk/english/archive/files/reports/DH_booklet_18-7-2013.pdf.

———. 2013b. "Export Control on Powdered Formula in Hong Kong." Powdered Formula Licensing Circular No. 1/2013. February 22. https://www.tid.gov.hk/english/import_export/nontextiles/powdered_formula/pf012013.html.

———. 2016. "Healthy Eating for Infants and Young Children—Milk Feeding." Family Health Service, Department of Health. https://www.fhs.gov.hk/english/health_info/child/12549.html.

———. 2017a. "Breastfeeding Survey." Family Health Service, Department of Health. https://www.fhs.gov.hk/english/reports/files/BF_survey_2017.pdf.

———. 2017b. "Hong Kong Code of Marketing of Formula Milk and Related Products, and Food Products for Infants & Young Children." Food and Health Bureau. https://www.hkcode.gov.hk/en/.

———. 2018. *The Smart City Blueprint for Hong Kong*. https://www.smartcity.gov.hk/doc/HongKongSmartCityBlueprint(EN).pdf.

Graham, Ben. 2017. "Frantic Shoppers Filmed Snapping up Scarce Baby Formula at Coles Store." News.com.au, October 19. https://www.news.com.au/finance/business/retail/frantic-shoppers-filmed-snapping-up-scarce-baby-formula-at-coles-store/news-story/b44728f3205526d29e770962679bf508.

Grant, Mark. 2000. *Galen, on Food and Diet*. London and New York: Routledge.

Grasseni, Cristina. 2009. *Developing Skill, Developing Vision—Practices of Locality at the Foot of the Alps*. New York: Berghahn Books.

———. 2011. "Re-inventing Food: Alpine Cheese in the Age of Global Heritage." *Anthropology of Food*, Volume 8. https://journals.openedition.org/aof/6819.

Greenhalgh, Susan. 2011. *Cultivating Global Citizens: Population in the Rise of China*. Cambridge, MA: Harvard University Press.

Greenhalgh, Susan, and Edwin A. Winckler. 2005. *Governing China's Population: From Leninist to Neoliberal Biopolitics*. Stanford, CA: Stanford University Press.

Greenwood. Bernard. 1981. "Cold or Spirits? Choice and Ambiguity in Morocco's Pluralistic Medical System." *Social Science & Medicine* 15 (3): 219–235.

Guha, Amala. 2006. "Ayurvedic Concept of Food and Nutrition." SoM Articles, Paper 25. http://digitalcommons.uconn.edu/som_articles/25.

Guilford, Gwynn. 2013. "Foreign Dairy Firms Are Going to Have to Start Helping Their Chinese Competitors." *Quartz*, July 9. https://qz.com/101344/selling-milk-to-china-is-about-to-become-a-much-trickier-business/.

Gussler, Judith D., and Linda H. Briesemeister. 1980. "The Insufficient Milk Syndrome: A Biocultural Explanation." *Medical Anthropology* 4 (2): 145–174.

Hannerz, Ulf. 1996. *Transnational Connections: Culture, People, Places.* London: Routledge.

Harbottle, Lynn. 2000. *Food for Health, Food for Wealth: The Performance of Ethnic and Gender Identities by Iranian Settlers in Britain.* New York: Berghahn Books.

Harney, Alexandra. 2013. "Special Report: How Big Formula bought China." Reuters. Accessed May 15, 2019. https://www.reuters.com/article/us-china-milkpowder-special report/special-report-how-big-formula-bought-china-idUSBRE9A700820131108.

Harris, Marvin. 1974. *Cows, Pigs, Wars & Witches: The Riddles of Culture.* New York: Random House.

———. 1979. *Cultural Materialism: The Struggle for a Science of Culture.* New York: Random House.

———. 1986. *Good to Eat: Riddles of Food and Culture.* London: Allen and Unwin.

Harris, Marvin, and Eric B. Ross, eds. 1987. *Food and Evolution: Toward a Theory of Human Food Habits.* Philadelphia: Temple University Press.

Harvey, David. 2005. *A Brief History of Neoliberalism.* New York: Oxford University Press.

Hastrup, Kirsten, Peter Elsass, Ralph Grillo, Per Mathiesen, and Robert Paine. 1990. "Anthropological Advocacy: A Contradiction in Terms?" *Current Anthropology* 31 (3): 301–311.

Hatton, Celia. 2013. "Baby Milk Rationing: Chinese Fears Spark Global Restrictions." BBC News. April 10. https://www.bbc.com/news/business-22088977.

Hawkes, David. 1985. *The Songs of the South: An Anthology of Ancient Chinese Poems by Qu Yuan and Other Poets.* Harmondsworth, Middlesex: Penguin Books.

Hays, Sharon. 1996. *The Cultural Contradictions of Motherhood.* New Haven, CT: Yale University Press.

Herskovitz, Stephen, and Malcolm Crystal. 2010. "The Essential Brand Persona: Storytelling and Branding." *Journal of Business* 31 (3): 21–28.

Hertzler, Steven R., L. Bao-Chau, B. L. Huynh, and Dennis A. Savaiano. 1996. "How Much Lactose Is Low Lactose?" *Journal of the American Dietetic Association* 96 (3): 243–246.

Hertzler, Steven R., and Dennis A. Savaiano. 1996. "Colonic Adaptation to Daily Lactose Feeding in Lactose Maldigesters Reduces Lactose Intolerance." *The American Journal of Clinical Nutrition* 64:232–236.

HKIYCNA. 2011. "The Hong Kong Infant and Young Child Nutrition Association Launches Code of Practice for the Marketing of Infant Formula." October 18. Accessed April 13, 2020. http://hkiycna.hk/downloads/English%20Press%20Release%20on %2018%20Oct%202011.pdf.

Ho, Louise. 2015. "Public Breast-Feeding Still Not Accepted by Chinese." *Global Times.* http://www.globaltimes.cn/content/955931.shtml.

Hohenegger, Beatrice. 2006. *Liquid Jade: The Story of Tea from East to West.* New York: St. Martin's Press.

Hsieh, Arnold Chialoh. 1982. "Speech at the 115th Congregation." University of Hong Kong. Accessed June 5, 2019. https://www4.hku.hk/hongrads/index.php/archive/graduate_detail/87.

Hsiung Ping-chen. 1995. *You You: Chuantong zhongguo de qiangbao zhi dao*. Taipei: Lian jing chuban shiye gongsi minguo.

Hu, Dinghuan, Ruiying Fan, Ting Lin, and Bing Liu. 2012. "Exploring the Causes of Rapid Development of China's Dairy Industry." Proceedings of a Symposium held at 15th AAAP Congress, Bangkok, Thailand. November 29. http://dairyasia.org/file/Proceedings_dairy.pdf#page=29.

Hu S. H. 1966. *Yin Shan Zheng Yao*. Taibei: Taiwan shang wu yin shu guan, Minguo.

Huang, Hsingtsung. 2000. "Fermentations and Food Science: Biology and Biological Technology." *Science and Civilization in China*, vol. 6, part 5. Cambridge: Cambridge University Press.

———. 2002. "Hypolactasia and the Chinese Diet." *Current Anthropology* 43 (5): 809–819.

———. 2008. "Early Uses of Soybean in Chinese History." In *The World of Soy*, edited by Christine M. Du Bois, Cheebeng Tan, and Sidney W. Mintz, 45–55. Urbana: University of Illinois Press.

Huang Jiahe, ed. 2011. *Chong chu Xianggang hao wei lai*. Xianggang: Jing ji ri bao chubanshe.

Huang, Yu. 2016. "Neoliberalizing Food Safety Control: Training Licensed Fish Veterinarians to Combat Aquaculture Drug Residues in Guangdong." *Modern China* 42 (5): 535–565.

Huitema, H. 1982. "Animal Husbandry in the Tropics, Its Economic Importance and Potentialities." *Studies in a Few Regions of Indonesia*. Communications—Royal Tropical Institute.

Hunt, Tristram. 2014. *Ten Cities That Made an Empire*. London: Allen Lane.

Hunter, William C. (1882) 1938. *The Fan Kwae at Canton before Treaty Days 1825–1844*. Shanghai: The Oriental Affairs.

Hutching, Gerard. 2018. "Milking It: The True Cost of Dairy on the Environment." Stuff Ltd, August 25. https://www.stuff.co.nz/business/farming/106546688/milking-it-the-true-cost-of-dairy-on-the-environment.

Inouye, Abraham. 2018. "Peoples Republic of China—Dairy and Products Semi-annual: Fluid Milk Consumption Continues to Increase." *GAIN Report* No. CH18028. May 15. https://apps.fas.usda.gov/newgainapi/api/report/downloadrepo rtbyfilename?filename=Dairy%20and%20Products%20Semi-annual_Beijing _China%20-%20Peoples%20Republic%20of_5-16-2018.pdf.

———. 2019. "Peoples Republic of China—Dairy and Products Semi-annual: Higher Profits Support Increased Fluid Milk Production." *GAIN Report* No. CH19042. July 17.

Itan, Yuval, Adam Powell, Mark A. Beaumont, Joachim Burger, and Mark G. Thomas. 2009. "The Origins of Lactase Persistence in Europe." *PLOS Computational Biology* 5 (8): e1000491.

Jacobi, Corinna, Stewart Agra, Susan Bryson, and Lawrence D. Hammer. 2003. "Behavioral Validation, Precursors, and Concomitants of Picky Eating in Childhood." *Journal of the American Academy of Child & Adolescent Psychiatry* 42 (1): 76–84.

Jing, Jun, ed. 2000. *Feeding China's Little Emperors*. Stanford, CA: Stanford University Press.

Kaimen, Johnathan. 2014. "Hong Kong's Umbrella Revolution—the Guardian Briefing." *The Guardian,* September 20. https://www.theguardian.com/world/2014/sep/30/-sp-hong-kong-umbrella-revolution-pro-democracy-protests.

Kaptchuk, Ted J. 2000. *The Web That Has No Weaver: Understanding Chinese Medicine*. New York: McGraw-Hill.

Katz, Cindi. 2008. "Childhood as Spectacle: Relays of Anxiety and the Reconfiguration of the Child." *Cultural Geographies* 15:5–17.

Ke Zhixiong. 2009. *Zhongguo naishang*. Shanxi: Shanxi jingji chubanshe.

Kerzner, B., K. Milano, W. C. MacLean Jr., G. Berall, S. Stuart, and I. Chatoor. 2015. "A Practical Approach to Classifying and Managing Feeding Difficulties." *Pediatrics* 135:344–353.

Kimura, Aya Hirata. 2013. *Hidden Hunger: Gender and the Politics of Smarter Foods*. Ithaca, NY: Cornell University Press.

Kleinman, Arthur. 2006. *What Really Matters: Living a Moral Life amidst Uncertainty and Danger*. Oxford and New York: Oxford University Press.

Kleinman, Arthur, ed. 1976. *Medicine in Chinese Cultures: Comparative Studies of Health Care in Chinese and Other Societies: Papers and Discussions from a Conference held in Seattle, Washington, USA, February 1974*, 241–271. Washington, DC: National Institutes of Health, Public Health Service, US Department of Health, Education, and Welfare (US Government Printing Office).

Knaak, Stephanie J. 2010. "Contextualising Risk, Constructing Choice: Breastfeeding and Good Mothering in Risk Society." *Health, Risk and Society* 12 (4): 345–355.

Kou Ping. 2015. *Quan you xin jin*. Beijing: Zhongguo zhong yiyao chubanshe.

Kuan, Teresa. 2015. *Love's Uncertainty: The Politics and Ethics of Child Rearing in Contemporary China*. Oakland: University of California Press.

Kukla, Rebecca. 2005. *Mass Hysteria, Medicine, Culture and Women's Bodies*. New York: Roman and Littlefield.

Lai, K. K. Y., J. L. Y. Chan, G. Schmer, and T. R. Fritsche. 2003. "Sir Patrick Manson: Good Medicine for the People of Hong Kong." *Hong Kong Medical Journal* 9 (2): 145–147.

Laland, Kevin N., John Odling-Smee, and Sean Myles. 2010. "How Culture Shaped the Human Genome: Bringing Genetics and the Human Sciences Together." *Genetics* 11:137–149.

Lane, Christopher. 2006. "How Shyness Became an Illness: A Brief History of Social Phobia." *Common Knowledge* 12.3:388–409.

Lau, Siu-kai, and Hsin-chi Kuan. 1988. *The Ethos of the Hong Kong Chinese*. Hong Kong: Chinese University Press.

Lawrence, Felicity. 2019. "Can the World Quench China's Bottomless Thirst for Milk?" *The Guardian,* March 29. https://www.theguardian.com/environment/2019/mar/29/can-the-world-quench-chinas-bottomless-thirst-for-milk.

Leach, Helen M. 1999. "Food Processing Technology: Its Role in Inhibiting or Promoting Change in Staple Foods." In *The Prehistory of Food,* edited by Chris Gosden and Jon Hather, 129–138. London: Routledge.

Lee, Ellie J. 2007. "Health, Morality, and Infant Feeding: British Mothers' Experiences of Formula Milk Use in the Early Weeks." *Sociology of Health and Illness* 29 (7): 1075–1090.

———. 2008. "Living with Risk in the Era of 'Intensive Motherhood': Maternal Identity and Infant Feeding." *Health, Risk and Society* 10 (5): 467–477.

Lee, Paul S., Clement Y. K. So, and Louis Leung. 2015. "Social Media and Umbrella Movement: Insurgent Public Sphere in Formation." *Chinese Journal of Communication* 8 (4): 356–375. doi:10.1080/17544750.2015.1088874.

Lee, Sing. 1999. "Fat, Fatigue and the Feminine: The Changing Cultural Experience of Women in Hong Kong." *Culture, Medicine and Psychiatry* 23 (1): 51–73.

Leong, Desiree. 2017. "The Days of Easy Money Exporting Baby Milk Powder Are Over." Vice Channel, July 28. https://www.vice.com/en_au/article/evde3p/the-days-of-easy-money-exporting-baby-milk-are-over.

Leung, Angela Kiche. 2009. *Leprosy in China: A History.* New York: Columbia University Press.

Leung, Sophie S. F. 1995. *A Simple Guide to Childhood Growth and Nutrition Assessment.* Xianggang: Xianggang Zhong wen da xue er ke xue xi.

———. 2005. *Ni ke yi bu yin niu nai.* Xianggang: Quan xin chubanshe you xian gong si.

Leung, Sophie S. F., and Susan S. H. Lui. 1990. "Nutrition Value of Hong Kong Chinese Weaning Diet." *Nutrition Research* 10:707–715.

Levenstein, Harvey. 2003. "Paradoxes of Plenty." In *Paradox of Plenty: A Social History of Eating in Modern America,* 237–255. Berkeley: University of California Press.

Levitt, Tom. 2018. "Dairy's 'Dirty Secret': It's Still Cheaper to Kill Male Calves than to Rear Them." *The Guardian,* March 26. https://www.theguardian.com/environment/2018/mar/26/dairy-dirty-secret-its-still-cheaper-to-kill-male-calves-than-to-rear-them.

Levy, Marion Joseph. 1968. *The Family Revolution in Modern China.* New York: Atheneum.

Li, Lillian M. 1981. *China's Silk Trade: Traditional Industry in the Modern World, 1842–1937.* Cambridge, MA: Council on East Asian Studies, Harvard University. Distributed by Harvard University Press.

Li Lingyun and Hua Xiaogang. 1925. "Ruer de rong yang fa." *Chenbaofujuan hao* 39 (August): 1–2.

Li, Sherry F., Elizabeth Haywood-Sullivan, and Lin Li. 2012. "Made in China: The Mengniu Phenomenon." *Management Accounting Quarterly* 13.3.

Li Shizhen. (1578) 2003. *Compendium of Materia Medica: Bencao gangmu.* Beijing: Foreign Languages Press.

Li, Wenhua, and Qingwen Min. 1999. "Integrated Farming Systems an Important Approach toward Sustainable Agriculture in China." *Ambio* 28 (8): 655–662.

Li, Yaochung A. 1981. *Against Culture: Problematic Love in Early European and Chinese Narrative Fiction*. Microfilm. Ann Arbor: University Microfilm International.

Liang Xingyi. 2014. "Pianshi naifen yi zhi pianshi." *MingPao Daily*, February 3.

Liao Xixiang. 2009. *Shunde yuansheng meishi*. Zhongguo: Qingzhou chubanshe.

Lieban, Richard. 1973. "Medical Anthropology." In *Handbook of Social and Cultural Anthropology*, edited by J. J. Honigman, 1021–1072. Chicago: Rand McNally.

Lindquist, Galina. 2001. "Wizard, Gurus, and Energy Information Fields." *Anthropology of East Europe Review* 19 (1): 16–28.

Ling, Amy, and Hardy Zhou. 2014. "China Continues Rural Support with Agribusiness Tax Incentives." *China Business Review*, October 16. https://www.chinabusinessreview.com/china-continues-rural-support-with-agribusiness-tax-incentives/.

Liong, Mario. 2017. "Sacrifice for the Family: Representation and Practice of Stay-at-Home Fathers in the Intersection of Masculinity and Class in Hong Kong." *Journal of Gender Studies* 26 (4): 402–417.

Liu Fang et al., eds. 2012. *You you xinshu*, Section 4, buer fa Part VI. Guangzhou: Guǎngdong kejì chubanshe.

Liu, Jenny. 2013. *Breastfeeding in China: Improving Practices to Improve China's Future*. UNICEF. https://www.unicef.cn/en/reports/improving-practices-improve-chinas-future.

Liu Shuyong, ed. 2009. *Jian ming Xianggang shi*. Xianggang: San lian shu dian (Xianggang) you xian gong si.

Lo, Shukying. 2009. "Mother's Milk and Cow's Milk: Infant Feeding and the Reconstruction of Motherhood in Modern China, 1900–1937." PhD diss., The Chinese University of Hong Kong.

Lock, Margaret. 1980. *East Asian Medicine in Urban Japan: Varieties of Medical Experience*. Berkeley: University of California Press.

Lock, Margaret, and Deborah Gordon. 1988. *Biomedicine Examined*. Dordrecht: Kluwer Academic Publishers.

Ma, S. C., J. Du, P. P. But, X. L. Deng, Y. W. Zhang, V. E. Ooi, H. X. Xu, S. H. Lee, and S. F. Lee. 2002. "Antiviral Chinese Medicinal Herbs against Respiratory Syncytial Virus." *Journal of Ethnopharmacology* 79 (2): 205–211.

MacCannell, Dean. 1973. "Staged Authenticity: Arrangements of Social Space in Tourist Settings." *The American Journal of Sociology* 79 (3): 589–603.

Mackie, W. W. 1903. "The Value of Oak Leaves for Forage." *California Agriculture Experiment Station* 150:1–21.

Macvarish, Jan, Ellie J. Lee, and Pam K. Lowe. 2014. "The 'First Three Years' Movement and the Infant Brain: A Review of Critiques." *Sociology Compass* 8 (6): 792–804.

Mak, Sau-wa. 2014. "The Revival of Traditional Water Buffalo Cheese Consumption: Class, Heritage and Modernity in Contemporary China." *Food and Foodways: Explorations in the History and Culture of Human Nourishment* 22 (4): 322–347.

———. 2016. "Digitalised Health, Risk and Motherhood: Politics of Infant Feeding in Post-Colonial Hong Kong." *Health, Risk & Society* 17 (7–8): 547–564.

———. 2017. "How Picky Eating Becomes an Illness—Marketing Nutrient-Enriched Formula Milk in a Chinese Society," *Ecology of Food and Nutrition* 56 (1): 81–100.

Man, P. 2012. "Plate of Problems for Young Fussy Eaters." *The Standard*, June 28, 12.

Manson-Bahr, Philip H., and A. Alcock. 1927. *The Life and Work of Sir Patrick Manson*. London: Cassell.

Marketline. 2017. *Market Industry Profile—Dairy in China*. Progressive Digital Media Limited, June.

Masson, Robert T., and Lawrence Marvin DeBrock. 1980. "The Structural Effects of State Regulation of Retail Fluid Milk Prices." *Review of Economics and Statistics* 62 (2): 254–262.

Mauss, Marcel. (1954) 2011. *The Gift*. Glencoe: The Free Press.

McCracken, R. D. 1971. "Lactase Deficiency: An Example of Dietary Evolution." *Current Anthropology* 12:479–517.

McDonald, Mark. 2012. "Carcinogen Found in Chinese Baby Formula." *New York Times*, July 23. https://cn.nytimes.com/china/20120724/c24formula/en-us/.

McIntyre, Bryce T., Christine Wai-sum Cheng, and Weiyu Zhang. 2002. "Cantopop." *Journal of Asian Pacific Communication* 12 (2): 217–243.

Meadjohnson. 2018. "Enfamama." Accessed August 10, 2018. https://www.meadjohnson.com.hk/products/enfamama.

Meulenbeld, G. Jan, and Dominik Wujastyk, eds. 1987. *Studies on Indian Medical History*. Groningen: Egbert Forsten.

Messer, Ellen. 1981. "Hot-cold Classification: Theoretical and Practical Implications of a Mexican Study." *Social Science & Medicine. Part B: Medical Anthropology* 15 (2): 133–145.

———. 1984. "Anthropological Perspectives on Diet." *Annual Review of Anthropology* 13:205–249.

Milktealogy. 2016. "Keung Hing Cafe." Accessed April 15, 2020. https://www.facebook.com/milktealogy/posts/712322378925347/.

Minchin, Maureen. 1985. *Breastfeeding Matters: What We Need to Know About Infant Feeding*. Melbourne: Alma Publications in association with George Allen & Unwin.

Ming Pao. 2011. "Gang xian naifen huang zhuoyue: Suo sheng wuji." January 4, B02.

———. 2013. "Nan di 'mama hui' gui jia jiceng tizao zhuan xi zhou." January 31. https://life.mingpao.com/general/article?issue=20130131&nodeid=1508261096500.

———. 2014. "Pianshi naifen yi zhi pianshi." February 3, A8.

Mintz, Sidney W. 1985. *Sweetness and Power: The Place of Sugar in Modern History*. New York: Viking Penguin.

Mintz, Sidney, and Cheebeng Tan. 2001. "Bean-Curd Consumption in Hong Kong." *Ethnology* 40 (2): 113–128.

Mok, Winston. 2015. "China's Central and Local Governments Must Seek a Fairer Share of the Fiscal Burden." *South China Morning Post*, September 29. https://www.scmp.com/comment/insight-opinion/article/1862356/chinas-central-and-local-governments-must-seek-fairer-share.

Morris, Carol, and Nick Evans. 2001. "'Cheese Makers Are Always Women': Gendered Representations of Farm Life in the Agricultural Press." *Gender, Place & Culture* 8 (4): 375–390.

Morton, Edouard. 2018. "Transparency International: China Climbs Two Places in Global Corruption Perception Ranking as President Xi Jinping Wages War on Graft." *South China Morning Post*, February 22. https://www.scmp.com/news/world/united -states-canada/article/2134145/transparency-international-china-climbs-two-places.

Moynihan, R., and A. Cassels. 2005. *Selling Sickness: How the World's Biggest Pharmaceutical Companies Are Turning Us All into Patients*. New York: Nation Books.

Murphy, Elizabeth. 2000. "Risk, Responsibility, and Rhetoric in Infant Feeding." *Journal of Contemporary Ethnography* 29 (3): 291–325.

National Bureau of Statistics of China. 2018*a*. *China Statistic Yearbook 1996–1999*. Accessed June 2, 2018. http://www.stats.gov.cn/english/statisticaldata/annualdata/.

———. 2018*b*. "Number of Refrigerators per 100 Rural and Urban Households in China from 1990 to 2016." Accessed June 13, 2018. https://www.statista.com /statistics/278747/number-of-refrigerators-per-100-households-in-china/.

National Dairy Council. 2017. "Health and Wellness." Accessed November 1, 2017. http://researchsubmission.nationaldairycouncil.org/Pages/Home.aspx.

Nestle, Marion. 2002. *Food Politics: How the Food Industry Influences Nutrition and Health*. Revised and expanded edition. Berkeley: University of California Press.

———. 2018. *Unsavory Truth: How Food Companies Skew the Science of What We Eat*. New York: Basic Books.

Nestlé Health Science. 2019. "Nitren Junior—About the Product." Accessed April 15, 2020. https://www.nestlehealthscience.us/brands/nutren-junior/nutren-junior.

New York City Department of Health and Mental Hygiene. 2015. "Breastfeeding Disparities in New York City." *Epi Data Brief* No. 57. Accessed April 11, 2020. https:// www1.nyc.gov/assets/doh/downloads/pdf/epi/databrief57.pdf.

New Zealand Herald. 2017. "The Interview: Fonterra Plays the Long Game in China." March 18. http://www.nzherald.co.nz/business/news/article.cfm?c_id=3&objectid =11820356.

Nicholls, Dasha, Rache Chater, and Bryan Lask. 2000. "Children into DSM Don't Go: A Comparison of Classification Systems for Eating Disorders in Childhood and Early Adolescence." *International Journal of Eating Disorders* 28:317–324.

Nicklas, Theresa A., Haiyan Qu, Sheryl O. Hughes, Sara E. Wagner, H. Russell Foushee, and Richard M. Shewchuk. 2009. "Prevalence of Self-Reported Lactose Intolerance in a Multiethnic Sample of Adults." *Nutrition Today* 44 (5): 222–227.

Ng, Brady. 2017. "Obesity: The Big, Fat Problem with Chinese Cities." *The Guardian*, January 9. https://www.theguardian.com/sustainable-business/2017/jan/09/obesity -fat-problem-chinese-cities.

Ng, Naomi. 2017. "Suicides among Hong Kong Children Accounted for Quarter of Unnatural Deaths in 2012 and 2013." *South China Morning Post*, September 2.

Ng, Yupina. 2017. "Children in Hong Kong Are Raised to Excel, Not to be Happy, and Experts Say That Is Worrying." *South China Morning Post*, November 25. https:// www.scmp.com/news/hong-kong/community/article/2121442/children-hong -kong-are-raised-excel-not-happiness-and.

Nutt, Helen H. 1979. "Infant Nutrition and Obesity." *Nursing Forum* 18:131.

Ortner, Sherry. 1984. "Theory in Anthropology since the Sixties." *Comparative Studies in Society and History* 26 (1): 126–166.

Orwell, George. 1946. "A Nice Cup of Tea." *Evening Standard,* January 12.

Osborne, Michael A. 2001. "Acclimatizing the World: A History of the Paradigmatic Colonial Science." *Osiris* 15:135–151.

Ouyang, Shijia. 2018. "Looks Build Brands and Careers Now." *China Daily,* January 22. http://www.chinadaily.com.cn/a/201801/22/WS5a6546cba3106e7dcc135ae0.html.

Ouyang Yingji. 2007. *Xianggang wei dao.* Xianggang: Wan li ji gou, Yin shi tian di chubanshe.

Oxfeld, Ellen. 2017. *Bitter and Sweet: Food, Meaning, and Modernity in Rural China.* Oakland: University of California Press.

Palmer, David, A. 2007. *Qigong Fever: Body, Science, and Utopia in China.* New York: Columbia University Press.

Park, Sohyun, Jae-Heon Kang, Robert Lawrence, and Joel Gittelsohn. 2014. "Environmental Influences on Youth Eating Habits: Insights From Parents and Teachers in South Korea." *Ecology of Food and Nutrition* 53 (4): 347–362.

Parreñas, Rhacel Salazar. 2001. "Mothering from a Distance: Emotions, Gender, and Intergenerational Relations in Filipino Transnational Families." *Feminist Studies* 27 (2): 361–390.

Patel, Raj. 2007. *Stuffed and Starved: Markets, Power and the Hidden Battle over the World's Food System.* London: Portobello Books.

Paxson, Heather. 2010. "Locating Value in Artisan Cheese: Reverse Engineering Terroir for New-World Landscapes." *American Anthropologist* 112 (3): 444–457.

Pease, Bob. 2000. *Recreating Men: Postmodern Masculinity Politics.* London: SAGE Publications Ltd.

Pei, Xiaofang, Annuradha Tandon, Anton Alldrick, Liana Giorgi, Wei Huang, and Ruijia Yang. 2010. "The China Melamine Milk Scandal and Its Implications for Food Safety Regulation." *Food Policy* 36 (3): 412–420.

Pelto, Gretel H., and Luis Alberto Vargas, eds. 1992. "Perspectives on Dietary Change: Studies in Nutrition and Society." *Ecology of Food and Nutrition* (Special issue) 27 (3–4).

Peters, Erica J. 2012. *Appetites and Aspirations in Vietnam: Food and Drink in the Long Nineteenth Century.* Lanham, MD: AltaMira Press.

Petryna, Adriana, and Arthur Kleinman. 2006. "The Pharmaceutical Nexus." In *Global Pharmaceuticals: Ethics, Markets, Practices,* edited by Adriana Petryna, Andrew Lakoff, and Arthur Kleinman, 1–32. Durham, NC: Duke University Press.

Peverelli, Peter J. 2006. *Chinese Corporate Identity.* London: Routledge.

Peynaud, Emile. 2005. "Tasting Problems, and Errors of Perception." In *The Taste Culture Reader: Experiencing Food and Drink (Sensory Formations),* edited by Carolyn Korsmeyer, 272–278. New York: Berg Publishers.

Pidgeon, Emily. 2017. "'It Was Chaos': Woman Claims Frenzied Asian Shoppers nearly Knocked Her Off Her Feet as They Sprinted through Coles Grabbing Baby Formula." *MailOnline,* October 19. https://www.dailymail.co.uk/news/article-4996438/Woman-claims-Asian-shoppers-knocked-feet-Coles.html.

Pingali, Prabhu. 2007. "Westernization of Asian Diets and the Transformation of Food Systems: Implications for Research and Policy." *Food Policy* 32:281–298.

Poitras, Geoffrey. 2012. "OxyContin, Prescription Opioid Abuse and Economic Medicalization." *Medicolegal and Bioethics,* November 22.

Porkert, Manfred. 1974. *Theoretical Foundations of Chinese Medicine: Systems of Correspondence.* Cambridge, MA: MIT Press.

Qian, Linhai, Wei Huang, and Hangen Ma. 2011. *Handbook of Yummy Shunde.* Shunde: Zhujiang Shang Bao Jingying Zhongxin.

Radbill, Samuel X. 1981. "Infant Feeding through the Age." *Clinical Pediatrics* 10 (10): 613–621.

Radio Television Hong Kong. 2012. "Floating and Opportunity." Episode 19 in *The Hong Kong Story—Our Brands* series, March 19. Accessed April 13, 2020. https://www.youtube.com/watch?v=BkxHuVnCIkE.

Relman, Arnold S. 2008. "Industry Support of Medical Education." *Journal of the American Medical Association* 300 (9): 1071–1073.

Ritzer, George. 2019. *The McDonaldization of Society: Into the Digital Age.* 9th ed. Thousand Oaks, CA: SAGE Publications, Inc.

Romagnoli, Amy, and Glenda Wall. 2012. "'I know I'm a Good Mom': Young, Low-Income Mothers' Experiences with Risk Perception, Intensive Parenting Ideology and Parenting Education Programmes." *Health, Risk & Society* 14 (3): 273–289.

Rosaldo, Michelle Z. 1984. "Towards an Anthropology of Self and Feeling." In *Culture Theory: Essays on Mind, Self and Emotion,* edited by Richard A. Shweder and Robert A. LeVine, 137–157. Cambridge: Cambridge University Press.

Rose, Nikolas. 2001. "The Politics of Life Itself." *Theory Culture & Society* 18 (1): 1–30.

Roseberry, William. 1996. "The Rise of Yuppie Coffees and the Reimagination of Class in the United States." *American Anthropologist* 98 (4): 762–775.

Sabban, Francoise. 2011. "Milk Consumption in China: The Construction of a New Food Habit." Paper presented at the 12th Symposium on Chinese Dietary Culture: Foundation of Chinese Dietary Culture. Okinawa, Japan, November 19–21.

———. 2014. "The Taste for Milk in Modern China (1865–1937)." In *Food Consumption in Global Perspective: Consumption and Public Life,* edited by Jakob A. Klein and Anne Murcott, 182–208. London: Palgrave Macmillan.

Sachse, William L., ed. (1659) 1961. *The Diurnal of Thomas Rugg, 1659–1661.* London: Royal Historical Society.

Sadock, Benjamin J., Virginia A. Sadock, Pedro Ruiz, and Harold I. Kaplan. 2009. *Kaplan & Sadock's Comprehensive Textbook of Psychiatry.* Philadelphia: Wolters Kluwer Health/Lippincott Williams and Wilkins.

Sahlins, Marshall. 1976. *Culture and Practical Reason.* Chicago: University of Chicago Press.

Sasson, Tehila. 2016. "Milking the Third World? Humanitarianism, Capitalism and Moral Economy of the Nestlé Boycott." *The American Historical Review* 121 (4): 1196–1224.

Sayer, Geoffrey Robley, and D. M. Emrys Evans. 1985. *Hong Kong 1862–1919: Years of Discretion.* Hong Kong: Hong Kong University Press.

Schafer, Edward H. 1977. "Tang." In *Food in Chinese Culture: Anthropological and Historical Perspectives,* edited by Kwangchih Chang, 85–140. New Haven, CT: Yale University Press.

Scheper-Hughes, Nancy, and Margaret M. Lock. 1987. "The Mindful Body: A Prolegomenon to Future Work in Medical Anthropology." *Medical Anthropology Quarterly* 1.1:6–41.

Scrinis, Gyorgy. 2008. "On the Ideology of Nutritionism." *Gastronomic* 8 (1): 39–48.

———. 2013. *Nutritionism: The Science and Politics of Dietary Advice.* New York: Columbia University Press.

Selwyn-Clarke, Sir Selwyn. 1975. *Footprints: The Memoirs of Sir Selwyn Selwyn-Clarke.* Hong Kong: Sino-American Publishing Co.

Shen Bao. 1929. "Kede Milk Advertisement." Supplement, April 21.

Sheng, S. Y., M. L. Tong, D. M. Zhao, T. F. Leung, F. Zhang, N. P. Hays, J. Ge, et al. 2014. "Randomized Controlled Trial to Compare Growth Parameters and Nutrient Adequacy in Children with Picky Eating Behaviors who Received Nutritional Counseling with or without an Oral Nutritional Supplement." *Nutrition and Metabolic Insights* 7:85–94.

Shih Ziggy. 2016. "Nushen Angelababy, Linxinru huaiyun yiran xianxi du bao biaopan dian nu xing yun ma mi yang tai bu yang rou mi zhao." *Cosmopolitan,* November 3. https://tw.news.yahoo.com/女神angelababy林心如懷孕依然纖細度爆表-盤點女星孕媽咪養胎不養肉秘招-125239130.html.

Showalter, Elaine. 1985. *The Female Malady: Women, Madness and English Culture, 1830–1980.* New York: Pantheon.

Shunde Longjiang Gazette. 1967. "Longjiang." Taibei: Chengwen chubanshe.

Silanikove, Nissim, Gabriel Leitner, and Uzi Merin. 2015. "The Interrelationships between Lactose Intolerance and the Modern Dairy Industry: Global Perspectives in Evolutional and Historical Backgrounds." *Nutrients* 7:7312–7331.

Simmel, Georg. (1903) 2002. "The Metropolis and Mental Life." In *The Blackwell City Reader,* edited by Gary Bridge and Sophie Watson, 11–19. Oxford and Malden, MA: Wiley-Blackwell.

Singer, Merrill. 1990. "Reinventing Medical Anthropology: Toward a Critical Realignment." *Social Science & Medicine* 30 (2): 179–187.

Singer, Merrill, and Hans Baer. 1995. *Critical Medical Anthropology.* Amityville, NY: Baywood Publishing Company, Inc.

Singtao Daily. 2015. "Lots of Anxiety for Hong Kong Students, Parents Must Reduce Pressure." March 27, F09.

———. 2018. "Aaron Kwok Played the Role of a Street Hawker in Order to Earn Money for Milk Powder." October 28. Accessed April 11, 2020. https://std.stheadline.com/instant/articles/detail/850720/即時-娛樂-老婆又大肚-郭富城為愛女甘願跕街扮小販-型男變大叔撲奶粉錢.

Smith, Carl T. 1995. *A Sense of History: Studies in the Social and Urban History of Hong Kong.* Hong Kong: Hong Kong Educational Publishing Company.

Smith, Richard D. 2006. "Responding to Global Infectious Disease Outbreaks: Lessons from SARS on the Role of Risk Perception, Communication and Management." *Social Science & Medicine* 63 (12): 3113–3123.

Solomon, Richard. 1971. *Mao's Revolution and the Chinese Political Culture*. Berkeley: University of California Press.

Solt, George. 2014. *The Untold History of Ramen: How Political Crisis in Japan Spawned a Global Food Craze*. Berkeley: University of California Press.

Sonobe, Teysushi, Dinghuan Hu, and Keijiro Otsuka. 2002. "Process of Cluster Formation in China: A Case Study of a Garment Town." *The Journal of Development Studies* 39 (1): 140–164.

South China Morning Post. 2010. "Lower Milk Standard to Ward Off Melamine Use." July 14. Accessed August 29, 2017. http://www.scmp.com/article/719620/lower-milk-standard-ward-melamine-use.

Spence, Jonathan. 1977. "Ch'ing." In *Food in Chinese Culture: Anthropological and Historical Perspectives*, edited by Kwangchih Chang, 259–294. New Haven, CT: Yale University Press.

Statista.com. 2019. "Global Consumption of Fluid Milk 2018, by Country." Accessed May 27, 2019. https://www.statista.com/statistics/272003/global-annual-consumption-of-milk-by-region/.

Stearns, Cindy A. 2009. "The Work of Breastfeeding." *Women Studies Quarterly* 37.3 (4): 63–80.

Stevenson, Rachel, and agencies. 2008. "China Milk Scare Spreads to 54,000 Children." *The Guardian*, September 22. Accessed April 22, 2020. https://www.theguardian.com/world/2008/sep/22/china.

Striffler, Steve. 2005. *Chicken: The Dangerous Transformation of America's Favorite Food*. New Haven, CT: Yale University Press.

Su Yu. 2005. *Bijiang jianggu*. Guangzhou: Huacheng chubanshe.

Sun, Jian, Benny K. H. Tan, Shanhong Huang, Matthew Whiteman, Yizhun Hiteman, and Yizhun Zhu. 2002. "Effects of Natural Products on Ischemic Heart Diseases and Cardiovascular System." *Acta Pharmacologica Sinica* 23 (12): 1142–1151.

Sun Xianhong and Zhiguo Zhang. 2005. *Mengniu neimu*. Beijing: Beijing University Press.

Sun, Yuelian, Hans Gregersen, and Wei Yuan. 2017. "Chinese Health Care System and Clinical Epidemiology." *Clinical Epidemiology* 9:167–178.

Swislocki, Mark. 2009. *Culinary Nostalgia: Regional Food Culture and the Urban Experience in Shanghai*. Stanford, CA: Stanford University Press.

Tadesse, K., D. T. Y. Leung, and R. C. F. Yuen. 1992. "The Status of Lactose Absorption in Hong Kong Chinese Children." *Acta Paediatrica* 81 (8): 598–600.

Talbot, Margaret. 2001. "The Shyness Syndrome: Bashfulness Is the Latest Trait to Become a Pathology." *New York Times Sunday Magazine*, June 24, 11.

Tam, Luisa. 2018. "Hong Kong's Schoolchildren Are Stressed Out—and Their Parents Are Making Matters Worse." *South China Morning Post*, July 16.

Tam, Siumi Maria. 1996. "Normalization of 'Second Wives': Gender Contestation in Hong Kong." *Asian Journal of Women's Studies* 2:113–132.

Tan, Sweepoh, and Erica Wheeler. 1983. "Concepts Relating to Health and Food Held by Chinese Women in London." *Ecology of Food and Nutrition* 13 (1): 37–49.

Tang, Kwong-Leung. 1998. *Colonial State and Social Policy: Social Welfare Development of Hong Kong 1842–1997.* Lanham, MD: University Press of America.

Tao, Vivienne Y. K., and Yingyi Hong. 2013. "When Academic Achievement Is an Obligation—Perspectives from Social-Oriented Achievement Motivation." *Journal of Cross-Cultural Psychology* 45 (1): 110–136.

Tarrant, Marie, Joan E. Dodgson, and Vinkline Wing Kay Choi. 2004. "Becoming a Role Model: The Breastfeeding Trajectory of Hong Kong Women Breastfeeding Longer than Six Months." *International Journal of Nursing Studies* 41 (5): 535–546.

Tarrant, Marie, Daniel Y. T. Fong, Kendra M. Wu, Irene L. Y. Lee, Emmy M. Y. Wong, Alice Sham, Christine Lam, and Joan E. Dodgson. 2010. "Breastfeeding and Weaning Practices among Hong Kong Mothers: A Prospective Study." *BMC Pregnancy and Childbirth* 10:27. doi.org/10.1186/1471-2393-10-27.

Tay, Vivian. 2018. "Indonesia Prohibits Brands from Marketing Condensed Milk and Derivatives as Milk." *Marketing Interactive.* Accessed July 6, 2019. https://www.marketing-interactive.com/indonesia-prohibits-brands-from-marketing-condensed-milk-and-derivatives-as-milk/.

Teets, Jessica C. 2015. "The Politics of Innovation in China: Local Officials as Policy Entrepreneurs." *Issues & Studies* 51 (2): 79–109.

Thai, Hung Cam. 2006. "Money and Masculinity among Low Wage Vietnamese Immigrants in Transnational Families." *International Journal of Sociology of the Family* 32 (2): 247–271.

Timimi, Sami, and Eric Taylor. 2004. "ADHD Is Best Understood as a Cultural Construct." *British Journal of Psychiatry* 184:8–9.

Topick. 2015. "Shenshui bu yi kuan mei su jia er naifen que huo lu yu 45%" (One product of Frisco formula milk in Shumshuipo is 45% out-of-stock). February 16. https://topick.hket.com/article/546280/.

Tsang, Steve Yui-Sang. 2004. *A Modern History of Hong Kong.* Hong Kong: Hong Kong University Press.

Tuo, Guozhu. 2000. "Retrospective and Prospective of 50 years of Chinese Dairy Industry." In *50 Years of Chinese Dairy Industry,* edited by Huaibao Wang, 3–13. Beijing: Ocean Press.

Turner, S. Byran. 2004. "Foreword." In *Remaking Citizenship in Hong Kong: Community, Nation, and the Global City,* edited by Agnes S. Ku and Ngai Pun, xiii–xx. London and New York: Routledge.

UNESCO. 2017. "Ben Cao Gang Mu" (《本草纲目》 Compendium of Materia Medica). http://www.unesco.org/new/en/communication-and-information/memory-of-the-world/register/full-list-of-registered-heritage/registered-heritage-page-1/ben-cao-gang-mu-compendium-of-materia-medica/.

Unschuld, Paul Ulrich. 2010. *Medicine in China: A History of Ideas.* 25th anniversary ed. Berkeley; London: University of California Press.

Valenze, Deborah. 2011. *Milk: A Local and Global History.* New Haven, CT: Yale University Press.

Van Esterik, Penny. 1989. *Beyond the Breast-bottle Controversy*. New Brunswick, NJ: Rutgers University Press.

———. 1997. "The Politics of Breastfeeding: An Advocacy Perspective." In *Food and Culture: A Reader*, edited by Carole Counihan and Penny Van Esterik, 370–383. New York: Routledge.

———. 2008. "The Politics of Breastfeeding: An Advocacy Update." In *Food and Culture: A Reader*, 2d ed., edited by Carole Counihan and Penny Van Esterik, 467–481. New York: Routledge.

Veblen, T. (1899) 1994. "The Theory of the Leisure Class." In *The Collected Works of Thorstein Veblen*, vol. 1. Reprint, London: Routledge.

Waldmeir, Patti. 2013. "Bribery Allegations Emerge over Imported Infant Formula in China." *Financial Times*, September 23. https://www.ft.com/content/e4b697e2 -2116-11e3-8aff-00144feab7de.

Waley, Arthur. (1919) 2005. *More Translations from the Chinese*. London: G. Allen & Unwin.

Wang, Dingmian. 2009. "Dairy Industry Loss 20 Billion because of Melamine Scandal: Mengniu and Yili Face Heavier Pressures." *South Metropolitan Newspaper*, October 31.

Wang, Jing. 2008. *Brand New China: Advertising, Media, and Commercial Culture*. Cambridge, MA: Harvard University Press.

Wang Mengying. 1990. *Lidai zhongyi zhenben jicheng, Book 19*. Shanghai: Sanlian shuju.

Wang, Yongfa, Yongshan Yan, Jiujin Xu, Ruofu Du, S. D. Flatz, W. Kühnau, and G. Flatz. 1984. "Prevalence of Primary Adult Lactose Malabsorption in Three Populations of Northern China." *Human Genetics* 67 (1): 103–106.

Wardle, Jane, Lucy J. Cooke, E. Leigh Gibson, Manuela Sapochnik, Aubrey Sheiham, and Margaret Lawson. 2003. "Increasing Children's Acceptance of Vegetables: A Randomized Trial of Parent-Led Exposure." *Appetite* 40 (2): 155–162.

Wardle, Jane, Carol Ann Guthrie, Saskia Sanderson, and Lorna Rapoport. 2001. "Development of the Children's Eating Behavior Questionnaire." *Journal of Child Psychology and Psychiatry* 42 (7): 963–970.

Watson, James, ed. 1997. *Golden Arches East: McDonald's in East Asia*. Stanford, CA: Stanford University Press.

Watsons Pharmacy. 2003. "Children's Health Not at the Top of Hong Kong Mothers' Concerns Even after SARS Outbreak." Press Release, July 12. http://www.hutchison -whampoa.com/en/media/press_each.php?id=1203.

Weenink, Don. 2008. "Cosmopolitanism as a Form of Capital: Parents Preparing Their Children for a Globalizing World." *Sociology* 42 (6): 1089–1106.

Wen, Hua. 2013. *Buying Beauty: Cosmetic Surgery in China*. Hong Kong: Hong Kong University Press.

White House, United States Government. 2013. "Baby Hunger Outbreak in Hong Kong, International Aid Requested." Accessed September 23, 2018. https:// petitions.whitehouse.gov/petition/baby-hunger-outbreak-hong-kong-international -aid-requested/xVSGJNN1.

Wiley, Andrea S. 2007. "Transforming Milk in a Global Economy." *American Anthropologist* 109 (4): 666–677.

———. 2011. *Re-imagining Milk: Cultural and Biological Perspectives.* New York: Routledge.

———. 2014. *Cultures of Milk: The Biology and Meaning of Dairy Products in the United States and India.* Cambridge, MA: Harvard University Press.

Windfuhr, Michael, and Jennie Jonsen. 2005. *Food Sovereignty: Towards Democracy in Localized Food Systems.* Rugby, Warwickshire: ITDG Publishing. http://www.ukabc.org/foodsovereignty_itdg_fian_print.pdf.

Wolf, Eric R. 1982. *Europe and the People without History.* Berkeley: University of California Press.

World Health Organization (WHO). 2003. "Summary of Probable SARS Cases with Onset of Illness from 1 November 2002 to 31 July 2003." Accessed April 21, 2020. https://www.who.int/csr/sars/country/table2004_04_21/en/.

———. 2013. "Country Implementation of the International Code of Marketing of Breast-milk Substitutes Status Report 2011." Geneva: World Health Organization.

———. 2019*a*. "Breastfeeding." Accessed November 5, 2019. https://www.who.int/topics/breastfeeding/en/.

———. 2019*b*. "Melamine." Accessed May 26, 2019. https://www.who.int/foodsafety/areas_work/chemical-risks/melamine/en/.

Wright, Peter. 1991. "Development of Food Choice during Infancy." *Proceedings of the Nutrition Society* 50:107–113.

Wu, Chun, Magen Xia, Youchi Kuo, and Carol Liao. 2014. "Capturing a Share of China's Consumer Health Market: From Insight to Action." Boston Consulting Group. February 25. https://www.bcg.com/publications/2014/center-consumer-customer-insight-globalization-insight-action-capturing-share-chinas-consumer-health-market.aspx.

Wu, David. 1997. "McDonald's in Taipei: Hamburgers, Betel Nuts, and National Identity." In *Golden Arches East: McDonald's in East Asia,* edited by James L. Watson, 110–135. Stanford, CA: Stanford University Press.

Wu, H., F. Yang, S. Cui, Y. Qin, J. Liu, and Y. Zhang. 2007. "Hematopoietic Effect of Fractions from the Enzyme-Digested Colla Corii Asini on Mice with 5-Fluorouracil Induced Anemia." *American Journal of Chinese Medicine* 35:853–866.

Wu Junxiong, Jiewei Ma, and Dale Lü, eds. 2006. *Xianggang, wen hua, yan jiu.* Hong Kong: Hong Kong University Press.

Wyeth Nutrition. 2015. "Why S-26® PE GOLD®?" https://www.wyethnutrition.com.my/en/products/picky-eater/s-26-pe-gold#.

Xinhua News Agency. 2015. "China Focus: Chinese Dairy Farmers Resort to Dumping Milk, Killing Cows." Accessed January 10, 2016. http://www.xinhuanet.com/english/indepth/2015-01/10/c_133910360.htm.

Xiu, Changbai, and K. K. Klein. 2010. "Melamine in Milk Products in China: Examining the Factors that Led to Deliberate Use of the Contaminant." *Food Policy* 35:463–470.

Xu, Fenglian, Liqian Qiu, Colin W. Binns, and Xiaoxian Liu. 2009. "Breastfeeding in China: A Review." *International Breastfeeding Journal* 4:6–21.

Xu Xian. 2007. *Gong xiang tai ping: Tai ping guan can ting de chuan qi gu shi*. Xianggang: Ming bao chubanshe you xian gong si.

Yan, Ruizhen, and Changbai Xiu. 2009. "Survey of Dairy Industry Development in Helinger County, Inner Mongolia." Unpublished technical report to *Evangelischer Entwicklungdenst e.v.*, Bonn, Germany.

Yan, Yunxiang. 2013. "The Drive for Success and the Ethics of the Striving Individual." In *Ordinary Ethics in China Today*, edited by Charles Stafford, 263–291. London: Bloomsbury.

Yang, Jie. 2010. "The Crisis of Masculinity: Class, Gender, and Kindly Power in Post-Mao China." *American Ethnologist* 37 (3): 550–562.

Yang Xiaofang. 2012. "Ying zai qipaoxian." *Xiaoxue kexue: Jiaoshi* 4. Accessed November 12, 2019. http://www.cqvip.com/qk/89687x/201204/42062863.html.

Yinlong yinshi jituan. 2013. *Gang ren fan tang, cha can ting*. Xianggang: Wan li ji gou, Yin shi tian di chubanshe.

Yu, Lea. 2012. "A Nation of Provinces." *CKGSB Knowledge*. Cheung Kong Graduate School of Business. http://knowledge.ckgsb.edu.cn/detail/a-nation-of-provinces.

Yu, Songlin, Huiling Fang, Jianhua Han, Xinqi Cheng, Liangyu Xia, Shijun Li, Min Liu, Zhihua Tao, Liang Wang, Li'an Hou, Xuzhen Qin, Pengchang Li, Ruiping Zhang, Wei Su, and Ling Qiu. 2015. "The High Prevalence of Hypovitaminosis D in China: A Multicenter Vitamin D Status Survey." *Medicine* 94 (8): e585.

Yu, Xiaochua. 2015. "China's Fight for Safe Food." *Caixin*, May 5. http://www.slate.com/articles/news_and_politics/caixin/2015/05/china_s_broken_food_safety_system_chinese_consumers_don_t_trust_the_government.html.

Yukio, Kumashiro. 1971. "Recent Developments in Scholarship on the *Ch'min* Yaoshu in Japan and China." *The Developing Economies* 9 (4): 422–448.

Yung, Vannessa. 2015. "Now with Video—Milktealogy: Twins Help Preserve Hong Kong's Tea Drinking Culture." *South China Morning Post*, February 17. https://www.scmp.com/lifestyle/food-wine/article/1714746/milktealogy-comic-strip-devoted-preserving-hong-kongs-tea.

Zeitlyn, Sushila, and Rabeya Rowshan. 1997. "Privileged Knowledge and Mothers' 'Perceptions': The Case of Breasfeeding and Insufficient Milk in Bangladesh." *Medical Anthropology Quarterly* 11 (1): 56–68.

Zetland Hall. 2020. "History of Zetland Hall." Zetland Hall Trustees and/or its suppliers. Accessed April 9, 2020. http://www.zetlandhall.com.

Zhang C. Z. 1978. *Ru men shi qin*. Section III. Taibei: Taiwan shang wu yin shu guan.

Zhang, Lixiang, et al. 2009. *Development Report on China Dairy*. Beijing: Zhongguo jingji chubanshe.

Zhen, Shihan, Yanan Ma, Zhongyi Zhao, Xuelian Yang, and Deliang Wen. 2018. "Dietary Pattern Is Associated with Obesity in Chinese Children and Adolescents: Data from China Health and Nutrition Survey (CHNS)." *Nutrition Journal* 17:68.

Zhong, Gonfu. 1982. "The Mulberry Dike-Fish Pond Complex: A Chinese Ecosystem of Land-Water Interaction on the Pearl River Delta." *Human Ecology* 10 (2): 191–202.

Zhou Shimí. 1990. *Yinger lun*. Shanghai: Shanghai kexue jishu chubanshe.

Zhu, Feng, Chouyong Yang, and Honghe Zhang. 2009. "Tracing Back to the Sanlu Poisonous Milk Powder: How Sanlu Glosses over the Fact." *China News,* January 4. Accessed May 13, 2018. http://www.chinanews.com.cn/cj/kong/news/2009/01-04 /1513271.

Index

About the Author

Veronica Sau-Wa Mak is assistant professor at Hong Kong Shue Yan University, teaching courses on food, gender and health, globalization, family, and heritage. Before joining Shue Yan University, she taught courses on advertising and marketing management in the Business Faculty at Chinese University of Hong Kong.

Before her training as a medical anthropologist, Mak was associate account director at Bates Advertising, and later a marketing consultant strategizing marketing plans for many food companies, including China Mengniu Dairy and Kikkoman. Formally trained in both marketing and anthropology, she has conducted more than a hundred consumer research projects and prepared numerous marketing plans for food companies. Since completing her PhD, Mak has published professional papers in academic journals, such as *Ecology of Food and Nutrition* and *Food and Foodways*, and contributed chapters to *Globalised Eating Cultures, Mediatization and Mediation*, edited by Jörg Dürrschmidt and York Kautt (2019), and *Chinese Food and Foodways in Southeast Asia and Beyond*, edited by Tan Chee-Beng (2011). She has also published more than a hundred articles on food culture in *Grocery Trade Magazine*, a Hong Kong–based food trading magazine.